I0061310

Migrant Resettlement in the Russian Federation: Reconstructing 'Homes' and 'Homelands'

Migrant Resettlement in the Russian Federation: Reconstructing 'Homes' and 'Homelands'

MOYA FLYNN

Anthem Press

This edition first published by Anthem Press 2004

Anthem Press is an imprint of
Wimbledon Publishing Company
75-76 Blackfriars Road
London SE1 0HX

© Moya Flynn 2004

The moral right of the author to be identified as the
author of this work has been asserted

All rights reserved.
No part of this publication may be reproduced,
stored in a retrieval system, or transmitted, in any form
or by any means, without the prior permission in writing of
Wimbledon Publishing Company, or as expressly permitted
by law, or under terms agreed with the appropriate
reprographics rights organization.

British Library Cataloguing in Publication Data
Data available

Library of Congress in Publication Data
A catalogue record has been applied for

1 3 5 7 9 10 8 6 2

ISBN   1 84331 116 X (hbk)
              1 84331 117 8 (pbk)

Designed by Abe Aboody
Typeset by Alliance Interactive Technology
Printed in India

Contents

List of Tables, Figures and Maps

The author and publisher wish to thank Frank Cass Publishers for kindly giving permission to reproduce Map 4.1.

Acknowledgements

The research for this book was partly funded by the Economic and Social Research Council (Research Studentship Award, Post-Doctoral Fellowship Award TO26 27 1017), and would have been impossible without its financial support. I am grateful also to friends and former colleagues at the Centre for Russian and East European Studies at the University of Birmingham. I would like to thank Hilary Pilkington, who provided me with the initial opportunity to pursue my interest in Russian migration, and who has consistently given me her encouragement and support. Thanks also go to Nigel Hardware, Mike Berry, Marea Arries, Tricia Carr and other colleagues at the Centre for their academic and technical assistance. Both during my time at Birmingham, and since, very special thanks go to Jon Oldfield for his comments on earlier drafts of chapters and for his continual support, enthusiasm and encouragement. At the Department of Central and East European Studies at the University of Glasgow, I would especially like to thank Rebecca Kay; her comments on earlier drafts of chapters are much appreciated, and our conversations about Russia and what the country has come to mean to us both provides a great source of motivation and inspiration. I would also like to extend special thanks to Kate Thomson, Denis Shaw, Erica Richardson, Annie Phizacklea, Alison Stenning, Mark McGuinness and Steff Jansen for their valuable thoughts and comments on my work at different points of time in its development.

In Russia, my deepest thanks go to the many friends and colleagues who provided me with emotional and practical support, and who demonstrate consistently to me the very special and positive sides of Russian life. In particular, Elena Omel'chenko, Guzel Sabirova, Ul'iana Bliudina and Natasha Goncharova, and all at the Centre 'Region' at Ul'ianovsk State University, Larisa Kosygina in

Novosibirsk, Katia Belova and Nadia Shapkina of (but no longer living in) Saratov, Irina Tartakovskaia in Samara, and Natal'ia Kosmarskaia in Moscow. Also in Moscow, Lidiia Grafova and Svetlana Gannushkina were willing to talk with me on many occasions, despite the great limitations on their time. I thank them for offering information, for sharing their opinions with me, and for providing me with an insight into the valuable work that they are doing. I am also grateful to Galina Vitkovskaia, Zhanna Zaionchkovskaia, Eloisa Siuch, Olga Salova, Richard Morris and Edwin McClain for providing me with expert insight into the complexities of studying and working in the Russian migration field. Above all, the research and the writing of the book would not have been possible without the many migrants with whom I was fortunate enough to talk, and I would like to thank them for giving me their valuable time; equally, the migrant associations in Saratov, Samara and Novosibirsk who on many occasions welcomed me back and answered my questions. I would especially like to remember Irina Fedotova who sadly died in August 2000.

Finally, I would like to say a very special thank you to my family, and to my friends both in the UK and Russia, for their love and understanding, and for being a constant source of support and diversion.

Moya Flynn
Glasgow, September 2003

NOTE ON TRANSLITERATION

The Library of Congress transliteration system has been used throughout the text, apart from frequently used Russian names, e.g. Yeltsin. Transliterated Russian words used in preference to the English translation in the text are:

Krai/a	Territory/Territories
Oblast'/oblasti	Region/s
Raion/y	District/s

Introduction

Following the collapse of the USSR in 1991, and the rapid political, social and economic change that ensued, widespread population movements took place across the former unitary territory of the Soviet Union. One of these movements has been that of the ethnic Russian and Russian-speaking populations in the Soviet successor states to the Russian Federation. In 1991, 25.3 million ethnic Russians were living outside the borders of the Russian Federation, along with 11 million members of other ethnic groups whose primary cultural affinity was to Russia, and who have become known as the 'Russian-speaking' populations.[1] Over the period 1991–2001, approximately 1.5 million individuals from these populations have been officially registered as 'forced migrants' or 'refugees' by the Russian government. However, it is estimated that as many as 8–10 million individuals have actually made the journey from the former republics and come to reside within the borders of the Russian Federation.[2]

The book explores the 'return' migration and resettlement experience of members of these ethnic Russian and Russian-speaking migrant populations who during the period 1991–2001 left their homes in the former republics of the Soviet Union to resettle on the territory of the Russian Federation, their 'historical homeland'.[3] In many ways this was a telling and significant time for both the subjects of the study – the ethnic Russian and Russian-speaking migrants – and for its geographical area – the newly independent Russian Federation. The mass displacement of peoples that occurred demanded speedy and radical responses from the individuals, states and governments involved; the newness of the situation that they faced must be considered in any critical analysis of the responses at both the individual and state level.

Significant changes have taken place in migration policy within the Russian Federation since 2000, and new levels and types of migration movements are leading to novel challenges at the local, regional and national level. Nonetheless, the experience of migration and resettlement of the ethnic Russian and Russian-speaking populations as revealed by this study remains a lived reality for those people who have moved, and may be equally so for the many who still wish to come. Although the book presents an incomplete picture of this migration movement and resettlement process, it provides a valuable insight into the lives of some of the individuals who migrated and who experienced in a very immediate way the social, economic and cultural displacement that many lived through in the first decade of post-communism. Yet the migrants' narratives which emerge throughout the book are also illustrative of the processes of re-location and re-creation of 'homes' and future 'homelands' that are taking place amongst many communities across the Russian Federation and wider post-Soviet space.

Central to the book is an examination of how the migration process (the migration movement and subsequent resettlement) and the space to which individuals arrive – the physical territory of the 'homeland' – are constructed by key actors (including state and government bodies, non-governmental organizations, the media) within the international, federal and regional migration regimes. The book compares and contrasts the ways in which the migration process and the space of 'return' are created at these different levels, and the way individual migrants are envisaged as fitting into this space: the wider 'homeland'. The migrant, and his/her experience of displacement, migration and re-settlement, is consciously moved to the centre of the debate. The book charts how migrants construct their own idea of 'home/land',[4] and asks how, despite displacement and the frequently constraining features of the surrounding migration environment, they begin to reconstruct their own sense of 'home' at the site of settlement. This dual approach reveals the discrepancy that can exist between state constructions of a migration process and actual migrant experience and understanding of the same process.

The aim of the book is therefore to present a picture of the migration and resettlement experience of the ethnic Russian and Russian-speaking 'returnees' that prioritizes their individual perspectives, but which at the same time accepts that these perspectives must be read within both the context of the wider social, economic, political and cultural environment and the surrounding global, national and regional migration regimes. In this study of migration and re-settlement in Russia, all these aspects are afforded equal attention. Understanding the historical specifics of the post-Soviet Russian context, within which the migration and resettlement process is taking place, is crucial to the study.

The migration process can be seen as the 'final stage' of a migration cycle, i.e. the 'return' back of the Russian populations from the 'empire' periphery to the central core.[5] This historical context is considered at both the Russian state and individual migrant level. In particular the study explores, and throws up further questions about, the experience of living in the 'borderlands' of the Soviet 'empire', and the effect this experience had upon the identities of the populations involved.

The insights that emerge at state, society and individual level, through the prism of the migration and resettlement process, also help to further our understandings of 'what is Russia' and 'how it works' in the contemporary period. The dual analysis of the micro-worlds of migrants and the wider macro-level structures of state, society, economy and polity provides room for representation of the alternative transformations that are taking place and being experienced at an individual/community level across the post-Soviet space.[6] The migration movement is occurring against a contemporary backdrop of mass social and economic upheaval and displacement – the experience of Russian migrants provides a stark representation of this reality. The arrival of the Russian migrant populations in different regions across the Russian Federation has presented a challenge to, amongst others, government policy makers and local communities, and has evoked a wide variety of responses. In addition, massive efforts of adaptation and survival have been demanded from those individuals who have experienced displacement. In particular, the everyday lives of migrants and the strategies they utilize reveal the central importance of kinship, friendship and wider migrant networks to the migration movement and resettlement process. The role of different levels of formal and informal networks for the migrants, and their interaction with and influence upon other structures within and beyond the regions of settlement, offer insights into the state/societal, public/private relations that exist in post-Soviet Russia, which may contribute a new dimension to frequently static and prescriptive debates over the nature of Russian 'civil society'.[7]

On a more conceptual but equally significant level, experiences of and responses to the migration movement inform discussions over the nature of Russian identity and Russian-ness in the post-Soviet period.[8] The Russian communities still resident in the other former republics of the Soviet Union have become a focus for state and non-state actors who, in the aftermath of 'empire' collapse, are contesting the boundaries and constitution of the contemporary Russian nation-state. The nature of both official and unofficial approaches towards the potential and actual migration of the Russian communities reveals the conflicting opinions that are present within Russia at both a political and a public level. At an individual level, migrants' own perceptions and experiences of the Russian 'homeland' contest the state and non-state frameworks through which they are positioned both prior to and upon 'return'. The hybrid and 'diasporic' identities of Russian migrants that emerge complicate the idea of their belonging to a bounded Russian 'homeland' and question the concept of any singular, homogenous ethno-national Russian identity in the post-Soviet period.

While exploring some of the specifics of post-Soviet Russia through the prism of migration, the book also provides an in-depth analysis of a contemporary migration movement and resettlement process. It does not suggest that due to the spatial or temporal (i.e. Russian/post-Soviet), context, the movement must be positioned or considered as 'unique'. Instead, the research aims to bring the relatively unexplored 'migration ' territory of Russia into wider migration theory and policy debates, at a time when, in a very real sense, it has become part of the wider European and global migration regimes. Due to the lack of Russian experience at both government and non-governmental level in dealing with mass (forced) migration flows, the book provides an account of precisely how migration regimes emerge, which informs thinking about responses to migration in other national and regional contexts. Through its theoretical and empirical approach, it attempts to reinforce existing efforts within the field of migration studies that aim to be both sensitive to and adequately represent the 'migrant perspective' to a greater extent than has been achieved before. Theories and concepts such as 'transnationalism' and 'diaspora' allow greater room to be given to migrant experience and identity; yet only through more empirically grounded study can the gap between theory and reality be bridged, and these often abstract concepts be more adequately utilized to represent the migrant voice.[9] This approach reflects calls in migration studies and in Russian studies, social anthropology and human geography, for the need to prioritize the individual and the 'everyday reality' in order to gain a more adequate understanding of the experience and nature of wider processes such as population displacement and regional economic, political, social and cultural 'transition' and upheaval.[10]

Two conceptual frameworks, that developed and emerged through the research, facilitate its broad aims and allow its thematic and geographical scope to be managed. These are a 'migration system' within which the interaction of 'agency' and 'structure' during migration and resettlement can be explored, and a 'home/land' framework which furthers understanding of what causes allegiances and attachments to place. These concepts helped to define, and were further shaped by, the empirical work that was conducted over the period 1997–2002.[11] The empirical study took place in three regions of the Russian Federation: Saratov and Samara *oblasti*, in the middle-Volga region, and Novosibirsk *oblast'*, in the Western Siberian region. Across the three regions, interviews were conducted with 72 migrant respondents in both urban and rural areas, and extensive field observations were carried out at different sites of migrant settlement. All but a handful of the respondents (who had been displaced upon the territory of the Russian Federation due to the conflict in Chechnia) had left the former republics – primarily Uzbekistan, Tajikistan, Kazakstan, as well as Azerbaijan, Georgia and Turkmenistan – between 1991 and 2001. Representatives of migrant organizations and official migration bodies at both a regional and federal level were also interviewed. The data collected from interviews and observation was used in combination with other secondary information and documentary materials (official legislation and policy documents, institutional documentation, newspaper articles), which were analysed over the period of research.

The original empirical data gathered are used throughout the text to both assess and critique existing theoretical and policy frameworks. The crucial interaction between data and theory in turn furthers understanding of the migration movement and resettlement process of the 'returning' Russians. It is particularly through the concept of 'home/land' that the book presents new understandings of the experience of migration and resettlement at the individual migrant level. The book reveals that the identification of the migration process taking place as either that of the forced migration or voluntary 'return' of an ethnic Russian 'diaspora' to its 'historical homeland', dominant in both state and non-state constructions of migration, can be challenged by an understanding of the process as one of the individual and collective migrant, displaced from a place they identified as 'home', and forced to renegotiate a relationship with what to many is a foreign territory rather than a welcoming 'homeland'.

The structure of the book reflects the theoretical and empirical aims of the study, and its organization attempts to further a holistic, yet complex, view of the migration process by moving between the different themes of analysis and locales of empirical focus. Chapter 1 introduces the focus of research. It firstly describes the migration movement of the ethnic Russian and Russian-speaking populations and locates these within the broader context of contemporary global and regional migration flows. It then introduces the two key conceptual frameworks – the migration system, and concepts of 'home' and 'homeland' – that shape the theoretical and empirical directions of the study. Through these frameworks, a number of key levels of empirical analysis are identified, which are focused upon in subsequent chapters: the global/international environment, state and non-state bodies, the regional context, the individual migrant and migrant networks. The conceptual frameworks, and their levels of analysis, point to the gap that exists between state constructions of the migration process and migrant experience and understandings of the same process.

Chapter 2 explores one of the key levels of empirical analysis identified in Chapter 1 – the Russian state and its response to the migration process and migrant resettlement. The chapter explores the three main state-led discourses that have developed since 1991 concerning the Russian communities resident in the former republics of the Soviet Union, and their 'return' to the Russian Federation. The exploration focuses in particular upon how Russia, as a 'homeland', is being constructed at the state level. To provide a context for the discussion of contemporary state response, the chapter details the historical migration of the Russian communities to the borderland regions during the periods of the Tsarist and Soviet empires. The chapter then concentrates on the three state-led discourses of diaspora, forced migration and repatriation. The discussion combines a more theoretical exploration of why such discourses have become prevalent, with specific references to institutional and legislative developments that have shaped the official migration regime in the Russian Federation. The chapter demonstrates how the Russian communities, while in diaspora and upon 'return', have become a crucial issue on the domestic political arena due to both internal socio-economic concerns and external foreign policy interests of the Russian state. The chapter thereby provides a comprehensive picture of the conflicting and ambiguous ideas of 'homeland' that are present within Russian state discourse and policy, which are challenged in later chapters through migrant narratives.

Chapter 3 shifts the level of analysis to that of the migrant and draws upon the empirical interview data gathered amongst migrant communities in the regions of Saratov, Samara and Novosibirsk over the period 1997–2002. An introduction to migrant understandings of 'home' and 'homeland' is provided through an exploration of the relationship of migrant respondents to their long-term place of residence – the former republic. Migrant narratives demonstrate how 'home' and 'homeland' often existed in tandem for the migrants in the former republics but reveals the subtle differences that differentiate understandings of the two concepts at this location. The chapter then explores how 'home' and 'homeland' were disrupted by the wider political and socio-economic upheaval that succeeded the collapse of the Soviet Union in 1991, and why, in the case of the individuals focused upon within the remit of the present study, this disruption led to the decision to migrate to the Russian Federation – the 'historical' homeland. The dichotomy of 'home' and 'homeland' that emerges provides a comparative framework within which the subsequent migrant experience of 'return' and resettlement is explored in subsequent chapters.

Chapter 4 brings together different interpretations and experiences of the migration and resettlement process at the site of settlement. It explores one aspect of the 'return' and resettlement experience of Russian migrants – their reception by and interaction with the Russian state. The chapter again draws upon the range of empirical data gathered in order to provide an in-depth picture of the operation of regional structures concerned with migration. Real-life migrant experiences of interaction with these structures are then traced to further develop this picture. A number of key spheres of the resettlement process that emerged during interviews with migrants – registration, employment and housing – are focused upon. The comparison of regional state practice and migrant experience reveals how 'confrontation' with state structures during resettlement may generate widespread disillusionment with – and frequent dissociation from – the Russian state amongst the migrant communities. This is shown to impact upon migrants' own understandings of Russia as a present and future 'homeland', and to influence their use of alternative strategies to facilitate the re-creation of 'home'.

Through analysis of the non-governmental migrant sector, Chapter 5 continues to challenge official frameworks and interpretations of the migration process that have started to emerge from migrant narratives; it concentrates upon the non-governmental migrant sector that has developed in the Russian Federation since 1991, and which has become crucial to the operation of the evolving Russian migration regime. Firstly it assesses the impact of international involvement upon the development of the official migration regime in the Russian Federation and upon other domestic non-governmental actors. Secondly, it explores the origins and growth of domestic non-governmental organizations in Moscow, and demonstrates how these actors have attempted to reshape dominant migration discourse and practice to provide Russian migrants with an alternative 'homeland' to that offered by the Russian state. The chapter then shifts the level of analysis to the regions and explores the development and activity of regional migrant associations in Saratov, Samara and Novosibirsk. These associations, which have emerged from within the migrant communities themselves, represent one strategy that returnees use to facilitate their resettlement. The relationship between the migrant organizations and other actors at the regional and federal level is explored, as are the ways in which these non-governmental actors have influenced government institutional and legislative structures, and how they attempt to reframe the 'space' of resettlement for the individual migrant.

Chapter 6 moves to a key level of analysis that emerges through the preceding chapters of the book – the importance of family, friendship and wider migrant networks for the individual migrant during the period of migration and resettlement. It demonstrates the centrality of immediate/primary and wider/secondary networks at all stages of the migration process – in the decision to move, the actual movement, and at the site of resettlement. An important component of this chapter is investigation as to how migrants 'outside of' the operating structures and remit of the migrant organizations relate to these bodies. These assessments are used to question the role of migrant associations and other wider migrant networks in the migration and resettlement process. The predominant migrant perspective demonstrates how returnees often choose to distance themselves from wider migrant networks, preferring to focus in the short term upon immediate circles of family and friends, which are found to best facilitate the process of resettlement and the re-creation of 'home'.

The concluding chapter reassesses the dominant discourses and central experiences of the migration process (return and resettlement) that run throughout the text of the book. The concept of the term 'homeland' to portray what Russia represents to the returning migrants is questioned again, by reiterating the alternative understandings of both 'homeland' and 'home' amongst the returnee communities. The conclusion re-addresses the discrepancy that is traced throughout the book – the gap that exists between the construction of the migration process, through political (and academic and media) discourse and policy making, and the perceptions and experience of the same migration process that emerge from migrants' narratives. Furthermore, it addresses the implications of this discrepancy. The experience and negotiation of the migration process by ethnic Russian and Russian-speaking migrants returning to the Russian Federation is found to contest interpretations of that same process by the Russian state. At the individual migrant level the priority of re-creating 'home' often engenders a withdrawal from the operation of the official migration regime, and the wider territory of 'homeland', to an immediate and supportive locale made up of close family and friendship networks. The debate is broadened out to assess the future implications of Russian state practice towards both the Russian communities who are still 'in diaspora' and those who have 'returned'. The question of whether the migrant communities will be employed in future 'theoretical' constructions of a Russian 'homeland', or whether their energies and resources will be engaged in a constructive way for post-Soviet Russian society, is assessed in the light of current developments in Russian government discourse and practice.

1
Understanding Migration in Post-Soviet Russia

This chapter introduces the research space and research focus, and the main theoretical approaches, which run throughout the course of the book. Firstly, the process of migration (the 'return' movement and resettlement) of ethnic Russian and Russian-speaking migrants from the former republics of the Soviet Union to the territory of the Russian Federation since 1991 is located within the context of contemporary global and regional migration processes, and the precise migration movements which are occurring into, within and out of the Russian Federation. Secondly, the chapter describes the conceptual frameworks – the migration system, and the 'home/land'[1] dichotomy – that shape the theoretical and empirical boundaries of the study. This enables a number of key levels of empirical analysis which are pertinent to the migration process in question to be identified: the global/international environment, the Russian state, the regional context, migrant networks and the individual migrant. The identification of these frameworks and levels of analysis reveals a key theme that is explored through the book – the discrepancy that can exist between state (and other 'official') constructions of the migration process and of the 'homeland', and actual migrant experience and understandings of the same process, and their priorities for the re-creation of 'home'. Finally, the empirical project that enabled the interrogation of (and further shaped) the conceptual frameworks and theoretical parameters of the study is described.

THE GLOBAL MIGRATION CONTEXT

The last decade of the twentieth century witnessed great political, economic and social upheaval and change, which had significant implications for contemporary

migration movements.[2] The changes in the character of migration flows have
led to the application of the term a 'new migration'[3], and for the period of the
late twentieth century and beginning of the twenty-first century to be labelled
by some as an 'age of migration'.[4] A number of characteristics of contemporary
migration are used to justify the application of the term 'new'. To a greater extent
than any other period, all areas of the globe have been drawn into both global
and regional patterns of migration. Since 1989, Europe has witnessed its most
intense migration movements since the Second World War, and such movements are increasing in volume in all major regions of the world. Individual
countries are affected by a greater range of migrants of different origins and
backgrounds than in previous periods. There has been an increase in the numbers of refugees and asylum seekers[5] and, with the shift to a post-industrial
global economy, new 'types' of migrants have emerged. These include highly
skilled, elite labour migrants, together with increased numbers employed in the
private service industries and domestic services. This latter trend has led to the
'feminization' of migration.[6] In response to contemporary migratory flows,
there has been a growing politicization of the issue, and a corresponding securitization and institutionalization of migration at the domestic and international
levels. Improvements in transportation and communication have meant that
migrants are increasingly able to sustain simultaneous, multi-stranded, transnational relationships that link societies. Multiple attachments to different lo-
calities have allowed the development of new and complex 'diasporic' identities
amongst migrant communities.[7]

THE FORMER SOVIET UNION: A NEW GLOBAL MIGRATION SPACE

Population movements across the former Soviet Union

One of the 'new' spaces of migration within the complex and changing global
migration environment is the territory of the former Soviet Union (FSU).[8] The
opening up of borders between east and west, and the relaxation of restrictions
on movement, meant that a previously isolated area was included within a wider
global migration system and became caught up in both regional and global migratory flows.[9] The emergence of fifteen independent states in 1991 transformed
the volume, direction and nature of previously internal population movement
into significant international migration flows. Millions of former Soviet citizens migrated within, between and out of the former republics of the Soviet
Union during the last decade of the twentieth century. The diverse reasons for
the migrations taking place include ethnic conflict and discrimination, severe

socio-economic and political collapse and environmental disaster. Central to understanding the complexity of the movements is the specific environment of political, social and economic change in which they are located, where processes of 'decolonization' and nation building are taking place concurrently. Many of the migration movements are motivated by the influences of nationalism and ethnic sentiments, which have brought about a return of groups of repatriates to their respective 'homelands' and the rehabilitation of formerly deported peoples.[10] The role played by issues of nationalism and ethnicity in influencing the migration movements means that they become inextricably related to wider issues of identity, citizenship and belonging for the individual and wider definitions of territory and nation for the state.[11]

Another result of the collapse of the Soviet Union and the opening up of its external borders has been the arrival in the territory of the Commonwealth of Independent States (CIS) and Baltic states of individuals from the 'far abroad'[12]; these include refugees in search of asylum or economic migrants seeking employment. The intended final destination of many of these migrants is the west; however, restrictive policies of western governments has meant that they frequently find themselves trapped on the territory of the FSU. The consequent challenge for all the former Soviet republics on an institutional and policy level has been immense. None of the present governments had any experience of dealing with the problems of mass migration, specifically the complex nature of the migration movements in question. Institutional and legislative structures have rapidly been created to manage the migration flows that are under way. Nevertheless, in most states these are still in an evolving form.[13]

The migratory processes on the territory of the former Soviet Union have also provided a policy challenge for the international community. As noted by Held *et al.*, within the global migration system there exists a 'hierarchy' of power between nation states where national governments possess varying capacities to control population movements, to maintain the integrity of their borders and to shape the structure of international migratory regimes.[14] At the present time, the west is dominant in this hierarchy. From 1989 the potential for a mass migration of people from the territory of the former Soviet bloc generated great concern at the international and particularly European level.[15] Although the west had called for the liberalization of emigration from the Soviet Union during the 1970s and 1980s, following the breakdown of borders between east and west from 1989 the west perceived the potential migration as a threat and used this to legitimate the policies of an increasingly 'Fortress Europe'.[16] Where previously migrants who arrived from the FSU had been unconditionally accepted as political refugees, now they were treated as ordinary, voluntary/economic immigrants and, as such, they faced increasingly severe entry restrictions. In many ways, movement between east and west was as restricted as it had been prior to 1989.[17]

The fear of a mass migration has not been realized. Just over two million individuals left the territory of the FSU for the far abroad during the period 1989–95, which was less than 1 per cent of the 1989 population.[18] Most of these were ethnic migrants moving to Israel, Germany and Greece.[19] Western government policy may have discouraged migration, but equally it has failed to move beyond the idea that the economically 'superior' conditions in the west are sufficient to generate mass migration, and ignores other essential factors influential in determining movement such as individual motivation, psychological readiness, adequate infrastructure and family and friendship networks in the destination country.[20] As Codagnone suggests, we must therorize not only why people move but also why people stay, despite the existence of strong socio-economic push and pull factors. Of significance to the present study is a need to understand why migrants choose to move within the territory of the FSU, i.e. from another former Soviet republic to Russia, rather than consider a possibly beneficial socio-economic move to the west.[21]

Migration flows to, and within, the Russian Federation

Individual regions within the territory of the FSU have experienced varying types and levels of migration. The Russian Federation is the successor state perhaps most affected by the population movements engendered by the social, economic and political changes of the 'transition' period, both in terms of migration into the territory from the 'near' and 'far' abroad, and by internal migration within its borders. The country is experiencing the arrival from the former Soviet republics of ethnic Russian and Russian-speaking 'returnees', other 're-turnees' belonging to ethnic groups of the Russian Federation, refugees and forced migrants, formerly deported peoples and economic migrants.[22] Amongst the arrivees are immigrants of former Soviet nationalities coming from their respective home countries, primarily Ukrainian, Armenian, Belorusian, Azeri, Georgian and Tajik. During the period 1989–96, 1 million of these immigrants arrived in the Russian Federation as a result of the push and pull of socio-economic factors and, in the case of Armenia, Azerbaijan, Georgia and Tajikistan, due to ethnic and civil conflict that forced the titular nationalities to leave.[23] In addition, the country is facing large-scale internal migration and displacement as a result of the Chechen conflict[24], and due to socio-economic out-migration from the North, Eastern Siberia and the Far East.[25]

As for the whole of the territory of the FSU, migration from the far abroad has increased. It is made up of refugees and undocumented migrants from Asia,

Africa and the Middle East – many of whom are using the Russian Federation as a transit region to reach Western Europe – and permanent and temporary economic migrants arriving primarily from China and Vietnam.[26] As Russia has become part of the global migration system, and a major 'receiving' territory, fears have increased about the 'threat' of 'illegal' migration. Particularly in recent years, the phenomenon of 'illegal' migration, and its related 'negative' consequences, is frequently spoken about both by government representatives and widely in the Russian press.[27] Estimates of the numbers of 'illegal' migrants vary widely, from 1.5 million up to 15 million.[28] Reflecting tendencies for the wider territory of the FSU, migration flows out of the Russian Federation consist largely of Greek, Jewish and German repatriates returning to their 'historical' homelands. Between 1990 and 1996, 86.3 per cent of emigrants from the Russian Federation went to Israel, Germany and Greece.[29] Over the period 1997–2001, this figure decreased to 64.6 per cent.[30] This shows an overall continuation in the dominant trend in emigration during the late Soviet period. From 1976 to 1990 nine out of ten emigrants were Jewish or German.[31]

The 'return' of the ethnic Russian and Russian-speaking populations of the successor states of the former Soviet Union

A population greatly affected by the upheaval and change in the FSU over the last decade has been the community of ethnic Russians who found themselves in the newly independent states following the collapse of the Soviet Union in 1991. According to the last Soviet census conducted in 1989, there were 25.3 million ethnic Russians living in Soviet republics other than the Russian Federation (see Table 1.1). In addition there were 11 million Russian-speaking (*russkoiazichnii*) members of the non-titular nationalities in the FSU whose primary cultural affinity is to Russia.[32]

The movement of Russians within the territory of the Russian and later Soviet 'empires' has dominated the nature and direction of migration flows since the sixteenth century.[33] However, it was during the Soviet period that the greatest number of Russians and other Slavic nationalities, involved in the drive for agricultural and industrial development, migrated out to the former republics of the Soviet Union (see Tables 1.2 and 1.3).[34] This movement peaked in the 1960s when the number of Russians in the republics as a whole grew by almost one third.[35] Yet, although the share of the Russian population in the eight southern republics of the FSU reached its optimum point in 1959, in the six European republics this only occurred in 1989.[36] The 'return' movement began at different times depending upon the republic in question: the number of Russians in Georgia and Azerbaijan started to decrease in the early 1960s and 1970s, in

TABLE 1.1 Russians in the other Soviet Republics, 1989

Republic	Total	As percentage of total number of Russians in republics of the FSU	As percentage of Republic's total population
Baltics			
Estonia	475,000	1.9	30.3
Latvia	906,000	3.5	34.0
Lithuania	344,000	1.4	9.4
Western			
Belarus	1,342,000	5.3	13.2
Moldova	562,000	2.2	13.0
Ukraine	11,356,000	44.9	22.1
Caucasus			
Armenia	52,000	0.2	1.6
Azerbaijan	392,000	1.6	5.6
Georgia	341,000	1.3	6.3
Central Asia			
Kazakstan	6,228,000	24.6	37.8
Kyrgyzstan	917,000	3.6	21.5
Tajikistan	388,000	1.5	7.6
Turkmenistan	334,000	1.3	9.5
Uzbekistan	1,653,000	6.6	8.3
Total	25,289,000		

Source: *Goskomstat SSSR* 1991, pp. 34–47 cited in Codagnone 1998a, p. 14.

Kazakstan at the beginning of the 1970s, while in the Central Asian republics a significant 'return' of Russians only occurred from the late 1970s.[37] The Baltic republics and Ukraine, however, continued to receive the immigration of Russians until the late 1980s.[38] Prior to 1989, processes of modernization in the former Soviet republics were seen as the primary cause of the return movements. The development of the education and training of members of the titular nationality increasingly brought competition for urban residence and employment opportunities in professional, management and skilled labour sectors.[39]

From the late 1980s and early 1990s the process of 'return' accelerated rapidly. Initially this was due to ethnic Russians and Russo-phones fleeing from former republics where there was civil war and ethnic conflict. Significant flows of Russian refugees occurred as a result of outbreaks of violence in Nagorno-Karabakh (Azerbaijan) and the Ferghana valley (Uzbekistan) in the late 1980s, in Baku (Azerbaijan) in 1990, and later conflicts in Georgia, Moldova, Tajikistan and the North Caucasus.[40] By 1994 the main regions of departure had shifted to Central Asia and Kazakstan, the movements being caused by the interplay of socio-economic and ethno-political factors.[41] By 2001 the highest levels of

TABLE 1.2 Soviet inter-republican net migration, 1961–89

Republic	1961–70	1971–80	1981–8	1989
Russia	−1,114,000	+673,000	+1,526,000	+79,000
Belarus	−160,000	−84,000	+3,000	+9,000
Ukraine	+530,000	+199,000	+132,000	+45,000
Moldova	+68,000	−58,000	−26,000	−21,000
Estonia	+93,000	+60,000	+43,000	+4,000
Latvia	+144,000	+104,000	+81,000	0
Lithuania	+49,000	+68,000	+85,000	+15,000
Azerbaijan	−69,000	−96,000	−217,000	−36,000
Georgia	−94,000	−162,000	−25,000	−37,000
Armenia	+144,000	+85,000	−289,000	−44,000
Kazakstan	+414,000	−562,000	−676,000	−24,000
Kyrgyzstan	+130,000	−99,000	−116,000	−24,000
Tajikistan	+120,000	+3,000	−77,000	−41,000
Turkmenistan	+10,000	−9,000	−70,000	+15,000
Uzbekistan	+414,000	+150,000	−465,000	−126,000

Source: Arutiunian 1992, p. 35; Subbotina 1992, p. 84 cited in Codagnone 1998a, p. 13.

TABLE 1.3 Percentage of Russians in the total population of the Soviet Republics 1926–89

Republics	1926	1939	1959	1970	1979	1989
Baltics						
Estonia	–	–	20.1	24.7	27.9	30.3
Latvia	–	–	26.6	29.8	32.8	34.0
Lithuania	–	–	8.5	8.6	8.9	9.4
Western						
Belarus	7.7	6.5	8.2	10.4	11.9	13.2
Moldova	8.5	10.2	10.1	11.6	12.8	13.0
Ukraine	9.2	12.9	16.9	19.4	21.1	22.1
The Caucasus						
Armenia	2.2	4.0	3.2	2.7	2.3	1.6
Azerbaijan	9.5	16.5	13.6	10.0	7.9	5.6
Georgia	3.6	8.7	10.1	8.5	7.4	6.3
Central Asia						
Kazakstan	19.7	40.3	42.7	42.4	40.8	37.8
Kyrgyzstan	11.7	20.8	30.2	29.2	25.9	21.5
Tajikistan	0.7	9.1	13.3	11.9	10.4	7.6
Turkmenistan	8.2	18.6	17.3	14.5	12.6	9.5
Uzbekistan	25.4	11.5	13.5	12.5	10.8	8.4

Source: *Goskomstat* SSSR 1972, 1981, 1991 and Kozlov 1982, pp. 80–83 cited in Codagnone 1998a, p. 12.

out-migration were to be found from Kazakstan, Uzbekistan and Tajikistan.[42] Out-migration of Russians from the Baltic States, Ukraine and Belarus in the 1990s for the first time replaced the in-migration of Russians that had been characteristic of the population exchange up to the end of the 1980s.[43]

The official registration of returnees from the former Soviet republics by the Federal Migration Service of the Russian Federation[44] began in July 1992; by 1 January 2002, 1,576,100 ethnic Russian and Russian-speaking forced migrants and refugees had been registered in the Federation (see Table 1.4).[45] The peak of in-migration was reached between 1993 and 1995; thereafter there has been a slow decline in numbers. However, these figures do not account for the total migration occurring between the former republics of the Soviet Union and the Russian Federation due to the high incidence of non-registration with the branches of the Federal Migration Service, and overall inconsistencies and ambiguities in the collection of data on migrants and refugees.[46] It is estimated that the actual number of returnees from the CIS states to date may be as high as 8–10 million (see Table 1.5).[47]

EXPLORING THE MIGRATION PROCESS – LOCATING A THEORETICAL AND EMPIRICAL CONTEXT

The migration of the ethnic Russian and Russian-speaking populations from the former republics of the Soviet Union to the territory of the Russian Federation provides a challenge to existing migration theories and their capacity to adequately conceptualize the character of migration flows, the nature of 'return' movements and resettlement processes, and the 'reality' of migrant experience. Furthermore, examination of the nature of, and response to, the migration movement informs debates concerning the constitution of the present-day Russian nation and Russian national identity. In-depth study of the process, at both the state and individual level, allows further complication of definitions of Russia and proves relevant to the contested question of the nature of 'Russia' and 'Russian-ness' in the contemporary period.[48] In order to negotiate the complexities of the theoretical and empirical field, two broad and interrelated conceptual frameworks are utilized: a migration system, within which the migration process (the movement and resettlement) takes place, and a 'home/land' dichotomy through which the migration process can be better understood.

The migration system

The migration system framework, which draws on Giddens' theory of structuration[49], attempts to further the resolution of 'structure' and 'agency' that has

TABLE 1.4 Annual registration of 'forced migrants' and 'refugees' by Country of Origin 1992–2001

Country	1992	1993	1994	1995	1996	1997	1998	1999	2000	2001
Belarus	–	17	108	188	119	45	4	0	0	0
Moldova	10,341	4,323	2,682	2,688	2,476	1,394	792	540	509	540
Ukraine	19	262	1,904	2,262	2,838	2,182	1,086	541	392	328
Central Asia/	69,929	115,153	182,223	197,226	122,484	99,132	94,129	59,539	43,159	33,323
Kazakstan	283	7,665	63,533	88,689	61,836	64,079	71,953	42,427	29,026	22,054
Kyrgyzstan	897	20,074	32,588	17,769	9,040	4,331	2,148	1,334	1,115	1,307
Tajikistan	65,448	68,598	24,320	26,982	20,796	12,903	7,431	4,326	3,387	1,794
Turkmenistan	54	450	2,208	4,574	6,867	4,560	1,168	525	279	216
Uzbekistan	3,247	18,366	59,574	59,212	23,945	13,259	11,423	10,927	9,352	7,952
The Caucasus	57,803	112,406	34,584	25,394	16,930	8,279	6,119	3,348	4,974	3,042
Armenia	126	1,864	3,382	1,653	755	361	124	168	58	36
Azerbaijan	32,860	44,479	13,751	12,963	9,300	4,682	2,056	1,173	619	238
Georgia	24,817	66,063	17,451	10,778	6,875	3,236	3,939	2,007	4,297	2,768
The Baltic States	189	5,716	9,903	9,317	7,380	4,591	1,590	685	255	141
Estonia	60	1,090	2,784	3,171	3,084	2,115	819	321	127	56
Latvia	85	4,160	5,929	5,427	3,856	2,198	603	296	106	51
Lithuania	44	466	1,190	719	440	278	168	68	22	34
Russian Federation	21,826	48,125	23,040	34,871	20,680	15,371	13,924	14,061	9,712	4,440
Area not indicated	234	690	74	31	19	73	79	31	195	144
Total	160,341	287,592	254,518	271,977	172,926	131,130	117,717	78,745	59,196	41,958

Source: *Goskomstat* 1998 cited in Vitkovskaia 1998a, p. 18, *Goskomstat* 2000, p. 113, *Goskomstat* 2002a, p. 128.

* It should be noted that only in 1998 did *Goskomstat* publish data that distinguished between refugees and forced migrants. Russian returnees would make up the large part of the figures shown, however, it is for the years 1998 onwards that figures for forced migrants only are shown. The problems associated with registration figures for forced migrants and refugees are discussed in Appendix 1.

TABLE 1.5 Total annual migration inflows to the Russian Federation from the CIS and Baltic States, 1992–2001

Country	1992	1993	1994	1995	1996	1997	1998	1999	2000	2001
Belarus	36,212	34,670	43,383	35,337	23,903	17,575	13,760	11,549	10,274	6,520
Moldova	32,340	19,344	21,364	18,715	17,847	13,750	10,762	9,037	11,652	7,569
Ukraine	199,355	189,409	247,351	188,443	170,928	138,231	111,934	81,297	74,748	36,503
Central Asia/Kazakstan	450,821	465,401	625,468	442,468	297,064	328,829	291,582	210,620	199,030	87,110
Kazakstan	183,891	195,672	346,363	241,427	172,860	235,903	209,880	138,521	124,903	65,226
Kyrgyzstan	62,897	96,814	66,489	27,801	18,886	13,752	10,997	10,370	15,536	10,740
Tajikistan	72,556	68,761	45,645	41,799	32,508	23,053	18,396	12,116	11,043	6,742
Turkmenistan	19,035	12,990	20,186	19,129	22,840	16,501	10,509	7,998	6,738	4,402
Uzbekistan	112,442	91,164	146,670	112,312	49,970	39,620	41,800	41,615	40,810	24,873
The Caucasus	139,940	154,424	162,822	128,966	104,280	73,518	60,049	50,205	51,070	21,075
Armenia	15,750	29,806	46,480	34,112	25,419	19,123	16,780	14,677	15,951	5,814
Azerbaijan	69,943	54,684	49,495	43,442	40,310	29,878	22,210	15,902	14,906	5,587
Georgia	54,247	69,934	66,847	51,412	38,551	24,517	21,059	19,626	20,213	9,674
The Baltic States	67,065	126,703	56,076	27,576	17,151	10,926	6,732	3,947	3,516	2,576
Estonia	24,440	14,340	11,250	8,591	5,869	3,483	1,771	852	786	535
Latvia	27,271	25,891	26,370	14,859	8,227	5,658	3,577	2,108	1,785	1,283
Lithuania	15,354	19,407	8,456	4,126	3,055	1,785	1,384	987	945	758
Total	925,733	922,886	1,146,349	841,505	631,173	582,829	494,819	366,655	350,290	186,226

Source: Goskomstat 1998 cited in Vitkovskaia 1998a, p. 19, *Goskomstat* 2000, p. 52, *Gosomstat* 2002b, p. 335.

* Vitkovskaia notes that these figures are likely to be incomplete due to the gradual dismantling of control over the movement of people, specifically the 'abolition' of the *propiska*, and the porous borders and lack of control over migration.

been addressed in both general migration literature[50] and with specific reference to the migration processes and developments of migration regimes in the former Soviet Union and post-Soviet Russia.[51] The system encompasses the migration flows made up of individual migrant and migrant networks and other institutions, political and non-political, of the surrounding migration regime (see Figure 1.1).[52] To understand the process and perpetuation of migration, the system is seen as a fluid framework, stretching between the regions of departure and site of settlement, which is under formation due to the interactive relationship of 'agency' and 'structure'. Key levels or locales of analysis – individual, household, network, the host society, state, the global environment – can be identified, allowing the production and transformation of the migration system to be explored.

Due to the attention to both human agency and structural determinants, the migration system approach enables the diversity of causation of migration to be considered.[53] Equally the approach allows the nature of relationships between individual migrants, other key actors, and the structural and institutional specifics of the wider national and global migration system, to be understood. Yet despite attention to this interaction, the consideration given to the properties of the migration system, specifically the institutional structures of the migration regimes and the way in which they impact *upon* and constrain the individual agent, acknowledges the 'analytical distinctiveness' of 'structure' and 'agency'.[54] Such an approach therefore avoids any latent tendency within structuration theory to collapse, rather than explore, the distinguishing characteristics of 'structure' and 'agency'. Furthermore, the identification of intermediary 'social phenomena' – migrant organizations, migrant networks, migrant households – and a detailed exploration of their activity, provides a way of illustrating just how 'structure' and 'agency' act upon each other. Again, this does not imply fusion. Indeed the present empirical study reveals a relative 'independence' of the 'agent' (migrant) as he/she withdraws from the structures of the surrounding migration regime.

The space of migration
The migration system stretches between the region of departure and that of settlement, both temporally and spatially, which in the present study is particularly pertinent. The regions of departure and those of settlement are connected via historical, political, social, economic and cultural links, which are presently undergoing transformation.[55] As states renegotiate their own national identities, inter-state level relationships are being reformulated. Equally, at the individual level physical and emotional attachments to the former republic are being renegotiated and reimagined in the adjacent 'ethnic' homeland, a process that is

**THE MIGRATION
SYSTEM**

**POLITICAL
FORCES**

**ECONOMIC
FORCES**

**THE CONTESTATION
AND EXPERIENCE OF
'RETURN' AND
RESETTLEMENT**

INDIVIDUAL MIGRANTS	POLITICAL AGENCIES
THE MIGRATION FLOWS	**THE MIGRATION REGIME**
MIGRANT NETWORKS	NON-POLITICAL AGENCIES

THE MIGRATION PROCESS

**THE SITE OF
DEPARTURE**

**THE SITE OF
SETTLEMENT**

**SOCIAL
FORCES**

**CULTURAL
FORCES**

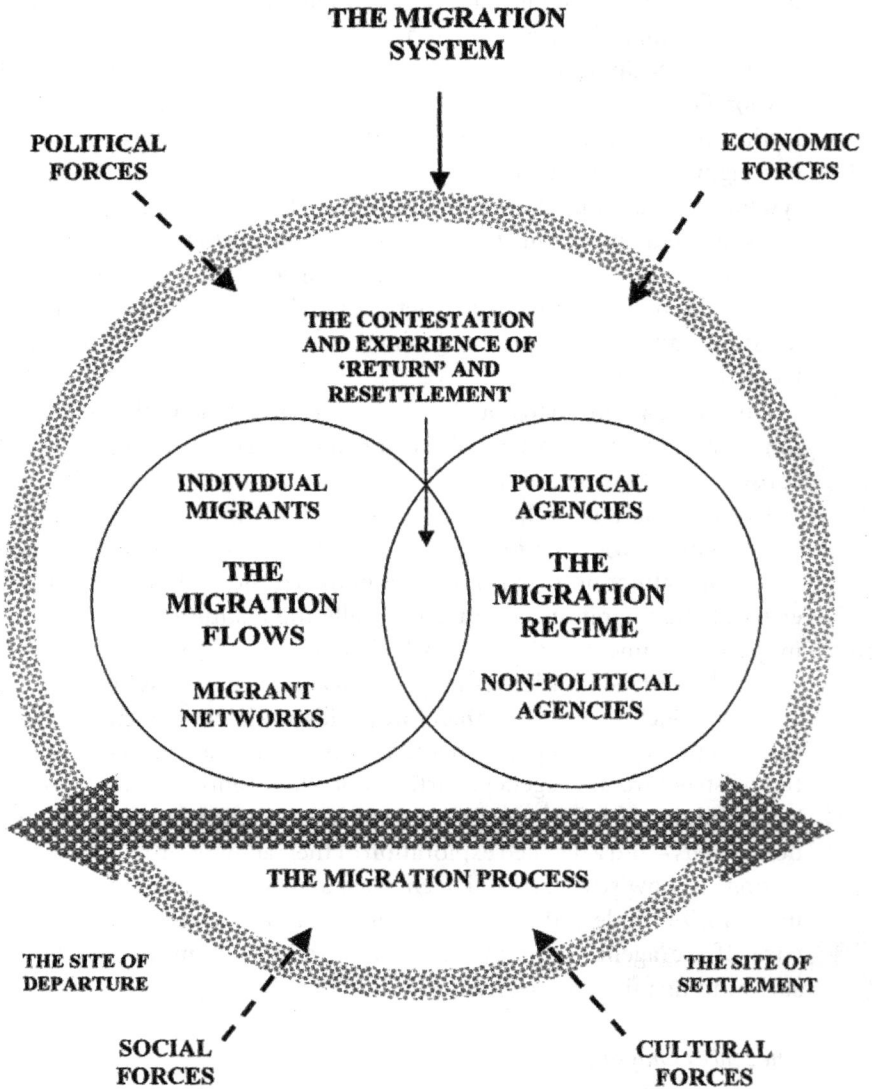

FIGURE 1.1 The migration system framework

often facilitated by personal (family or friendship) connections. However, the existence of past physical and emotional ties in the former 'homeland' can problematize the migrants' connection, for example via ethnicity, to the Russian 'homeland'. The relevance of these emerging personal 'transnational' spaces and connections is explored in more detail below.

Attention to the temporal roots of the migration movement, i.e. seeing the movement as the 'final stage' of a migration cycle – the 'return' of the Russian populations from the 'empire' periphery to the central core – helps to contextualize the present-day response to the new Russian 'diaspora' and the possibility of their 'return'. Such a view provides a means of tracing the historical connections between the Russian state and the Russian communities in the Soviet successor states, and of understanding the centrality of the communities to present-day attempts by both political and non-political forces to redefine the nature of the Russian nation. Both within academic theory and political commentary, the movement of Russians back to the Russian Federation is often identified as a continuation of a repatriation or decolonization movement that had already begun from the late 1960s.[56] However, it is acknowledged that the political, social and economic environment in which the migration is taking place has radically changed to cause an intensification and acceleration of the process of 'repatriation'.[57] The distinction is therefore clearly made between the prior voluntary and predominantly socio-economic nature of the movement prior to the breakup of the Soviet Union, and the more 'forced' and ethnically rooted nature of the migration processes currently under way.[58] This interpretation places the migration movements of Russians within a wider structural relationship of colonialism that existed between Russia and the former Soviet republics during the Tsarist and Soviet periods and which initially impelled out-migration to the periphery of the 'empire'. With 'decolonization' the migration flows have reversed, producing the 'return' of the Russian populations.

The historically rooted nature of the out-migration of the Russian communities, the multi-levelled connections that have bound them to the Russian state, and their subsequent importance within contemporary Russian society, are important at the levels of both the Russian state and the individual migrant. Yet, attention focused at the individual level enables a move away from the tendency for both the Russian communities 'in diaspora', and those communities who 'return', to be treated *primarily* within (political, academic and media) frameworks that prioritize issues of repatriation and decolonization. Equally, analysis at the individual level problematizes frameworks which prioritize Russian national and ethnic identity, the political significance of the Russian 'diaspora', and its centrality to the development of the wider Russian nation.[59] At the individual level, the environment of 'decolonization' and economic and political transformation within which the migration movement is taking place cannot, and should not, be ignored. Yet migrants are moving between and within wider structural forces at a very personal level. The movement and resettlement of migrants reveals the practical process of re-creating 'home' within the socio-economic and political realities of post-Soviet Russia that is not adequately conceptualized using, for example, the framework of an ethnic repatriation to an 'historical homeland'. The dichotomy of 'home/land' that emerges must be interweaved with any analysis of the wider structural environment of the migration process.

The migration flows: origins and causes
Understanding the position of the potential migrant at the site of departure, and the reasons for migration, is central to any comprehension of the whole migration process and informs analysis at the site of resettlement. The migration is a journey, in which the circumstances of leaving and those of arrival and settling down are equally important. Consideration is needed for the intersection of the different stages of the journey on both a temporal and spatial level.[60] However determining cause, and the position of the individual at the site of departure, must be approached in a fluid manner. Evidence of the complex interaction of ethno-political with socio-economic concerns and fears that lead to the decision by the Russian returnees to move,[61] reflects observations which have been made of the situation in the present global migration environment where the constant interplay of political and economic causal factors can be observed.[62] The combination of causes that has encouraged the migration of the 'returning' Russians impedes any neat typology of the returnee population. The problems of distinguishing between migrant 'types' increase in the post-Soviet context due to the coincidence of widespread socio-economic crisis, the outbreak of ethnic and civil wars, and the simultaneous processes of empire breakup and the birth of 'new nationalizing states' in which national minorities find themselves disadvantaged. Thus, a strict categorization of Russian returnees as 'repatriates', 'forced migrants' or 'economic migrants', which are the typologies often suggested, is problematic.[63]

This complexity reinforces the need for a move away from the forced/voluntary dichotomy long held in academic debate and policy-making; a move that is occurring in recent studies of migration that interrogate the conceptual bases upon which the division continues to be made. Koser suggests it may not be accurate to distinguish between political and economic migrants because of the need to recognize that nearly all migrants move for mixed motivations, including social reasons.[64] Economic forces and motivations may be the immediate reason for displacement, but the root causes may be political factors shaping the migration process.[65] Prior research of the Russian case has questioned the possibility of strictly defining the movement as either 'forced' or 'voluntary'.[66] Attention to different levels of analysis within the migration system – the individual, the group, the state, wider environment – allows the false dichotomy of voluntary and involuntary migration to be further broken down, and points to the discrepancy that exists between policy labelling and migrant reality.

An exploration of the intertwining of ethnic and socio-economic motivations is needed directly at the individual level.[67] Within the newly independent states the introduction of government policies concerning the official state language and citizenship rights initiated a process of the institutionalization of ethnic dominance of the titular nationalities over the new minority groups. The response to these official policies at the individual level, and their immediate translation into concrete concerns about future employment, social and political status, education and the futures of children, inform the migration decision-making process. The movement is inspired by individual consideration of the 'push' factors rooted in both ethnic discomfort and socio-economic concerns, and the relative 'pull' factors rooted in 'ethnic' affinity and socio-economic prospects. The ethnic affinity is heightened by the experienced ethnic discomfort, and the movement may be undertaken as much to avoid downward mobility as for increased opportunity.[68] Migration cannot be an assumed outcome, however. The individual consideration of the political, socio-economic, cultural and psychological advantages and disadvantages of movement may result in a decision to stay, as evidenced by the relatively small outflow of Russians from the Baltic Republics despite the existence of anti-Russian sentiment and language and citizenship legislation.[69]

The site of resettlement and the migration regime
The exploration of the ethnic and socio-economic motivations for migration is valuable when considering the nature of 'return' and the expectations that are held upon 'return'; it also demonstrates how 'push' factors in the place of residence interact with 'pull' factors in the Russian Federation. Yet personal motivations and the presence of push and pull factors do not sufficiently explain the 'process' of migration – the continuation and perpetuation of migration beyond the site of departure to that of resettlement. The movement of people does not occur in a vacuum but within the system, through which it is organized and coordinated across time and space.[70] Specific institutions and networks develop within the system, which encompass both the region of departure and the site of resettlement. These institutions and networks may be formal (state) or informal (migrant), and their presence may enable or restrict the possibility for initial migration to take place. A key level of analysis is the formal process of

institutionalization that has occurred in reaction to the migration flows in question, which has resulted in the formation of a 'migration regime'.[71] The wider migration regime is a multi-layered structure made up of political and non-political agencies at the local, national, transnational and international level. The creation of institutions to 'manage' the migration, and accompanying discursive and legislative frameworks – particularly at the domestic (national and regional) level – plays a central part in defining the nature of the migration that is taking place, in shaping responses to the migration and in defining the 'space of settlement'.[72]

Within the migration regime, policy decisions are made by institutions, e.g. national governments, based upon assumptions stemming from the interpretation of the migration flow and the perceived implications of movement or lack of movement.[73] Nagel suggests that in western countries the treatment of immigrants reflects two contradictory impulses of the modern political economy: (i) the need for labour and (ii) the need and ability of the nation-state to police boundaries, to maintain sovereignty over national territory, and to define and restrict membership to the national society through citizenship and other legal categories.[74] These contradictory 'needs' of the nation-state are relevant to the Russian case and the emerging migration regime. As will be shown in Chapter 2, the response of the Russian government to the return of the Russian communities has been partly determined by political and strategic desires to redefine a relationship between the Russian state and 'diaspora' communities; yet equally significant have been economic concerns about the capability of state resources to provide for a large influx of migrants, fears for domestic political and economic stability and, latterly, hopes that in-migration might solve the national demographic 'crisis'. The development of policies to migrant return is further complicated at the regional level by socio-economic and political factors of concern to local authorities, that may succeed in shaping a regional migration policy in conflict with both federal directives and migrants' needs (see Chapter 4). Migration and the wider geopolitical and (national/regional) domestic concerns of the state must be seen as a single rather than separate topic of study. Interrogation of this relationship is central to understanding the process by which the migration movement, and the space of settlement that the migrant confronts, is constructed.

The development of migration legislation and policy is one mechanism through which national and regional governments can influence and control migration flows. A further mechanism is the control and provision of information to potential and arriving migrants. The channels of information that extend between the constituent parts of a migration system are key to its development, and to the operation of the migration regime. In his analysis of the role of information in shaping 'repatriation' processes, Koser shows how the transfer of information is one medium of connection between the individual migrant and the wider structural environment, is key to individual decision-making, and is important in subsequent stages of the migration process.[75] The source and type of information is a vital factor. If there is a possibility of concrete assistance then migration may be encouraged, however, if knowledge of restrictive or limited policies is gained, then migration may be deterred. A 'mediator' supplies the information. Amongst possible mediators are the home government, another institutional body or the media; each of these agents has the power to distort the information which the potential returnee receives, depending on their own motivations and interests in the possibility of large-scale migration. Since the transfer and availability of information is a major component in the way the return movement and resettlement process is framed and experienced, the individual needs to be aware of distortions and gaps in the information. There is also the possibility of personal information channels opening up as bridges are developed between those individuals who have already migrated and potential returnees. The present study explores how the presence and absence of information from both official and non-official sources at the site of departure and arrival impacts upon the process of migration and resettlement.

The Russian migration regime must also be placed within the context of wider European and global migration regimes.[76] The inclusion of Russia within the global system ensures that actions at the Russian state level are mediated by other connections that transcend state borders, such as required adherence to international agreements and conventions. Equally, within the domestic migration regime, international and domestic non-governmental organizations are operating; these agencies are able to establish relationships and networks with both their target population and other non-governmental actors, which may bypass the regional or national government.[77] The attitude of western governments to the migration situation on the territory of the Russian Federation, and the way western powers perceive Russian territory in migration terms, is also significant. Since 1991, initial enthusiasm to invest in the migration space of the FSU, and facilitate institutional and legislative development across the territory, seems to have waned in the face of national self-interest and fluctuating political significance, especially as the awaited outflow of migrants from the territory did not occur. Changing external perceptions of, and responses to, the Russian 'migration space' impact upon both the internal nature of this space and the development of the national level migration regime.[78]

The individual and collective migrant
Integral to understanding the wider migration system and the nature of the

migration regime is an analysis of the discrepancy – and in some cases conflict – between official definitions of the migration movement and constructions of the space of settlement, and migrant understandings of the migration movement, migrant needs and priorities, and migrant perceptions of the space of settlement. Migrant response to displacement and contribution to resettlement is an area often neglected in migration and especially refugee literature.[79] To avoid this absence, the present study identifies the individual as an independent actor who is capable of strategic action within the system. The extent to which an agent (in this case the migrant) has the possibility to change social systems must be questioned[80], and there are instances where action is not possible – in which case people might distance themselves from the rules that they find oppressive.[81] However, 'the distancing from rules' may be reinterpreted as a strategy of alternative action at the level of the migrant. Research has demonstrated that despite the increasingly restrictive and controlled environment in which individuals move, migrants are increasingly responding and developing alternative self-strategies to cope with the surrounding regime and forming other relationships within the migration regime that enable action.[82] The following chapters demonstrate how migrants, displaced from their former 'homes' and confronted with an often hostile and unwelcoming reception in the 'homeland', the Russian Federation, are still able to shape to varying extents the nature of the migration process and subsequent resettlement.

Hence, empirical analysis is required at the individual and collective migrant level to explore whether migrants gain the capacity to influence the environment around them through direct negotiation with the state, or whether they exclude themselves from the action of the state and/or develop group strategies by drawing upon alternative resources and networks of power within the migration regime, to facilitate their priorities of resettlement. In certain cases, returnees might reject the 'label' that is applied to them and their migration movement by the Russian government. Of importance, therefore, is the relevance the migrants attach to the status of 'forced migrant', and the way they 'use' this official category, or displace it with their own definition. In other cases migrants might withdraw from interaction with the surrounding official migration regime and negotiate the migration process, and the re-creation of 'home', within personal networks made up of family, friends and other migrants.[83] The family, and the growth of friendship and social networks developing between regions of departure and sites of settlement, and at sites of settlement, are central to the present process of migration and resettlement.[84] However, the nature of relations within these social units, individual perceptions of their role and feelings of inclusion or exclusion from the different levels of group networks require empirical analysis.

THE 'HOME/LAND' FRAMEWORK

If the migrant is recognized as an 'active' rather than a 'passive' social agent in the processes of migration and resettlement, then analysis of migrant experience of, response to and re-reading of these processes as represented in other discursive fields is essential. Hence, the migrants' narratives that retell these experiences must be explored. The 'migration system' approach allows consideration to be given to individual migrant agency, while taking into account broader structures, to reveal the contested nature of the migration process under way and the presence of alternative migrant narratives.[85] By affording adequate attention to individual agency, simplistic identifications of the migration process taking place as either that of the forced migration or voluntary 'return' of a Russian 'diaspora' to its 'historical homeland' are displaced. Instead, an attempt can be made to understand the process as one of the individual and collective migrant, displaced from a place they identified as 'home', and forced to renegotiate a relationship with what to many is a foreign territory rather than a welcoming 'homeland'.

Attention to the discrepancies between the construction of the migration process and actual migrant experience is central to the other conceptual framework that shapes the overall theoretical and empirical approach of the study: understandings of 'homeland' and 'home' and, integral to this, what causes and impedes allegiances and attachments to place. This conceptual framework acknowledges the relevance of transnational ties for migrants – whether concrete, or as argued in the present study rooted in the memories and identities of migrants, i.e. a type of 'consciousness'.[86] These ties extend beyond the 'local' to previous homelands and disrupt the idea of 'belonging' to an identified bounded space – i.e. the nation-state. In turn, the existence of such ties fosters new forms of 'diasporic' and hybrid cultural identities that influence the social reality of the locality in which migrants live.[87] Concepts of 'transnationalism' and 'diaspora' provide the room within which migrant/refugee experiences, social relationships and attachments to place/s can be more adequately interrogated, precisely because they allow the emphasis of agency and the value of studying people in their own right. However, as suggested within recent migration research, these concepts must be explored through grounded empirical study.[88]

The dichotomy of 'home/land' that is employed emerged to a great extent from the narratives of migrants themselves during the process of research. The key linguistic terms used by migrants that feed into this framework were *rodina* ('homeland') and *doma* ('at home'). Although any attempt at representation of the 'reality' of migrant experience by the researcher is problematic, the 'home/land' dichotomy is one mechanism through which the researcher can more adequately understand the reality in which migrants are living. The persistence of 'home' helps to overcome the artificial before/after distinction often applied to migration by the observer, and succeeds in drawing on migrants' own understanding of their situation, where the previous 'home/land' and present 'home/land' constitute the continuous and lived experience of the individual.[89] Through the 'home/land' framework, the experience of migration is opened up and alternative, migrant-centred understandings are allowed to emerge. These understandings reveal grounded comprehension of ideas of home and homeland against the background of an often cited 'generalized condition of homelessness'.[90] Against this background of increased fluidity of movement and emerging 'diasporic' attachments that construct allegiances 'elsewhere', absolute and fixed ideas of 'home' and 'homeland' are increasingly difficult to determine.[91] Yet it is precisely the contested nature and experiences of 'home' and 'homeland' that make any analysis of them all the more relevant. As Clifford suggests, mobility and the deterritorialization of identity leads to the question of 'what' constitutes a native land, and enables the creation of multiple allegiances outside the 'nation state'.[92] Both these questions are interrogated at an empirical level in relation to the understandings of 'home' and 'homeland' amongst the returning Russian communities. Firstly, what constitutes a 'native land'? Secondly, what is the nature of the 'multiple allegiances', i.e. what facilitates attachment to a specific territory or place?

'Homeland', and to a lesser extent 'home', are both territorializing metaphors which suggest something to which one is 'naturally tied'.[93] The movement of the ethnic Russian and Russian-speaking populations back to the Russian Federation is particularly useful for investigating such ideas of 'home nation/homeland' as it technically represents a 'return' movement to an 'ethnic homeland'. Therefore, the example could be adopted as a case to reinforce ideas of a primordial attachment to a bounded territory – the fusion of blood and land – yet a 'natural' attachment to an ethnic homeland cannot be assumed. As earlier studies of identity formation amongst Russian-speaking forced migrants have shown, the centrality of 'ethnicity' to understandings of 'homeland' is problematized by the ideas of native land amongst the Russian migrants themselves, since migrants do not necessarily identify their 'homeland' as the 'historical homeland' – Russia.[94] The present study accepts the importance of ethnicity as one of the central strands in understanding the movements of the Russian-speaking populations; however, as Pilkington suggests, 'blood and earth do not necessarily have to be fused for territory to have significance'.[95] 'Homeland' for the individual migrant is frequently not associated with the 'ethnic' homeland. By concentrating on understandings of 'home' and 'homeland' at the micro-level, the present study finds an alternative way of disrupting the idea of an unproblematic native land.

In addition to questioning ideas of 'homeland', the duality of the 'home/land' framework allows a deeper interrogation of the idea of 'home'. There is a danger that attention to 'home' within studies of migration can be lost both within the narratives of 'homelessness', or within wider narratives that prioritize national identity and attachments to bounded 'homelands'. As Morley suggests, 'whilst the processes that go to consolidate a country or nation are seen worthy of study, the solidarity of the home is somehow often taken for granted'.[96] However, the 'rootlessness' engendered by displacement both allows, and necessitates, greater attention to the question of 'what makes a place home'? Initially, analysis of migration allows us to acknowledge that the roots established at the location of 'home' and 'homeland' are in a state of flux, and not necessarily 'rooted' in one place.[97] Furthermore, it enables us to understand the process by which roots may be re-established as new places – i.e. 'homes' and 'homelands' – are produced and reproduced. The relocation of 'home' through migration represents the beginning of a longer process and is itself multi-faceted and gradual. As Douglas argues, 'Home is located, it is not necessarily fixed in space – rather home starts by bringing space under control'.[98] This focus on renewal allows a move away from tendencies within transnational theory that prioritize migrant relationships to distant homelands, while failing to take account of the reality of living within the structural context of the society of settlement – the importance and concerns of the 'concrete locality', the desire to put down roots and to be included within the operating structures at this locality.[99]

Brah's suggestion of two meanings of 'home': (i) 'an invocation of narratives of the 'nation' or (ii) 'home as a site of everyday lived experience', feed usefully into the 'home/land' framework.[100] The 'returnee' can be seen to have suffered the loss of both – the wider 'homeland' of the Soviet Union or national republic and the immediate surroundings of their physical 'home' in the former republic. With 'return' and resettlement, as the process of renegotiation of both 'homeland' and 'home' is undertaken, the subtleties of both concepts emerge. Despite displacement and a loss of a 'home' and 'homeland', the individual prioritizes relocation and a re-creation of 'home'. The desire for relocation, however, may not be rooted in a wish for a distinct 'homeland', i.e. attachment to a nation-state, but rather in a 'homing desire' – the need to 'feel at home' in the new location.[101] Nevertheless, the space created as 'homeland' by other key actors (e.g. the state) may not facilitate (and in fact may constrain) the re-creation of feelings of home. The 'home/land' framework therefore contributes further to bridging the theoretical and empirical gap that exists between migration discourse and migrant reality. It reveals the conflict that often exists between the way in which the migration process and the space of 'return' – the historical 'homeland' – are constructed through political and non-political discourse and practice, and migrants' understandings and experiences of the same process and their expectations of 'return'.

THE EMPIRICAL PROJECT[102]

The design of the empirical project took into account the uncertainty and changing nature of the topic and research environment: the spatial and temporal displacement experienced by migrants, the complex process of resettlement, the evolving nature of the migration regime in the Russian Federation and the surrounding fluidity of Russian society. In addition, it enabled the migrant voice to be heard, while engaging with both the micro and the macro levels and with the different actors involved in both the construction and experience of the migration process. A qualitative, ethnographic approach was adopted and, in particular, critical approaches to ethnography were drawn upon. These share with conventional ethnography an emphasis on the use of an extensive fieldwork approach where the researcher is located 'within' the context of what they are studying, and in addition stress that research is an interactive and reflective process between the observer and observed, and that the micro-location of a study can inform theoretical understanding of the wider 'whole'.[103]

A case study approach ensured that the researcher was immersed within the context of study. This approach enabled the evolution and operation of the migration system to be observed; specifically the way in which the process of migration, and subsequent resettlement, were constructed by certain key actors (regional governments, migrations services) and experienced and negotiated by the individual migrant. Pilot visits were made to the two main case study regions of Saratov and Samara *oblasti* in 1996, 1997 and 1998; the main period of fieldwork in these regions took place from June to September 1999.[104] Both the key concerns of the research project, and particular themes that had emerged from the principal study, were explored at the further case study site of Novosibirsk *oblast'* during the summer of 2002.[105] A follow-up trip to Samara was also conducted during this period. A final site of research was Moscow, where the activity of federal and international actors and their interaction with the regions were examined. The three case study regions were not chosen in order to present singular examples of distinct migration environments and migrant experiences of resettlement; instead, they were used to provide insight to differences in the construction and experience of the migration process, to inform analysis at the wider regional and federal level, and to refine theoretical explanation of the broader migration process and migration system.[106]

The empirical project applied a combination of qualitative research methods in triangulation: in-depth, semi-structured interviews with individual migrants; expert interviews with representatives of migrant associations, local, national and international NGOs and relevant government bodies; and field observations at different sites within the regional migration regimes. All the migrant interviews, and the majority of expert interviews, were taped, later fully transcribed and analysed in Russian. The choice of methods aimed to understand the different perceptions and priorities of the migration process, at varying levels of analysis and at different points in time, and to reveal the contradictions and inconsistencies existing between them. Points of contention and interest in one sphere were noted and tested in another sphere. The data collected from interviews and observation was also used in combination with other secondary information and documentary materials such as official legislation and policy documents, institutional documentation and newspaper articles.[107] The 'grounded' nature of the approach, and the time period of the study, meant that the parameters of the research and its theoretical frameworks were constantly reviewed, redefined and focused over the whole course of the research process.[108]

A total of 72 migrants were interviewed in the three regions. 44 respondents were interviewed in Saratov *oblast'* and 18 in Samara *oblast'*. 17 of the migrant respondents were interviewed as part of the pilot study in Saratov *oblast'* in September 1997. The remaining respondents were interviewed during the main period of fieldwork, from June to November 1999. A further ten respondents were interviewed in Novosibirsk *oblast'* in July 2002. All respondents had arrived in the Russian Federation over the period 1991–2001. Migrants were interviewed at a number of settlement sites located in urban, semi-urban and rural areas.[109] Although the respondents were not sampled according to socio-demographic characteristics, socio-demographic data were gathered for each individual and entered into an ACCESS database.[110] The majority of the respondents stated their nationality as Russian (82 per cent); the other stated nationalities were Ukrainian, Chechen, German, Uzbek, Tajik, Tatar, Chuvash and Moldovan. 53 female migrants and 19 male migrants were interviewed. Reasons for the higher incidence of female respondents were that female migrants were easier to access, they were generally more available than male migrants, especially at the rural resettlement sites, and were more willing to talk. In addition, the migrant associations used to access some respondents were predominantly run by women, who themselves had more contacts with other female migrants and found it easier to approach them. The respondents were also accessed through the territorial migration services and by using snowballing techniques beginning with migrant contacts.

A conscious attempt was made in the theoretical and empirical design of the project to allow the migrant voice to come through; this is continued through the structure of the book. Yet the difficulty of adequately articulating migrant agency and of representing migrant reality and experience is acknowledged. The book attempts to move away from prioritizing state (and academic and media) discourses that often frame migrant experience, by offering an alternative framework. The empirical approach that was adopted, particularly the use of in-depth interviews, attempted to prioritize the migrant subject. It has been suggested that in-depth interviews best cope with questions of identity and subjectivity, and reveal the 'empirical disjuncture' between expectations of migration and actual experiences of it.[111] The interviews provided access to the past experiences and changing identities of the respondents, essential to the study, and allowed their opinions about the wider institutional features of the surrounding migration regime, and Russian society, to be elicited. The data then enabled wider critiques of dominant assumptions being made of the migration processes under way, i.e. at the state level, by drawing on the reinterpretations of the process amongst the migrants themselves.[112]

By structuring a number of the chapters according to themes that arose from the migrant narratives and by using direct citations, the use of the data in the book aims to focus upon understandings of the migration and resettlement process by the individual. This approach allows analysis of individual experiences of migration and resettlement to be interweaved with analyses of larger frameworks; it also seeks to highlight the importance of understanding at the individual level, and to reinforce the contrast between individual perceptions and experiences of migration and resettlement, and how the process is constructed *for* the migrant at the level of the migration regimes. However, such an approach allows the voices of only a small number of individuals to be represented, and the data presented hides the process of research behind it.[113] The researcher approached the subjects, set the tone for and structured the conversations, translated the data and chose the quotes. These and other biases and subsequent limitations are acknowledged. However, the alternative framework that is presented must be seen to have equal validity with others which prioritize different actors, levels of analysis and fields of discourse.

CONCLUSION

This chapter has introduced the key locales of analysis at which the experience of migration and resettlement is negotiated – individual, household, social network, state/institutional (regional, national, global) – which takes place within the surrounding migration system. It has also introduced the dichotomy of 'home/land' which is central to the migration and resettlement process, and allows alternative understandings of the process to emerge, particularly at the individual migrant level. The book continues to prioritize understanding of the nature and experience of migration and resettlement at the micro-level, where the focus is that of the individual migrant's perspective. However, it accepts that the experience of migration and resettlement is shaped by – and must be read within the context of – the global, national and regional migration regimes. This chapter has also suggested how the approach adopted – simultaneous attention to migration discourse and policy, and migrant agency and 'reality' – can interrogate both the viability of official policy and the validity of dominant characteristics that are often applied to the migration process in question: for example, the 'ethnic' nature of the migration, the 'forced' versus voluntary nature of the migration, and the assumption that it is a post-colonial 'return' to 'homeland'. This interrogation is given substance through empirical analysis in the following chapters.

2

Constructions of the 'Homeland' by the Russian State

This chapter explores the way in which a key actor in the migration process – the Russian state – through government discourse, legislation and policy, constructs the territory of the Russian Federation as a 'homeland' for the Russian communities still resident in the former republics of the Soviet Union, and for those members of the communities who have 'returned'. It begins with an examination of the historical migration of the Russian communities to the 'borderland regions', and explores the relationship that existed between the migrating communities and the Russian centre during the periods of the Tsarist and Soviet 'empires'. This provides a background within which the 'return' movement of the populations, and responses to migration and resettlement at both the state and individual levels, can be better conceptualized. The remainder of the chapter concentrates on the three dominant state-led discourses that have developed since 1991 vis à vis the Russian communities and their possible migration: those of 'diaspora', 'forced migration' and 'repatriation'. It demonstrates how the Russian communities, while 'in diaspora' and upon 'return', have become an important issue in the domestic political arena due to the internal socio-economic concerns and external foreign policy interests of the Russian state; and furthermore, a focus for debates over the nature of post-Soviet Russian national identity. A preliminary picture emerges of the conflicting and ambiguous constructions of 'homeland' that are present within the three state discourses and resultant policy. The picture suggests that the territory of the Russian Federation is not represented as a real 'homeland' to which the communities may 'return', and indicates the limited positive response of the Russian state to their resettlement.

HISTORICAL CONTEXTS: THE MIGRATION AND SETTLEMENT OF THE RUSSIAN POPULATIONS

The movement towards the periphery prior to 1917

Although the Russian Empire was not formally established until 1721, the birth of a multi-national Russian empire, the beginnings of rapid territorial Russian expansion and the significant movement of Russians beyond the borders of the present-day Russian Federation may be traced to the conquest of Kazan in 1552.[1] The nature of the migration taking place, the causes of migration and the role of the settler communities in the peripheral regions of the empire influenced both the development of the character of the Russian communities outside the present borders of Russia and their identity and relationship vis à vis the Russian state.

The territorial expansion of the Tsarist empire was accompanied by the out-migration of increasingly large numbers of Russians from the centre of the empire to the outlying borderlands, whose settlement became a key factor in the consolidation of the power of the imperial state.[2] State policies both encouraged and restricted movement depending upon priorities and concerns at government level. The migration of Russian settlers was promoted to increase security and to raise the material and cultural levels of the populations in the border regions of the empire. However, the existence of serfdom impeded free movement, and even after its abolition in 1861 migration was still controlled through a state policy that branded 'irregular', spontaneous migration as a punishable offence. During earlier periods the state restricted migration when it feared this would lead to revolutionary feelings; later it promoted migration as a method of diluting revolutionary ferment. In the late nineteenth century a more active state policy to encourage migration was pursued due to increased demographic pressure in European Russia, when incentives were offered for individuals to settle in the border areas of the empire. Yet, as in other parts of Europe, for the individual the prospect of increased economic opportunities, religious or political freedom and free land played an important part in the large-scale out-migration. Although state policy legitimized the migration that was taking place, these processes were often already under way.[3]

Whatever the primary cause of the movement, the presence of the Russian settlers in the border regions played a central role in the expansion of the Russian state and provided a means of unifying a diverse empire.[4] The migration and settlement of Russians facilitated the imposition of political control and the introduction of a distinct Russian culture to the outer borderlands. During the later nineteenth century, policies of russification increased. Yet although

Russian identity was central to the expansion of the imperial order, the priority was the consolidation of the 'empire-state' rather than the development of a Russian 'nation'.[5] Despite the imposition of the Russian language, policies of russification did not have an ethnic focus but were an attempt to generate identification of the minority communities with the tsarist system and inclusion within a broad civic Russian national identity.[6] A Russian empire where a commitment to the Russian 'state' displaced a commitment to a 'nation' or 'homeland' (*rodina*) impeded the development of an ethnic Russian national identity or politicized Russian ethnic consciousness.[7]

Russian migration and settlement under the Soviet regime

The Soviet period saw the continued out-migration of Russians from the central Russian republic to the other ethno-republics of the Union. Between 1897 and 1970 the Russian population outside the area of the Russian Soviet Federated Socialist Republic (RSFSR) increased by more than 15 million. Migration was the main reason for the increase.[8] The out-migration is identified as a continuation of the already established migratory processes that had been under way since the sixteenth century, and were to continue to the 1960s when a significant reverse movement was first apparent.[9] During the Soviet period a number of factors influenced and stimulated the migratory movements including the Soviet industrialization drive and urbanization, the collectivization of the rural economy which led to famine and rapid out-migration from the countryside, the Second World War and the movement of large industrial enterprises to the east, and the 1959–70 campaign to develop the virgin lands in Kazakstan.

There has been much debate concerning the underlying causes of the mass movement of Russians to the non-Russian republics of the Soviet Union. A socio-economic model places the movements within wider processes of modernization; and an ethno-political model prioritizes the role of the state and the desire for either 'russification' of the populations in the other republics or the promotion of migration as part of a 'transcendence of nationality' to result in the creation of a 'de-nationalized' Soviet man.[10] Both models have come under criticism: the former for ignoring the ethnic (and sometimes forced) nature of the mass migration of many different nationalities in the Soviet Union, and the latter for its assumption that the state could control phenomena on such a scale. Furthermore, the actual impact of migration on nationality relations and processes of 'russification' in the former republics may be questioned.[11] State policies were employed to encourage migration, whether for political or economic reasons, although movement was also highly restricted by the state through the operation of the internal passport system. Yet, in spite of the state promotion and restriction of migration, there is also evidence of large-scale spontaneous movement rooted in individual volition.[12] As Kolstø suggests, both models provide important insights into the nature of the movements, and whether influenced predominantly by the specific ethno-political motivations of the state or by wider processes of economic development and modernization, the migration of the Russians was central to the Soviet agricultural and industrial drives and the consolidation of territory.[13]

As was the case during the period of the Tsarist Empire, the Russian communities in the non-Russian Soviet republics were closely associated with the 'imperial' power that was now the Soviet state and dominant Communist ideology. Although widely debated by Soviet, Russian and western scholars, there is little doubt that the Russians held a privileged position within the Soviet Union; they occupied top posts in the state and party apparatus at both the central and republic level and enjoyed both linguistic and cultural privileges which other non-titular groups did not possess.[14] During the Stalinist period, Russian superiority was promoted and Stalin declared the Russians to be 'the guiding force of the Soviet Union'.[15] The Russian populations were concentrated in the major industrial cities and administrative centres of the Soviet republics, where they enjoyed a higher standard of living and professional status than that of the indigenous populations.[16] Although their position of superiority lessened towards the end of the Soviet era as educational and employment advances were made by the titular populations, the Russian populations were still seen as the 'glue' which held the Soviet Union together and were often perceived by the titular nations as representatives of a Soviet 'empire'.[17]

Yet although the specific role the Russians occupied ensured the strengthening of the Soviet state and its institutions, at the same time it impeded the development of a distinct Russian ethnic and national identity. The communities instead developed a social and cultural identity, rooted in their position within the Soviet political and economic system.[18] The lack of national institutions within the Russian republic also impeded its development as a central 'national homeland' for the Russian communities.[19] The Soviet Union was never organized as a Russian nation-state despite the dominance of the Russian nation within it; an imperial nation was rather substituted by an imperial party.[20] In the other ethno-republics of the Soviet Union, national identity was organized on the basis of territoriality and defined through the creation of national institutions.[21] This did not occur with the Russian republic, or Russian 'national identity'. The lack of this 'homeland', and the unique position of the Russian populations within the Union, meant that rather than identification with their 'native land' – the Russian republic – they more frequently thought of the entire Union as their 'national homeland'.[22]

The collapse of the Soviet Union in 1991 impacted upon the situation of the Russian populations possibly more than any other nationality group; crucially, it greatly affected the relationship between the central Russian 'core' and the borderland settler communities that had existed since Tsarist times. The communities were no longer representatives of the 'imperial' power and had become 'ethnic minorities' overnight; their previous wider 'homeland' – the Soviet Union – was now defunct, and they were located outside what was technically their 'ethnic homeland' – the newly formed Russian Federation – which for many was a highly ambiguous and unknown concept.[23] Apart from their own self-identity, which was in a state of redefinition, both the host nations of the newly independent states and the government of their ethnic 'homeland' (the Russian Federation) were redefining their national identities. In the newly independent states, government-level policies would threaten the previously dominant position of the settler communities; while at the popular level the settlers were increasingly branded as 'occupiers' and representatives of a now compromised former colonial power.[24] Meanwhile, the Russian Federation had emerged as an independent state following the collapse of the Soviet Union, but not necessarily as a Russian 'homeland'.[25] As part of the search for a 'new' national identity, the Russian government would attempt to redefine the relationship of the settler communities to the Russian state and nation, which had been severed with the collapse of the Soviet Union. The question of the position of the Russian communities in the former republics, and their possible 'return' to their 'historical homeland', thus became crucial both on the individual, personal, and the state political level.

STATE CONCEPTIONS OF 'HOME' AND 'HOMELAND'

The changing relationship between the Russian state and the Russian communities in the 'near abroad' has therefore become an issue of significant political debate. Of importance here is the way in which this relationship impacts upon the response of the Russian state to the 'return' of these populations and how, at the state level, a 'homeland' is constructed. The nature of a 'return' migration is influenced by key actors who hold varying degrees of power to shape the space of 'return' and the identities of those involved in the process of 'return'.[26] As identified in Chapter 1, a key actor involved in defining migration movement and resettlement experience is the 'host' nation and particularly its government. Since 1991 a dual policy has emerged on the part of the Russian government towards the Russian communities. One side of the policy upholds the right of the communities to remain in the former republics and constructs them as part of the Russian nation, but 'in diaspora' from the Russian state. The other side of the policy accepts the 'return' and resettlement of the Russian communities on the territory of the Russian Federation, but positions them as 'forced migrants' within the Russian state. A third and more marginal discourse is that of 'repatriation'. This discourse has been prevalent at certain periods over the last decade and provides an additional insight into how the Russian state *might*, depending upon other internal and external factors, construct itself as a 'homeland' for the Russian communities.

'Diaspora' discourse – the location of 'homeland' in the newly independent states

Since 1991, the location of the Russian communities outside the borders of the Russian state has led to increasing speculation and suggestion that the communities may constitute a new Russian 'diaspora'. In fact, it was in the late 1970s that an interest first developed in the specific identity of the Russian populations located beyond the borders of the Russian republic, as distinct from the core group of 'central' Russians.[27] This identity was seen as rooted in the nature of the position the 'peripheral' Russians occupied during the Soviet Union, the experience of living in another cultural environment and the adoption of traditions and customs of the nationalities living in the republic.[28] The proposal of the term 'diaspora' was to move from being purely figurative to gain wider political, and academic, significance after the breakup of the Soviet Union. Although the use of the term to describe the Russian communities in the 'near abroad' is contested, an interrogation of its usage can serve to question the relationship of the Russian 'diaspora' to the former republic, and the Russian Federation, on both a theoretical and empirical level.[29]

On a theoretical level the question of the applicability of the term 'diaspora' to the case of the Russian populations in the 'near abroad' has received considerable attention in western academic literature since the mid 1990s.[30] This attention has been facilitated by the wider return to the question of 'diaspora' in the light of increasing concern with transnational movement and, especially from postmodernist perspectives, its implications for identity. Russian academic literature has engaged with these debates, and has sought both to refine the use of the term 'diaspora' and to critically evaluate its applicability, both in general conceptual terms and with relation to the Russian-speaking communities.[31] It is difficult to locate the Russian 'diaspora' within the frameworks that traditional understandings of the concept offer. However, as the central pillar of diasporic identity is the question of the relationship to 'homeland', the majority of the studies usefully address the emerging relationship between the Russian 'diaspora' resident in the former republics and the Russian state/homeland. This book in particular draws upon critiques of traditional notions of 'diaspora' and their interrogation of the idea of a single 'homeland'. As Clifford suggests, 'the empowering paradox of diasporas is that dwelling here assumes a solidarity and connection 'there'. But 'there' is not necessarily a single place or exclusivist nation'.[32]

On an empirical level, the term has been widely adopted in post-Soviet Russia by politicians and the media but is often used in an indiscriminate and insufficiently analytical way.[33] As Kolstø notes, the 'terminological anarchy' surrounding the diaspora debate demonstrates the political confusion on the issue, and the difficulty of defining who makes up this 'diaspora' and its relationship to the Russian state.[34] The term is frequently used in a general, all-encompassing manner with no critical analysis of what constitutes this diaspora. Kosmarskaia comments that politicians and journalists (and academics) have tended to use 'diaspora' simply as a synonym or descriptive label for all the Russian-speaking populations in the newly independent states.[35] However, via these different discourses the Russian communities have become an object of 'diasporization'. The chapter now addresses the process of, and reasons for, the political 'diasporization' of the Russian communities in the former republics by the Russian state, and the implications this has for the construction of the Russian Federation as 'homeland'.

Russia's relationship to the communities still located in the successor states underwent a process of redefinition over the period 1991–2002 and is still under negotiation. The development of the policy took place against the background of a political battle between competing post-Soviet Russian elites over the future nature of the Russian state and nation, and its redefinition at both the regional FSU and global levels.[36] As suggested, in 1991 post-Soviet Russia was faced with a 'non-coincidence' of state and nation.[37] The legacy the Russian Federation inherited was a country whose national self-understanding spread beyond its present day territorial and institutional borders[38] – a legacy embodied physically in the present by the Russian communities. As different opinions emerged, at both a political and popular level, concerning what should territorially and 'spiritually' constitute the Russian nation, the Russian communities located beyond the borders of the Federation became a logical focus for the debate. Over the period of the 1990s, as part of the search for a new national identity, the need to re-establish links between Russia and its 'compatriots' – and in fact for Russia to protect these communities – became gradually accepted.[39]

In 1991, President Yeltsin and the Russian government were looking westwards to develop Russia's foreign policy and standing on the international stage. With the legitimacy and standing of the new Russian state uncertain following the end of the Soviet Union, they wished Russia to gain immediate international acceptance and to ensure its worldwide recognition as a member of the 'civilized'

European community. With regard to the other former republics of the Soviet Union, Russian leaders hoped to develop a relationship of cooperation within an international context, and to further this relationship they supported the ethnic Russian and Russian-speaking communities becoming citizens of those states. This initial anti-Soviet political movement within the Russian Federation, which saw the Russian nation contained 'within' the Russian Soviet republic, severed the historic connection that had existed between the Russian communities and the centre of political power in Moscow.[40]

However during 1992, as the 'near abroad' came to be seen as a key area of national Russian interest, certain political groupings – particularly within the Russian parliament – began to dispute the policy of conciliation. Following the December 1993 parliamentary elections there was a shift to the right as the 'near abroad', and the protection of the 'compatriot' communities, gained greater relevance. The creation of a Governmental Commission on the Affairs of Compatriots in December 1994 reflected the increased concern. The Commission, which included representatives of most governmental, presidential and parliamentary bodies related to the question of the Russian communities in the 'near abroad' along with representatives of Non Governmental Organizations (NGO), was given responsibility for coordinating activity and the realization of policy with regard to 'compatriot' issues.[41]

Prior to the formation of this body, the first specific legislation in relation to the communities had appeared. This included a Presidential decree on the 'Basic Conception of a Programme to Help Compatriots' and the accompanying resolution of the Russian Government on 'Measures for the Support of Compatriots Abroad', introduced in August 1994. The programme prioritized the integration of the Russian communities in political, economic and socio-cultural terms, but was unsupported by any significant action.[42] The programme also supported the idea of dual citizenship, which was seen as a solution to the 'discrepancy between the boundaries of the newly emerging state and those of the newly emerging nation'.[43] According to Russian government officials, the main advantages of dual citizenship were that it represented a more 'civilized' approach towards the issue of 'compatriots' in the 'near abroad', that it would help to discourage inmigration, and that it could serve as a possible lever of influence to represent the interests of the Russian state in the 'near abroad'.[44] However, the majority of governments of the other successor states were opposed to the idea, fearing that it would undermine their nation-building efforts. The Russian state subsequently accepted that such agreements could only be concluded in cases where there was a small Russian population. Dual citizenship agreements were concluded between the Russian Federation and Turkmenistan (1993) and Tajikistan (1997).[45]

The more interventionist stance towards the question of the Russian communities from 1992 was championed particularly by the Russian parliament. Neo-nationalist and neo-Soviet factions promoted the expansion and strengthening of a Russia to bind together the Russian people as one, and advocated the active involvement of the Russian state in deciding the fate of the 'compatriot' communities. The Parliamentary Committee on CIS Affairs and Relations with Compatriots was created to further this policy, and a sub-committee of the body was subsequently formed – the Parliamentary Commission on Refugee and Forced Migrant Affairs – which combined parliamentary and NGO forces.[46] At the time of the parliamentary elections in December 1995 a powerful bloc of support for the Russian communities seemed to have developed in the form of the Congress of Russian communities. However, their showing in the elections was poor and following this there was an apparent decline in parliamentary interest concerning the fate of the Russians in the 'near abroad'. However, the decline in interest may reflect the consensus that had been reached by 1995 between government and parliamentary bodies over the need to develop official government policy towards the Russian settler communities.[47] The consensus was consolidated by Democratic Statist forces within the Russian parliament, which succeeded in combining the 'return to empire' stance with the previously more liberal approach. It recognized the physical boundaries of the new Russia, but upheld the idea that the Russian state was organically linked to the settler communities and bore responsibility for their well-being.

The major piece of legislation that has been developed with respect to the Russian communities is the law 'Concerning the State Policy of the Russian Federation in Relation to its Compatriots Abroad', adopted in March 1999. The main responsibility for the development of the law lay with the Parliamentary Committee on CIS Affairs and Relations with Compatriots. The law defines who are 'compatriots', outlines the responsibility of the Russian state to its 'compatriots abroad' and details measures of support in the political, social, cultural, economic, linguistic and educational spheres.[48] Significantly, rather than the attachment between Russia and its communities being rooted in an 'ethnic' identification, it is located within a broader identification with the Russian state. Although the Russian Federation is talked about as the *istoricheskaia rodina* (historical homeland), the term used in relation to those within the 'diaspora' is *sootechestvenniki* (compatriots) and does not confine the 'diaspora' to ethnic Russians (*russkie*) or the Russian-speaking populations (*russkoiazichnie*). The term *sootechestvenniki* is commonly taken to include those who may not hold Russian citizenship but who have hereditary links with Russia or the FSU, and who possess cultural and spiritual links with Russia.[49] The broader 'cultural and spiritual' (as opposed to 'ethnic') basis for the Russian 'diaspora' in the law reflects the historical-political element that previously defined the Russian communities' relationship to the Russian state.[50] By deflecting attention away from the 'ethnic' axis of 'homeland' usually contained in definitions of 'diaspora', to an extent it more successfully characterizes the relationship that might exist between the Russian communities and the Russian Federation. Liberal politicians, academics and journalists have also avoided the term 'ethnic Russians' when referring to the 'diaspora' in an attempt to dilute the high degree of politicization of diaspora discourse and to counter the tendency among the nationalist camp to 'over-ethnicize' the term.[51] However, the inclusive definition of 'compatriots' in the law also demonstrates the difficulty faced by the Russian state in defining exactly who constitutes the 'diaspora', due to the 'multiethnic, multiconfessional and multilingual population' that has emerged as a result of centuries of imperial expansion and out-migration.[52]

Any practical implementation of the policies towards the Russian communities in the 'near abroad' has been limited.[53] However, through the wider policy of diasporization, there has been a rediscovery or 'reinvention' of the Russian communities as a defined group that continues to be identified by different actors as being in need of protection by the Russian state.[54] The identification of, and subsequent responsibility for, the 'diaspora' served to unite disparate political forces and provided a focus for developing Russia's post-Soviet identity: as a 'great power' with legitimate concerns towards an ethno-cultural community resident beyond its borders.[55] Both political discourse and subsequent policy served to legitimize and consolidate the attachment of the Russian state to the Russian communities in the 'near abroad', and through this policy their 'right' to remain in 'diaspora' has been normalized and upheld. This stance reflected a myriad of state interests which go far beyond any 'humanitarian' concern for the Russian communities including: the strength of a rightist parliamentary agenda that called for greater attention and concrete action with regard to the compatriot issue, coinciding foreign policy and geo-political priorities of the Russian government that redirected attention away from the west towards the former Soviet republics from 1992 onwards, and domestic socio-economic and security concerns about the impact of an influx of migrants from the 'near abroad' (see below).

Yet for the settler communities themselves, Russia is a removed or virtual 'homeland' and the reality of 'return' is not as firmly established. Furthermore, as the difficulty in defining the parameters of the diaspora suggests, the political 'diasporization' of the Russian communities does not necessarily result in the development of a 'diasporic' identity amongst the Russian populations in the 'near abroad'. Although it is undoubtedly true that a greater awareness of themselves as 'Russians' is experienced by the Russian-speaking communities in the former republics as a result of the 'nationalizing nationalisms' of their host countries,[56] the degree of that awareness is dependent not only on the policies of individual newly independent states or on the 'diaspora politics' of the Russian state, but also on the form of settlement that had developed in particular regions while under imperial Russian and then Soviet rule: size, ethnic composition[57], history of migration to the region, the socio-economic position of the settlers within each society and the degree of cultural cleavage with the indigenous community.[58] As suggested earlier, the identity of the Russian-speaking communities was primarily defined and experienced in socio-cultural rather than ethnic terms, and the connection to the 'homeland' expressed in their economic and political placement within All-Union structures controlled from Moscow, rather than in any longing for 'return'.[59] Furthermore, the degree of differentiation amongst the Russian communities, as Graham Smith observes, meant that they showed little sense of transnational solidarity linking their diasporic communities, either symbolically or through established social networks. Even within any Soviet successor state, Russian minorities displayed a weak sense of communal identity and thus a low level of collective action.[60] Therefore, any homogenous 'diasporic' identity, or common desire to return to the Russian Federation, cannot be assumed.

Forced migration discourse – the location of 'homeland' on the territory of the Russian Federation

The second strand of the dual policy towards the Russian communities, that accepts and shapes their 'return' to the Russian Federation, is embodied in the migration discourse and policy of the Russian government towards returnees and is enacted through relevant state institutions and legislation that have emerged since 1991. The policy reflects the political 'diasporization' of the Russian communities, and is also indicative of wider developments in the Russian migration regime and approaches to other forms of migration in post-Soviet Russia. The discussion here addresses precisely how migration policy, and the forced migration discourse around which it is constructed, has affected the returning migrant population, and the nature of their 'return' and the space of settlement.[61] Figure 2.1 shows the main institutional bodies, reaching down to a regional level, that constitute the official Russian migration regime, and have been influential over the period 1991–2002. It also depicts those government bodies that have been central to the formation of policy towards Russian communities still resident in the 'near abroad', and the non-governmental structures that have become significant actors within the Russian migration regime (see Chapter 5).

The complete absence of administrative structures or legislation to deal with any uncontrolled movement of peoples during the Soviet period meant that a rapid response was required when large-scale 'forced' migration began at the start of the 1990s. In 1992 the Russian Federation joined the international migration regime when it acceded to the 1951 UN Convention and 1967 Protocol Relating to the Status of Refugees. An institutional body, the Federal Migration Service (FMS), was established by presidential decree in July 1992 and held responsibility for affairs pertaining to migration until its abolition in May 2000.[62] As this study covers the period 1991–2002, and the interaction of migrants with state structures that occurred primarily prior to 2000, the FMS and its regional branches, the Territorial Migration Services (TMS), is the chief institution that is focused upon throughout the book. However, more recent institutional and legislative developments and their significance are also dealt with.

The two pieces of legislation that, when introduced in February 1993, applied to the 'forced movement' of the Russian communities were the Russian Federation laws 'On Forced Migrants' and 'On Refugees'.[63] A number of other laws influencing migration and resettlement were also passed, including the law 'On Citizenship' (November 1991, amended in February 1992) and the law 'On the Right of the Citizens of the Russian Federation to Freedom of Movement and Choice of Residence within the Russian Federation' (June 1993). The principal difference between qualification for refugee or forced migrant status was rooted in the possession of Russian citizenship. The law on forced migrants applied only to Russian citizens or those entitled to citizenship,[64] covered the reception, allocation of status and resettlement of those individuals and, in theory, guaranteed additional benefits and rights for their resettlement on Russian territory.[65]

The initial character of the Russian migration regime that emerged in 1992 appeared to reflect a tolerant approach towards in-migration. The FMS was mandated to 'protect the rights of refugees and forced migrants and help in their resettlement', while the introduction of the fairly liberal legislation was inspired by the western-oriented Ministry of Foreign Affairs, headed by Andrei Kozyrev, and was rooted in a desire for international recognition in the field of human rights.[66] However, from 1993 government priorities, and consequently the policy agenda towards the return migration of the Russian communities, began to shift. The difficulties of an inexperienced migration service, with legislative support of little practical use and suffering from severe financial constraints, were compounded by the concurrent politicization of the question of the Russian communities in the 'near abroad' and the economic and social crisis being faced on the territory of the Russian Federation. By the end of 1995, the initially liberal approach to 'return' had been replaced by support of their right to 'remain', which was accompanied by an increasing 'securitization' of the migration

STATE DUMA

Parliamentary Committee on CIS Affairs and Relations with Compatriots
Parliamentary Commission on Refugees and Forced Migrant Affairs
Council of Compatriots
Parliamentary Commission on Migration Policy
Council of Migrant Associations

GOVERNMENT

Governmental Commission on the Affairs of Compatriots
Governmental Commission on Migration Policy

PRESIDENTIAL APPARATUS

SECURITY COUNCIL

FEDERAL MIGRATION SERVICE OF RUSSIA (abolished May 2000)
MINISTRY OF FEDERATION AFFAIRS, NATIONAL AND MIGRATION POLICY (abolished October 2001) AND REGIONAL BRANCHES

MINISTRY OF INTERNAL AFFAIRS

REGIONAL LEVELS OF THE MINISTRY

REGIONAL ADMINISTRATIONS

RUSSIAN NON-GOVERNMENTAL ORGANIZATIONS:
THE CIVIC ASSISTANCE COMMITTEE
CCARFM
FORUM OF MIGRANT ASSOCIATIONS
THE COMPATRIOTS FUND

REGIONAL MIGRANT ASSOCIATIONS

INTERNATIONAL ORGANIZATIONS:
UNHCR
IOM
THE RED CROSS
CARITAS

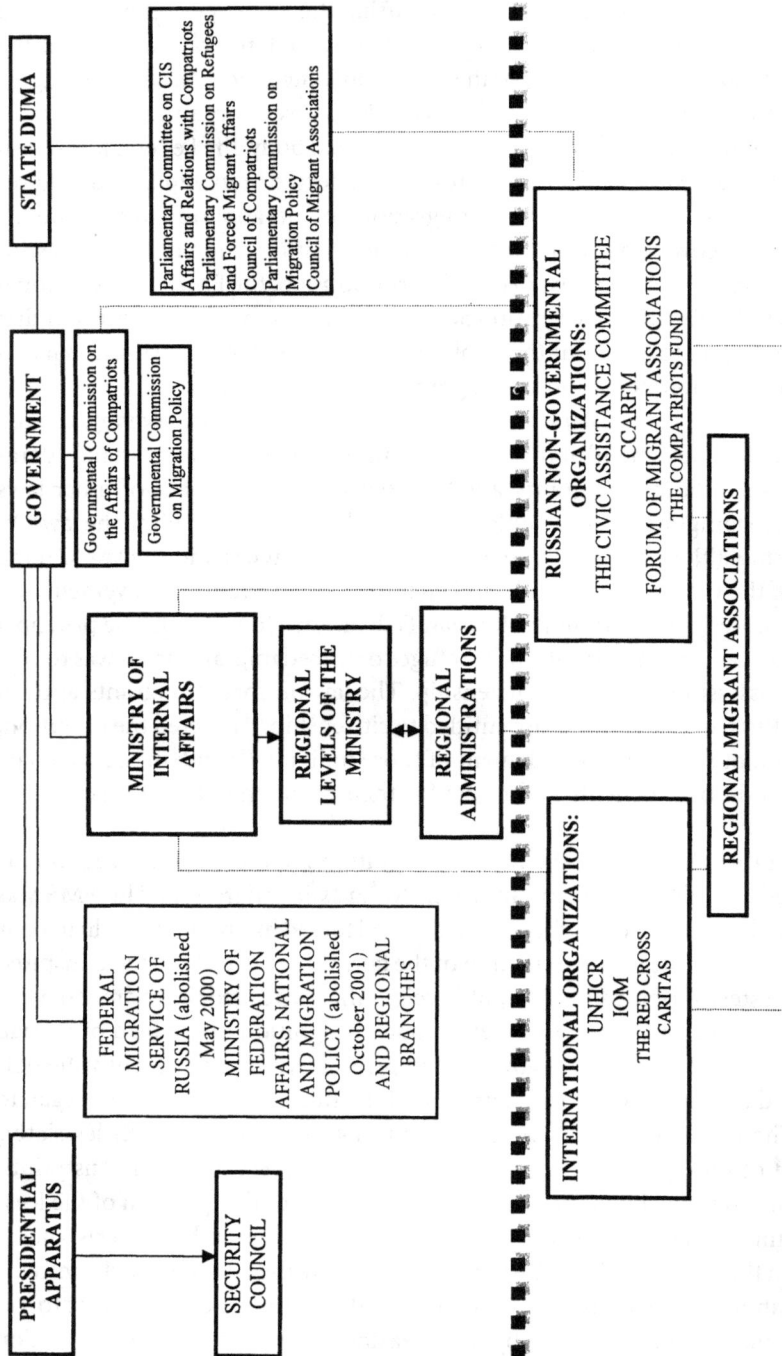

FIGURE 2.1   The institutional framework of the Russian Migration Regime 1992–2002

issue within the Russian Federation and the prioritization of 'control' over 'provision'. The shift reflected the governmental consensus over the need to 'protect' the Russian communities and their right to remain in the 'near abroad', and to encompass them as part of the Russian nation's sphere of influence.

Political support of the Russian communities' 'right to stay', and the accompanying desire to deter their return, both justified and facilitated corresponding changes in the institutional and legislative framework of the still embryonic migration regime. The FMS drew back from its responsibility for the social provision of migrants and adopted a wider, more regulatory role to control and manage migration. This shift in role was accompanied by demands for the service to gain ministry status, led by the then head of the service, Tat'iana Regent. The FMS felt that the absence of a single structure to fully coordinate migration policy, and the lack of cooperation and coordination between the different ministries and departments regarding resettlement and migration flows, hindered successful policy fulfilment.[67]

The proposal proved untimely as it coincided with severe criticism of the FMS for its infringement of the rights of refugees and forced migrants, and for the failure of the service to create a successful 'vertical management structure' with sufficient central control over regional branches. A report was carried out in 1997–8 by an inter-departmental commission of the Security Council. The Council, part of the presidential apparatus, saw migration as a matter of security and national interest; its report suggested that the FMS's lack of control over the activity of its regional branches had resulted in the distortion of state national policy. The FMS had been unable to prevent the adoption of damaging legislative acts at the local level, which prevented the execution of one of the basis tasks of the service – the provision of the relevant status to forced migrants and refugees.[68] The reasons lay in a combination of local mismanagement, lack of accountability, inexperience and financial negligence in a number of territorial migration services, and the dual subordination of the territorial migration services to both the FMS and individual *oblast'* governmental departments of heads of local administrations.[69]

Thus, over the period 1997–9, the increasingly broad agenda of the FMS, its monopoly as a single body over the rights of thousands of migrants and its failure to provide adequate social provision in the areas of employment, housing and compensation was increasingly questioned.[70] Although reform was attempted during 1999, the service was abolished on 17 May 2000 and incorporated into the Ministry of Federation Affairs, National and Migration Policy. The abolition was interpreted by many as the further withdrawal of the state from provision for refugees and forced migrants, and the lowering of the status of the problem of migrants within government priorities. The transition of the service to an institution that prioritizes control and management over protection and assistance was finally completed in October 2001 when the Ministry was itself abolished and responsibility for migration issues was handed over to the Ministry of Internal Affairs (MVD). The MVD is a prominent member of what can be termed Russia's 'power ministries'.[71] The decision led to outcry from some government officials, Russian parliamentary deputies and human rights and migration rights groups.[72] The primary fear was that by placing migration within the remit of the Ministry of Internal Affairs, vulnerable migrants would be forgotten and the ministry would interpret migration policy as only 'the struggle with illegal migration'. Andrei Chenenko, then head of the migration service within the Ministry of Internal Affairs, confirmed these fears to an extent when he said that the 'romantic period' with regard to migration was over, and that now the time had come when 'the Russian state must protect itself'.[73] Chernenko however also defended the move, stating that in other 'civilized' countries such as Britain, Finland and Germany migration is the responsibility of the equivalent of the Ministry of Internal Affairs.[74] However, as migration commentators in Russia have pointed out, the nature of the ministries in other countries is very different; traditionally they, unlike the MVD, fulfil not only 'power functions' and are civilian-led.[75]

The gradual shift from 'provision' to 'control' during the 1990s with respect to the 'return' of the Russian communities is also reflected in legislative frameworks and migration programmes. Amendments introduced to the law 'On Forced Migrants' on 22 November 1995 reinforced the framing of the 'return' of the Russian communities, within a discourse of 'forced migration'. A separate article (Article 2) included in the law defined those who *could not* qualify for forced migrant status, with a clear distinction between economic and political migrants, excluding economic migrants from forced migrant status.[76] The amendments demonstrated the desire of the Russian state and the Federal Migration Service to discourage migration through a tightening of definition of status and a reduction in social provision.[77] The attempt to clarify the term 'forced migrant' and distinguish between 'economic' and 'political' migrants was widely interpreted by non-political actors as a politically influenced effort to discourage the movement of Russians to the Russian Federation and to encourage their continued residence in the countries of the 'near abroad'.[78] The introduction of a new Citizenship Law in May 2002 also affected the implementation of forced migrant legislation. Under the new law, migrants who arrive without Russian citizenship face a wait of five years before they are able to make an application for citizenship. As Russian citizenship is required for an application for forced migrant status to be made, then this will significantly reduce the numbers of arrivees able to apply.[79]

The implementation of migration legislation and associated migration pro-grammes also shapes and constrains the 'return' and resettlement of those rec-ognized by the 'homeland' state as 'forced migrants'. The contradiction between government programmes and the requirements of the migrant populations is brought out further in the book by drawing directly upon migrant experience. However, an initial example – the Federal Migration Programme (FMP) – may be given here. The first Federal Migration Programme (*Migratsiia*) that was de-veloped by the FMS in 1993 was directed to the solution of the resettlement problems of migrants from the 'near abroad'.[80] However, in the later pro-gramme for the period 1998–2000[81] a move was made away from providing assistance to forced migrants and, as stated by the head of the FMS at the time Tat'iana Regent, towards 'the regulation of migration flows in accordance with the socio-economic and geo-political interests of the Russian state'.[82] This was demonstrated by the inclusion in the programme of a policy of resettlement of migrants in rural, depressed and scarcely populated regions of the Russian Fed-eration. Although individual regions were not listed, the introduction of a dif-ferentiated loan system[83] was designed to influence the choice of resettlement of forced migrants and, along with other economic stimuli noted in the pro-gramme, to encourage resettlement in areas favoured by the state as part of an attempt to achieve repopulation and regeneration. The policy is a demonstra-tion of the wider priorities of the government, and their perception of what role the returning communities could play in the economic revival of the Russian Federation. It failed to address the specific make-up of the migrant population that is predominantly urban, with a high proportion of highly educated and qualified specialists. A lack of in-depth research into the regional suitability for the resettlement of migrants meant there was a danger of pushing migrants into unsuitable regions where they did not wish to settle.[84]

The discourse of 'forced migration', and its translation into policy and prac-tice, fails to recognize the complexity of different factors affecting the Russian communities resident in the 'near abroad', which are experienced in diverse ways by the individuals within these communities. The legal category of 'forced migrant' is a peculiarity of the Russian context and reflects the contentious na-ture of the position and possible 'return' of the Russian communities. The initial legislation on forced migrants and refugees in 1993, which separated 'forced mi-grant' from 'refugee', recognized the responsibility of the Russian Federation, as a post-imperial state and legal successor to the Soviet Union, to provide for its 'compatriots' who were forced to 'return' from the 'near abroad'.[85] However, the term 'forced', reiterated in the 1995 amendments, stresses the involuntary nature of the movement and rejects it as being a natural and voluntary 'repatriation'. Although forced migrants are legislated greater rights regarding residence and assistance than non-Russian refugees, from the outset the legislation did not provide for the possibility of state assisted large-scale 'repatriation'.[86] Russians living in the 'near abroad' who wish to obtain assistance in resettling on the territory of the Russian Federation are not protected by any legal acts unless they can show evidence of clear discrimination.[87]

Through the prioritization of the 'forced' nature of the movement, the government is suggesting that under normal circumstances the Russian communities would stay; a position that is central to the policy towards the communities in the newly independent states and their construction as a Russian 'diaspora'. Yet, as will be shown, the close interplay of political, economic, social and cultural forces affecting the decision making of the potential migrant renders it difficult to define a predominant cause of migration. The use of the term 'forced migration' in Russian political discourse and administrative practice needs to be questioned; in practice only a minority of returnees have experienced 'immediate force'.[88] Codagnone suggests that many of those who receive the status are indeed better defined as 'repatriates'.[89] The discrepancy does not suggest that those 'repatriates' who return are not in need of government assistance, or that the severity of their life situation in the former republics was not sufficient to necessitate migration, but rather reveals the difficulties in labelling diverse movements in a uniform way at a policy level. To an extent the lack of any alternative legislation contradicts the Russian state policy of 'diasporization' that constructs the Russian Federation as the natural/historical 'homeland' of the Russian communities. Yet the right of the 'diaspora' to return to this 'homeland', with the assistance of the state, is limited to those returnees able to prove they were 'forced' to move.

Finally, it is useful to place the shift in approach towards the migration of the Russian communities, and the changes in the institutional and legislative frameworks of the migration regime, within the broader context of a move towards the 'securitization' of Russia's post-Soviet borders.[90] This process took place on two levels. Firstly, as suggested above, the securitization of the wider borders of the Russian 'nation' took place where the previous 'imperial' lands of the Russian and Soviet 'empires', and particularly the Russian 'diaspora' resident there, came to be seen as an integral part of reconstructing a post-Soviet Russian national identity that reached beyond the confines of the present-day borders of the Russian Federation. Secondly, the securitization of the internal borders of the Russian 'state' occurred; this was seen as necessary to protect domestic socio-economic and political stability and to isolate the Russian state from external 'threats' – e.g. migrants. Present government migration debate and policy has been criticized in particular for identifying the threat of 'illegal' migration, primarily of non-ethnic Russian migrants, as a major threat to the security of the country and individual regions, as have certain politicians and the mass media for the 'demonizing' of other 'ethnic minority' migrants.[91] With particular regard to the ethnic Russian and Russian-speaking forced migrant populations, this dual 'securitization' meant that an initial willingness to accept their return and provide for their resettlement was slowly replaced by increasing restrictions on in-migration and a reduction in assistance at the sites of settlement on Russian territory, so that a reluctant rather than a welcoming 'homeland' met the majority of 'forced' migrants upon their 'return'.

Repatriation discourse – encouraging a 'return' to 'homeland'

The dominant 'diaspora' and 'forced migration' discourses, and their translation into legislation and policy, have been accompanied over the past decade by another more marginal discourse relating to the Russian communities and their possible 'return' migration. Over the period 1991–2002, certain actors identified the lack of alternative legislation to allow the voluntary return of the Russian communities to the Russian Federation, particularly during the development of the policy towards the Russian communities in the 'near abroad'. During 1996–7 'repatriation' entered the mainstream migration debate, and calls were made for the introduction of a 'repatriation' law.[92] Amongst its main advocates were representatives of the democratic camp and the growing non-governmental sector. The Parliamentary Committee on CIS Affairs and Relations with Compatriots proposed a bill on repatriation with significant input from the non-governmental sphere.[93] The bill suggested a shift away from 'forced migration' as the central concept of the legislative framework in an attempt to establish a fundamental right to return irrespective of the reason for departure for citizens of the Russian Federation and Russian compatriots. The draft bill tried to bridge the artificially created gap between economic or political migrants that was encoded in forced migrant legislation by instilling the 'right' to return, and not concentrating on the reason for departure. The NGOs promoting a repatriation bill were also attempting to increase aid to a larger number of migrants in the face of the increasingly restrictive attitude of the Russian state, and to reframe the 'return' as a positive movement where the returning migrants would be seen as a beneficial population influx to help rebuild the Russian nation. Despite support from certain sectors of the government, there was no legislative outcome and a 'repatriation' discourse faded from the migration agenda.

Nevertheless, towards the end of 2000 the possibility of the state encouragement of repatriation re-emerged amongst government circles. The change is rooted in the increasing significance of the demographic question for post-Soviet Russia. By the end of 2000, the Russian population had suffered a negative natural population growth of 6 million since 1992 due to rising death rates and falling birth rates. Levels of in-migration from the 'near abroad' had compensated for this loss; however, those migration flows have been continually falling since 1995.[94] In November 2000, President Putin suggested that increased immigration from the former Soviet republics to Russia might solve the country's demographic problems. It is highly probable that Putin had in mind the 20 million ethnic Russians in the former republics, rather than the non-Russian populations from these countries.[95] A number of parliamentary deputies, particularly members of centrist factions, also called for the state-sponsored repatriation of the Russian communities to solve the demographic crisis.[96] In addition to the government revival of interest, actors within the non-governmental sector – who had been particularly vocal during earlier debates – renewed their support for a repatriation law, in some cases in collaboration with government deputies (see Chapter 5).[97]

However, there has been criticism of the implications of pursuing such a policy. Encouragement by the Russian state of the mass migration of 'ethnic' Russians from the former republics would problematize the future residence of those who wish to remain, may prevent the communities from attempting to fully integrate, and would affect Moscow's relations with the states it had long declared its primary foreign policy focus. It is likely that the policy would be accompanied by the increased restriction of the in-migration of non-ethnic Russians. There are already signs within Russian official discourse of a clear division of migrants into two groups: 'desirables' and 'undesirables', where 'quality' immigrants (i.e. 'compatriots' from the other former republics) are seen as beneficial, while migrants of other ethnic groups (Chinese, African, Roma, Central Asian, Caucasian) are seen as a threat.[98] Doubts have also been expressed about the capabilities of the Russian state to find the funds needed for such an effort in the current economic climate, taking into account the fact that the Russian government has failed to meet its obligations to those who have already returned, and that it liquidated the federal migration programme in June 2001 by excluding it from a list of financed programmes. Finally, changes to the Law on Citizenship problematize such proposals for 'repatriation'. As noted above, the new citizenship law passed in May 2002 states that persons are eligible to apply for citizenship only if they have lived in Russia for five years from the time of gaining permission for permanent residence. In contrast to the previous citizenship law of 1993, there are no special conditions for former citizens of the Soviet Union, apart from those born on the former territory of the RSFSR, and, following amendments to the law, for those who are already on Russian territory and who arrived prior to 1 July 2002 (see note 79). Thus, any real state support for a formal process of 'repatriation' continues to be restricted to the level of discourse.[99]

Nevertheless, 'repatriation' discourse has been significant for its attempt to reframe the nature of the 'return' of the Russian communities to the Russian Federation. It recognizes the need for a distinction between the different types of migration that inevitably occur with the collapse of a multinational empire and reflects the widespread interpretation by western and Russian academics, and some Russian non-governmental and governmental experts, of the migration processes going on between the Russian Federation and the 'near abroad' as a continuation of those which began before the breakup of the Soviet Union. If 'repatriation' discourse was translated into actual policy, the movement of the Russian communities would be legislatively reframed as the official 'return' to homeland, rather than a forced movement away from a territorial but not, according to the 'diasporization' policy, 'historical' homeland. However, repatriation is in danger of assuming an unproblematic collective view of Russia as a natural 'homeland' and a common desire to 'return' on the side of the Russian communities regardless of their personal current environment. How many of the returnee community who would have chosen to move if they had not suffered discrimination is open to debate.[100] Absent from this discourse is consideration of those who wish to remain, many of whom regard their former places of residence as their home and do not feel a 'natural' attachment to Russia. The gaps in the debate, as in the 'diaspora' and 'forced migration' cases, highlight the need to move away from state-constructed discourse concerning the migration process to the understandings of the process amongst individual migrants.

CONCLUSION

Government policy towards the 'return' and resettlement of the Russian populations demonstrates the ability of key state actors to frame a potential migrant population and their arrival in a particular way. Discourse and policy at the state level, rooted in domestic socio-economic concerns and external geo-political priorities, determines the way in which the migration process is constructed, and shapes policy towards both the potential migrant communities and those who have 'returned'. Comprehension of the historical contexts of the migration and settlement process is central to present understandings of reaction and response, at both the state and the individual level. The political 'diasporization' of the Russian communities in the successor states maintains a connection from the past between the Russian centre and its 'borderland' populations – a connection that came increasingly to be seen as necessary for the emerging identity of the Russian state and nation in the post-1991 period. Both the debates and the legislative initiatives that have emerged during the process of political 'diasporization', however, reveal the divisions that continue to exist within the post-Soviet Russian state over the question of 'what is Russia?' and 'who are the Russians?'

In real terms, the 'homeland' created through this policy of 'diasporization' for the Russian communities in the 'near abroad' is a virtual 'homeland' removed from their immediate reality, the priority of the Russian government being to uphold their right to 'remain'. The migration regime that developed on the territory of the Russian Federation is centred around a discourse of 'forced migration', is often restrictive and does not necessarily reflect the reality and needs of the returning individuals. Official Russian state discourse and policy that has developed towards the Russian communities both in 'diaspora' and after migration has not constructed the territory of the Russian Federation as 'homeland'; in fact, for those who 'return' it would appear to impede a sense of 'homeland' and 'home' from developing. Throughout this chapter, the deficiencies of government policy and discourse have been hinted at. Subsequent chapters, through an examination of migrants' own perceptions and experiences of being 'in diaspora' and of subsequent migration and resettlement, will both disrupt, and further reveal the inadequacies of, official discourse and policy.

3

Leaving 'Home' and 'Homeland'? The Decision to Migrate

The previous chapter demonstrated how through discursive, legislative and policy frameworks, the Russian government has been influential in constructing the nature of the territory of the Russian Federation for both the Russian communities in 'diaspora' and the 'returning' migrants. The tendency has not been to construct the Russian Federation as an accessible and welcoming 'homeland' for the 'returning' Russians, but to discourage movement to the territory and to restrict resettlement and provision opportunities upon arrival. However, the construction of the Russian 'homeland', via government discourse and policy, cannot be assumed to primarily determine the experience of 'homeland' by returnees. To appreciate the reality of this 'homeland' for those returning, it is necessary to understand the direct effect of government discourse and policy upon migrants, and to comprehend their response. It is also necessary to access migrants' own perceptions of 'home' and 'homeland', and to explore how these relate to how Russia has been – and is now – imagined. Such a framework provides a basis for comprehending how Russia as 'homeland' is then experienced upon 'return'.

The present chapter therefore shifts the level of analysis to that of the individual migrant and their parameters of 'home' and 'homeland'. Whereas the previous chapter demonstrated the historical and contemporary significance of the territory that stretches between the present day regions of departure and arrival, and how past and present connections at the state level impact upon governmental responses to migration and resettlement, this same approach is now initiated at the individual level. The chapter is structured around migrant narratives of their lives prior to the move to the Russian Federation, and their understandings of 'home' and 'homeland' at their long-term place of residence: the former Soviet republic. It firstly demonstrates how 'home' and 'homeland' existed in tandem for the migrants in the former republics, but reveals the subtle differences that differentiated understandings of the two concepts at this location. Secondly, it furthers understanding of the two concepts by exploring how 'home' and 'homeland' were disrupted by the wider political and socioeconomic upheaval that succeeded the collapse of the Soviet Union in 1991, and why this disruption led to the decision to migrate to the Russian Federation – the 'historical homeland'. Integral to the analysis is an exploration of migrants' connections to and perceptions of the Russian 'core' territory, the former national republic, and the Soviet Union within narratives of their past lives, and how these are starting to be renegotiated in the contemporary period. In the light of empirical evidence, the chapter revisits the strict and simplistic labelling of the communities as a 'diaspora' separated from their 'historical homeland', or as a 'repatriate' community willing to return or refugee type movement forced to flee. The dichotomy of 'home' and 'homeland' that emerges through the chapter provides an essential comparative framework within which the subsequent migrant experience of 'return' to the Russian Federation and resettlement on this territory can be explored in subsequent chapters.

MEMORIES OF 'HOME/LAND'

As introduced in Chapter 1, the two key linguistic terms employed by migrants that shape the 'home/land' framework are *rodina* ('homeland') and *doma* ('at home'). These terms may be loosely associated with the two meanings of home suggested by Brah (see Chapter 1): *rodina* as the wider 'narrative of the nation' (the former Soviet Union, or national republic, or the ethnic Russian homeland), and *doma* as the 'site of everyday lived experience' (the immediate physical surroundings of the physical 'home' in the former republic). Migrants' use of the term *rodina* in particular contrasts with its usage in Russian political, academic, media and political discourse, where the term *istoricheskaia rodina* (the Russian 'historical homeland') prioritizes the 'ethnic' and wider basis of belonging to the 'homeland'. Instead, by uncovering the additional concept of *doma*, empirical analyses of migrant understandings of *rodina* challenge the assumption of a natural attachment to a single 'homeland'. Both terms encompass associations with a place where ethnicity is not prioritised – *doma* referring to the immediate physical and social relations within the prior locality, and *rodina* stressing the wider and at the same time more 'rooted' attachment to the locality and surrounding territory, a place where they were born, have grown up, have family connections. When migrants spoke of their lives in the former republics, the terms were frequently used in tandem and their meanings often overlapped. However, the specific associations of either term can be distinguished to demonstrate the different nature and levels of their attachment to that place and time.

The former republic as 'homeland'

Rodina was a key term applied by migrants to their former Soviet republic of residence, which is perhaps logical as linguistically the term *rodina* fixes homeland as the 'place of birth'.[1] Out of the 72 migrant respondents the majority were either born (or had spent the vast majority of their lives) outside the borders of the present-day Russian Federation; only 11 of the respondents were born on Russian territory. Thus, many of the respondents placed *rodina* 'there' (in the former republic), in the territory where they were born:

> I consider that my *rodina* is where I was born, if nothing had happened, we would have lived in that place, our parents are buried there.
>
> *10, Saratov, 1997*[2]

The importance of establishing some sense of family 'rootedness' over a period of time was demonstrated by migrants when they spoke about *rodina* as the territory where they were born, where their parents were buried, and to which their ancestors had arrived. In this sense the former republic was quite explicitly the land of their kin, their people (*rod-ina*).[3] Individuals narrated how they, or their ancestors before them, were born in the former republic; they located their ancestral roots as being there:

> I was born in Tashkent, in Uzbekistan. My parents were also born there. It is a long story. My ancestors settled there for different reasons. My grandfather and grandmother, from both sides. On my father's side, they ended up there after the war. I can't say exactly how, but they ended up there. My grandmother after the revolution with her parents also turned up there for some reason. And I was born there too.
>
> *19, Saratov, 1999*

This ancestral attachment to the land was highly significant for some of the migrants. Although the breakup of the Soviet Union had altered the political 'ownership' of the territory, there was still a sense amongst migrants that this was and would always be 'their space'. This very personal attachment to the land was often expressed through references to ancestors who were buried on the territory:

> My mother is still there, she doesn't want to go anywhere, you see, all of her relatives are still there, and. . .how could she? All of her ancestors are buried there.
>
> *64, Novosibirsk, 2002*

Katherine Verdery discusses in depth the political power of 'dead bodies', specifically with reference to the post-Yugloslav space and the close connections that persist between territories, ancestors, memories and kinship, despite the redrawing of nation-state borders. She explores the interlinked effects of the politics of national conflict, the creation of new states and the 'concomitant reconfiguring of space and time', on 'altering the significance of territory and on rewriting history'. She also highlights that 'temporal conceptions are crucial elements of human experience'.[4] The narratives of respondents in the present study demonstrate the very real significance of these disruptions of both space and time for individuals, one example being the enforced displacement and separation from the territory of their ancestors. A female migrant from Kazakstan now living in Novosibirsk reiterated the significance of attachments to the land, through ancestors, when she spoke about the importance of and desire to 'return' to the former republic where her relatives where buried, and the distress she felt when such a visit was not possible:

> I want to go back so much. It's ten years since my husband died. . .and I can't go, I haven't got enough money, it's an impossible situation with money. Tickets have become so expensive. And everyone is buried there, my mother, father, husband, grandmother. Of course we really want to go, but it's impossible.
>
> *65, Novosibirsk, 2002*

The Soviet Union as 'homeland'

Rather than confining *rodina* to the territory of the former republic, a number of the respondents in the study related 'homeland' to the temporal and spatial territory of the former USSR as a whole. This association supports evidence that the Russian communities more than any other national group during the Soviet period identified with a Soviet rather than a Russian homeland; they saw the entire Union, not only the Russian Republic, as 'their' national territory.[5] Although the creation of a Soviet national identity, and the existence or survival of a *Sovietskii narod*, is questioned[6], the narratives of these migrants demonstrate that for some it was not an 'empty ideological shell' but a 'lived reality'.[7] Identification with the Soviet Union as a 'homeland', membership of a multinational community, and also considerable mobility within this 'borderless' space, was clearly expressed by a number of respondents:

> My understanding of *rodina* is all of the Soviet Union. My mother was Belarusian, my father Ukrainian. I was born in Alma Ata, Kazakstan, in my passport it is written I am Russian. My husband is Mordvin, we lived in Tajikistan.
>
> *1, Saratov, 1997*

. . .At that time, before *perestroika*, we lived in Kazakstan. But we didn't think then that we lived in a foreign country, abroad. It wasn't like that. We lived, everything was good, there were no differences. A single economic zone, a single currency – everything was the same. It wasn't a problem for me to travel eight hours from the Urals to Saratov, to call on my people there. My mother was buried here in Saratov, my sister lived in Saratov. . .And now what? Earlier we thought that Kazakstan, Belarus, Ukraine – all of that, not the Russian Federation, but the Soviet Union was our homeland. And now of course, now alas, my wife can't even go to her home there, where she was born. Her sister, mother, were buried there, her father, everyone. But it is not conceivable anymore – now it isn't possible. . .earlier there wasn't a difference, and everyone was happy.

31, Saratov, 1999

This identification with the Soviet Union as a 'homeland' was interspersed with narratives describing respondents' family histories of migration, and how this individual/group movement interweaved with the overall Soviet socio-economic and political project. Two female migrants, both born in Ukraine, and having lived most of their lives in Tajikistan and Kazakstan prior to their move, relate family stories which demonstrate how their personal pasts are deeply entwined with the wider historical pasts of the Soviet Union:

My family are from Ukraine. I was born in Poltava in 1945, in November, right after the war. My father was a chief engineer, he graduated from two institutes in Moscow, and as a chief engineer he was sent to Central Asia as part of the industrialisation drive (*podnimat' promyshlennost'*). There was no industry to speak of; there was only agriculture there. At the beginning he was director of *Rudnik* in Turkmenistan. But at the start of 1937 he was repressed, my mother returned from Turkmenistan to Poltava, she lived there during the war, after the war my father went to Tajikistan. In Tajikistan he became a director of a factory, then an engineer, so he was working according to his profession. Because our roots were there, we did not plan to move anywhere. You know, the national question was not an issue. . . some of us were Ukrainains, some Russians, some Tajiks, some Uzbeks, we all lived peacefully. But then unfortunately this nationalism began.

69, Novosibirsk, 2002

I have an interesting past, during the war my mother was repressed and was sent from the Volga to Kazakstan, to a Kazak village called Kazbek. She was 15, and lived there till she was 30. In 1956, when she was 29, it was the time when people were being sent to the virgin lands in Kazakstan. My father came to the virgin lands as part of a team, and they met there, he was from Ukraine. After that they got married, they went back to Ukraine, to his parents. I was born there, but when I was two months old we returned to Kazakstan, to the village of Kazbek, where my father had worked on the virgin lands.

63, Novosibirsk, 2002

These quotes demonstrate how individuals and families moved to often neighbouring former republics, both due to forcible deportation or through migratory processes encouraged as a means of securing the expanding industrial and agricultural expanse of the Soviet Union.[8] However, the 'borders' between republics, which were crossed during the period of the Soviet Union, were often not perceived by respondents in any strict physical sense. This particular overland formation of the Soviet Union (and also the earlier Russian Empire) is seen to mark out the Russian settlers as different from other colonial settler groups, and to have had an impact on the development of their national or – in terms of the Russian core as 'homeland' – 'diasporic' identity. As Brubaker notes, the original migration from core to periphery involved no crossing of state borders; thus migration was not only legally and politically defined as internal migration but was psychologically experienced as such.[9] Instead, the contiguous nature of homeland and hostland, and their common statehood for a significant period of time, disrupted the 'classic relationship' of a diaspora 'cut off' from its 'homeland' for the Russian-speaking communities in the former republics. A diasporic relationship to Russia 'as homeland' was rarely experienced. Instead, as has been shown here, for many identification with Russia was displaced by a 'Soviet' identity and security within a wider Soviet homeland.

Locating a 'home' within the 'homeland'

The memories of *rodina* ('homeland'), whether perceived at the level of the multinational state (the Soviet Union) or the former republic, were closely associated with the immediate locale where the individual lived, and what the time spent in this place represented. When individuals spoke of this 'time' and 'place', then 'homeland (*rodina*) and being 'at home' (*doma*) were spoken about in terms of each other. The rooted existence of a home in the former republic allowed the wider territory (republic, or Soviet Union) to become that of their 'homeland'.

To appreciate what made this immediate lived locality 'home', consideration of both the physical and social aspects of the place of residence is needed.[10] Doreen Massey suggests that a 'place' is formed out of the particular set of social relations, which interact at a particular location.[11] Participation within the socio-economic structures of that location would facilitate the formation of such social relations, as would more personal friendship and family networks. In addition, the location may be seen as an extension of the immediate 'home'; an area where the individual feels 'at home' due to a familiarity with the area and its physical environment.[12] Social relations present within these spatial regions contribute to a 'sense of belonging' in this area. However, the secure spatial identity of the individual, their knowledge of, movement within and memories of the physical space are equally as important. A quote from a female migrant who had moved from Uzbekistan to Novosibirsk demonstrates such a sense of a secure spatial identity:

> Tashkent was much more beautiful than here. It is more compact. You know, on the whole I like small cities. I knew every alleyway, every street, I would come home late, sometimes even at midnight, in the dark, and I could go through the whole of the city by foot, I was never scared. . .
>
> *70, Novosibirsk 2002*

The narratives of migrants demonstrate the multi-layered practical and emotional attachment to the locality of 'home'. Much was attributed to 'home' being where a person had feelings of stability and belonging, when there had been employment, housing, friends and community. The presence of family, material objects, everyday routines, social relations, and their continuity over time, had created a sense of 'home' in that particular spatial region, and had generated a deeper sense of belonging to a wider 'homeland'.[13] The narratives of this time were firmly grounded in a sense of the security, safeness and completeness of life, based upon well-established networks, connections and roots, which had been built up often over generations. Migrants spoke of growing up, getting married and having children there. Their work, flats and summer houses (*dachas*) were located there. These articulations clearly indicate that not only did the former republics constitute respondents' 'homeland' (*rodina*) but also where they were 'at home' (*doma*):

> I was born there, grew up there, I had an apartment, I got married, my daughter was born there. I was born there. Everything was good, everything was good, I mean, we lived normally there. And then, when it all started, how do you call it, that nationalism. I don't understand where it came from. We lived all our lives there, we studied together, friends of mine got married to Kazaks, and everything was okay. Why did it all happen? After all, people lived there for so many years, we had 'warmed' our place. I had an apartment there, a summer house (*dacha*). . .
>
> *68, Novosibirsk 2002*

Alongside these expressions of having lived 'well', of security and normality, there was an absence of any remembered desires to 'return' home, or of feelings of being separated at that time from their ethnic 'homeland', i.e. Russia. To many, Russia was an unknown territory prior to 1991. The decision to 'return' to the Russian Federation was made by the majority of migrants in direct response to the disruption of the security of the life they had enjoyed in the former republic. Until this security was challenged, they had not imagined Russia as a lived alternative:

Up until those events in the nineties in Kazakstan, we lived very well. We did not even think we would go anywhere. I had a four roomed apartment, excellent work, my husband worked, we were well-provided for.

59, Samara, 1999

The memories of 'homeland' and 'home' provide an initial picture of the relationship that existed between the individuals, their former place of residence and the wider territory of the Soviet Union. However, it is the narratives that relate the 'disruption' of 'home' and 'homeland' which enable a further and more detailed picture to be gained.

THE DISRUPTION OF 'HOME' AND 'HOMELAND'

I was born there in 1940. I always lived there in the same place, only in Kazakstan, I studied in Kazakstan, received my education in Kazakstan, you know, it is my *rodina*. We lived well there, my father was born there, and my father's mother. My ancestors went there to serve the Tsar, they were Cossacks, they protected the borders. That is why it is our *rodina*, it was good for us there, but, we left, because there was nowhere to live, nowhere to work, nowhere, everything was over, civilisation ended, and that was all, the small town where we lived, everything, the railway stopped working, everything, no organisations, no enterprises, nothing was left, everything was finished, everything lost its status, its meaning, and the people themselves, what can you do? So we decided, in order not to perish, that we had to leave.

65, Novosibirsk, 2002

The statement of this female migrant from Kazakstan demonstrates how it was the immediate disruption of their 'homes', lived out in their everyday lives and rooted in the social, political, economic and ethnic security that they had experienced under the Soviet system, which led to the decision to migrate. The reasons given by migrants for moving are significant in terms of understanding how a previous 'home' and 'homeland' had been disrupted, and serve to further reveal the relationships and connections people had to their former place of residence. Socio-economic securities of life – employment, education, everyday practices – had been threatened. However, the underlying reasons for the disruption were often identified as ethnic, political causes. The migrants' narratives thus provide an insight into the complex interplay of economic, social and ethno-political forces, and the powerful blend of motives, that influence the personal and group decision-making process. Such complexity further disrupts the strict 'economic' or 'political'/ 'forced' or 'voluntary' dichotomy that is embedded in Russian migration legislation. However, in addition to indicating the reasons for movement, the experiences at the site of departure equally demonstrate why Russia is imagined as the most logical and viable solution when the decision to migrate is made.

The most frequent reasons for departure given by migrants were: socio-economic and material difficulties; a concern for the safety and future of the children; the actual threat to personal safety and lives from disorder and conflict; and isolation from their 'own' culture and people. These were rooted in the rise of 'nationalism', including discrimination on the basis of language and ethnicity and everyday displays of nationalist feeling. Migrants spoke about these factors simultaneously and in relation to one another. A growing 'ethnic discomfort' was interwoven with other socio-economic and material factors that influenced the decision-making process.[14] The unconscious merging of motivations demonstrates the interplay of political, social, economic and ethno-cultural factors at the site of departure, how the previous existence of these factors in some kind of equilibrium had ensured a sense of security and normality, and how this equilibrium had been unbalanced by recent events. The disruption took place at a number of different but connected levels and scales, which again feed into the 'home/land' framework.

Disruption of the 'everyday'

'Home' located at Brah's 'site of everyday lived experience' was increasingly under disruption due to the encounter of ethnic discomfort in daily socio-economic practices. Discrimination on the basis of language and ethnicity was talked about in the sphere of employment and had led to increases in levels of insecurity and uncertainty about the future. A female migrant of working age from Uzbekistan stated:

> We only moved to Russia in August 1998. But such a situation had arisen that we were forced to move. All the family were affected by nationalism. We had to learn the language, and it was already impossible to learn the language. . .there was no work, and if there is no work then of course there is no money, and you have to exist on nothing. Therefore we left.
>
> *29, Saratov, 1999*

Socio-economic factors and material difficulties, such as lack of jobs and money, were rarely mentioned in isolation as a factor in the decision to migrate; these material difficulties were rooted in an ethnic context and the nationalist tendencies at the wider level of society. Although in most cases actual ethnic conflict or disorder were not being experienced, and it was the immediate threat to socio-economic security that forced the decision to migrate, ethnic discomfort experienced at the level of the everyday had destroyed the security and stability of previous years. The situation generated feelings of uncertainty and a lack of hope in the future. A female migrant and mother spoke of her individual experience in Tajikistan:

> You cannot say that nationalism is propagandised in Tajikistan, that does not exist, but there is everyday nationalism on a juvenile level, and this is frightening because it is the prospect for the future, it is already on an unregulated level, when it flares up spontaneously, all of this together creates such premises that firstly there is no future for your children, and secondly there is no future for you because in essence there is nowhere to work. . .
>
> *62, Samara, 1999*

The experience of ethnic discomfort was not confined to the work sphere. Of concern to respondents was its growing presence in everyday routines; daily activities such as shopping, public transport or walking down the street were no longer 'safe' and unproblematic. The ability to move freely within the surrounding environment, i.e. the possession of a secure spatial identity within that locality, had been disrupted:[15]

> . . .there we were restrained, our freedom, even when we went into the town, on public transport we weren't allowed through. Even when I was pregnant no one offered me a seat, even when I was with a small baby.
>
> *57, Samara, 1999*

The expressions of insecurity about the present socio-economic reality and the disruption of daily routines and familiar practices within the surrounding environment not only demonstrate how feelings of being 'at home' at the 'site of the everyday' had been disrupted, but indicate the clear concern amongst migrants that at this locality such securities could not be guaranteed or regained in the future. Such a perception contributed to the decision to leave.

Disruption of the family

As shown above, the narratives of 'home' and particularly 'homeland' located in the former republics demonstrated the central importance of establishing the continuity and security of a family over generations, the perpetuation of *rod* (kin). Therefore, when the children's security, lives and futures were threatened, the former republic was lost as a *rodina* in this sense, as a place where the continuity and security of a family could be guaranteed. In its stead, the Russian Federation was perceived as the place where a future 'homeland', especially for the children, might be secured. The threat to their children's security was rooted in a combination of ethnic and socio-economic factors.[16] The most predominant concern was for the short-term educational prospects of children due to the decline of adequate educational facilities for Russian speaking children in the former republics.[17] A young female migrant and mother who had arrived from Tajikistan to Saratov *oblast'* expressed these concerns:

> Recently there has been a large outflow of the Russian-speaking population from Tajikistan. All Russian specialists have begun to leave. There are no schools left for us. And we have a child, a daughter, she is thirteen. She has to study, and on the whole the schools are without teachers. . .we left because of this.
>
> *27, Saratov, 1999*

Concerns were also expressed for the long-term educational and professional prospects of the children, and the growing isolation of the children from their 'own' culture. A female migrant and mother, also from Tajikistan, who arrived in Samara *oblast'* in 1998, articulated these fears and the part they played in making the decision to migrate:

> The primary reason [for migration] was most of all the children, the fact that there was no future for them. It was impossible for them to study, impossible even to receive elementary education. Then there is the problem of the isolation of the children from their native culture, from its roots, in Tajikistan. It would be impossible for our children to receive higher education in Russia because they study according to a different programme, which means they lag behind. That would mean that they are denied higher education. Then there is the problem of teachers, there has been a constant outflow of the population and this has naturally lowered the standard of teaching.
>
> *62, Samara, 1999*

Children are seen as an essential part of a family network that can be used as a base to re-establish roots in the new place of residence. After arrival a number of individuals spoke of how Russia had provided the chance to initiate the process of securing their children's future. The primary concern of these respondents was clearly not their own security and well-being but that of their offspring. Thus the purpose of migration was seen through the eyes, and the future, of their children. Two female migrants from Tajikistan and Uzbekistan demonstrated this concern:

> They [our children] were receiving no sort of education. Basically we left for the children. Because, we, as you say, have had our day. But we must get our children established, that is the most important thing.
>
> *21, Saratov, 1999*

> . . .I wouldn't have come here if it had been possible not to worry about the future of my children. The schools closed, or as they say there, united, Russian and Uzbek together. There was trouble between the Russian people and the indigenous population. Children would throw stones at one another – what good is there in that? Of

course it was terrible. The best option was to come here. The children study at the gymnasium, my daughter has gone into the eleventh class.

70, Novosibirsk, 2002

DISRUPTION OF NETWORKS

The security of an established community, and the social network which formed this community in the former republics, were other key components of understandings of 'home'. The presence of a familiar and rooted set of social relations within a particular locality contributes to a 'sense of belonging' and a feeling of group identity situated at that locality. With significant changes in this environment, disruption of a secure sense of individual/group identity centred on both immediate and wider stable social networks can occur.[18] As the Russian population began to leave, social networks started to break down, and Russians who remained increasingly felt the lack of supportive social structures. A migrant from Uzbekistan spoke of this:

> All the Russians are leaving. Conditions there do not allow you to live. Everything is in Uzbek. And most of all what frightens you is that Russians are leaving. Only a few Russians are left. Living conditions of course are terrible. Even though here it is not much better, we are living amongst Russians, in Russia, all of us have Russian citizenship.

42, Saratov, 1999

The effect of other members of their family or close friends leaving also had a significant influence upon feelings of security. An elderly male migrant from Uzbekistan stated:

> We took the decision to leave, we spoke a lot about it, you know we started to panic, our family, all of our relatives, all the people close to us had begun to leave, it influences your psyche, so we thought it over and decided to leave.

54, Samara, 1999

The gradual breakup of a previous network of family and friends threatened one of the factors of stability that had rooted their lives in the former republics. The centrality of these networks to a sense of 'home', and the deep sense of loss felt due to a separation from them, was clearly expressed by many migrants:

> You know, all our friends and relatives are still there; they haven't got any money to move. It is difficult in your soul – do you understand? In your soul you yearn for that place, for your *rodina*, but you also know that a lot of your close acquaintances have left, it is difficult for the soul, because you remember everything, how we all lived together, there is such nostalgia, but I know that only a few people are still there, of those that we were close to.

64, Novosibirsk, 2002

The importance of such networks to feelings of 'home', and on a practical level to survival, is apparent in the desire to utilize, preserve or re-create such networks in the later stages of the migration process: the actual move, and at the site of settlement. This is explored in detail in Chapter 6.

A LOSS OF 'HOMELAND': DISRUPTING THE CONCEPT OF 'DIASPORA'

Rejection by the territorial 'homeland'

Although the majority of the respondents located their homeland (*rodina*) in the former republic, and did not demonstrate any clear 'ethnic' attachment to the 'historical homeland', a consciousness of 'being Russian' was heightened by the experiences of ethnic discomfort in the former republics. In these cases, Russia was rediscovered or uncovered as the 'ethnic homeland'.[19] Through their experiences in the former republics, the respondents were confronted with an 'ethnic' identity which many of them had previously not prioritized but were now forced to come to terms with. Therefore, a possible 'diasporic' identity was engendered because of their experience. Many respondents spoke of the verbal abuse they received in public on the grounds of their ethnicity, and of being told to 'return' to 'their Russia':

> It was difficult. They said to us 'your homeland (*rodina*) is Russia – you are Russian – go back to your Russia.'
>
> *42, Saratov, 1999*

Migrants also received these demands from within the immediate local community and social networks of which they had previously felt a part. A female migrant spoke of a particularly distressing moment when a lifelong friend with whom she had grown up told her:

> It is time for you to go to Russia, there is nothing for you to do here, this is *our land*.
>
> *35, Saratov, 1999*

This 'rejection' by the territorial homeland, on both a public and more personal level, was then countered by the perception of Russia as a solution to this 'ethnic' discomfort. A female migrant in Novosibirsk related how a friend who had already made the move to Russia, upon returning to Kazakstan for a holiday insisted that she (the respondent) should move to Russia precisely because she would be 'amongst other Russians'. The fact of being ethnic Russian (*russkii*) was initially identified as the problem, and subsequently Russia as the ethnic homeland was identified as the solution, principally for the normality it was hoped it would ensure:

A friend of mine who worked at the chemist with me, she moved here (Novosibirsk), and then came back on holiday, and said to me 'people live a completely different life there. Russians live amongst Russians, they speak Russian, no one oppresses anyone. What sort of life is it for you if you and your children are mocked, scorned, why are you living here? It is already impossible to live here. Everything, homes are deserted, children don't go to school, there is nowhere to study, no coal, no firewood, no work. Why are you sitting here, what are you waiting for? You are Russian, Russians live there, they get up, go out to work, perhaps they don't live well, but they live.'

65, Novosibirsk, 2002

Such experiences of 'ethnic discomfort', and the perception of Russia as the solution, therefore increased the ethnic consciousness of the potential migrants. Due to the context of the movement, for some respondents migration to Russia was directly perceived at this point as a return to an ethnic homeland:

We are Russian (*russkie*), we have come to our Russian brothers, we have not just moved anywhere, we have come to our native Russia.

35, Saratov, 1999

The sense of rejection by the new 'territorial' homeland on the grounds of ethnicity was heightened when migrants spoke of how they no longer felt 'needed' in the country where they had once felt valued. The role they considered that they had fulfilled during the time of the Soviet Union, and the socio-economic identity this had provided them with – of a valuable force for change, improvement and development in the former republics – had been challenged and displaced. Both a 'homeland' and 'home' that had been created was being broken down:

. . .everyone started to leave, everything became so bad there, there was no work, no future for the children. Everything went into Kazak, there was already nothing for us – although our parents had gone there to open up a new land, to build everything, but we turned out to be, how to say, redundant.

34, Saratov, 1999

Everything happened all of a sudden. . .we didn't have time to collect ourselves. Russians were told, 'Get out of here, you Russians, you are nobody.' But how are we nobody? We built the town, it was built mainly by Russians, Russians made up 80 per cent of the population there, and 20 per cent Kazak. Now, everything is the other way around. Immediately, at the beginnings of the 90s, specialists began to leave, doctors, professors, all the Russians began to leave.

68, Novosibirsk, 2003

Research on the situation of ethnic Russian and Russian-speaking communities in the former republics has noted the effect on individuals who have experienced a loss of meaning in life, self-confidence and self-respect due to feelings of not being needed in a country which was once considered their *rodina*. Although economic and material factors are recognized as being significant in the decision to migrate, the movement is also seen as an important way out of a crisis of ethnic, social and personal identity, where the new place of settlement (the Russian Federation) is perceived as the place where it is possible to recover personal self-respect and a sense of positive ethnic and social identity.[20] However, as will be demonstrated in later chapters, upon arrival migrants' understanding of both their 'newly discovered' Russian ethnic identity and their desire to restore a stable socio-economic identity is challenged, through interaction with the state during their resettlement and with the local community. This makes the recovery of a positive sense of either identity problematic.

Loss of the wider 'homeland'

Although the loss of 'homeland' was experienced at the territorial level of the former Soviet republic, its loss or disruption was also related directly by some migrants to the political and physical collapse of the Soviet Union. This again demonstrates the multi-layered understanding of 'homeland' amongst the returning migrants. With the collapse of the USSR and the redrawing of political borders, this wider 'homeland' was lost and could never be returned to either temporally or spatially. This reflects what Jansen terms the 'contradictory nature of movement' where even when people 'stay at home', they can find themselves displaced since borders are 'travelling' as well.[21] The wider 'homeland', which had ensured the Russian communities their secure socio-economic and political identity, had disappeared. The 'homeland' embodied in the Soviet Union was rooted in both memories of a time and experiences of a place, neither of which any longer existed. It represented a territory and wider 'homeland' which could not be returned to. A female migrant from Uzbekistan expressed this when she said:

> Of course I miss it, because all the best things remain there, of course I miss it. Not the Uzbekistan that exists now, no, not that, but, how can I say, that time, the Union.
>
> *70, Novosibirsk, 2002*

A comparison can be drawn with experiences of displacement in the former Yugoslavia. In a study located in this territory, Jansen shows how the private narratives of certain individuals and their sense of belonging to the 'former Yugoslavia' have been displaced by war, an event which led to a breaking point both in the grand narrative of Yugoslavia and in the narration of individual identities. A 'return' to this 'homeland' is no longer possible, since it would involve not a spatial but a temporal journey.[22] Although the circumstances of the breakup of the Soviet Union were very different, the relationship between the former Union and the individual sense of belonging to this Union have been broken. A number of migrants were clearly aware of the irony of their situation, prior to leaving their former homes – the fact that although they had remained stationary, political borders had moved 'over them' making them 'immigrants' within what they still identified as 'their own country', but this country (the Soviet Union) in fact no longer existed:[23]

> . . .Do you understand? We don't even understand ourselves what happened to us. We were all Soviet, we all just got on with living. And suddenly we found ourselves to be immigrants within our own country. But how? Within *our own* country [*svoei strane*], we were still in *our* own country.
>
> *65, Novosibirsk, 2002*

> Generally we lived peacefully. I went to Ukraine for four months to study – that was when it was the Soviet Union, I knew that I was still in my country. Do you understand? What did I have? – It was a security, that I had everything, it was all mine, wherever I went.
>
> *64, Novosibirsk, 2002*

These migrant narratives disrupt any simplistic labelling of the Russian communities resident in the other former Soviet republics as a Russian 'diaspora'. Indeed, if the label is applied then firstly it must be associated not with any initial movement away from a 'homeland' but with a clear lack of movement; what moved in 1991 were the borders of the Soviet 'homeland', not the specific ethnic communities. A number of studies have tried to conceptualize the peculiarity of the 'diasporic' status of the Russian communities. Robin Cohen classifies the Russians in the Soviet successor states as a 'stranded minority', akin to Hungarians 'stranded' across a number of other European countries upon the breakup of the Austro-Hungarian empire, while Emil Payin calls them an 'imperial minority'.[24] In a similar fashion, David Laitin refers to ethnic minorities who become a diaspora as a result of boundary shifts as 'beached' diasporas[25], while Rogers Brubaker refers to them as 'accidental' diasporas.[26] On the same grounds – that the 'diaspora' was a result of the collapse of empire rather than flight from the homeland – Graham Smith refers to the Russian 'diaspora' as 'borderland Russians', suggesting thereby that they are bound together only by their similar geographical location vis à vis the homeland – Russia – rather than any common identity.[27]

However, although these terms more closely represent how the possible 'diaspora' came about, perhaps they still assume too great an automatic attachment to the 'severed' homeland – the Russian core. The migrant narratives represented here suggest that many members of the Russian communities in 1991 felt displaced within a 'homeland' (the Soviet Union, the former Soviet republic) that no longer exists, rather than feeling suddenly physically separated from a long-imagined Russian 'homeland'. Although changing experiences vis à vis their new territorial 'homeland' foster a rediscovered awareness of their Russian-ness, it is difficult to position individuals firmly within a diaspora framework or to comprehend their move to the Russian Federation as an unproblematic 'return' to 'homeland'. The move to Russia was rarely a positive response by a 'diaspora' to a call from their 'historical homeland' – in fact any mention of such a call was completely absent from the respondents' narratives.[28]

FUTURE IMAGININGS OF 'HOME' AND 'HOMELAND'

The migrants' reasons for leaving their former places of residence, and choosing to move to the Russian Federation, demonstrate the disruption of both a sense of immediate lived 'home' and wider-rooted 'homeland'. With the political, social, economic and cultural changes brought about by the collapse of the Soviet Union, the security of both 'home' and 'homeland' had been disrupted and disconnected from one another. At this point, Russia was imagined as providing a possible return to both, as a place where they could be re-created and as the logical solution to the displacement felt. Yet, as argued above, this 'imagining' of Russia cannot be translated into a representation of the Russian communities as a 'diaspora' longing to return to an 'ethnic' historical homeland. Instead the 'logic' of choosing Russia should be seen in more practical and personal terms. Firstly, the presence of historical, political, social and economic institutional links between the former republics and the Russian Federation, and in particular the personal links that existed for many of the migrants with relatives or friends who were long-term residents of Russia, or other family and friends who had moved, meant the move was achievable.[29] Secondly, as a site of settlement Russia was a place where the future might be imagined, a place which would enable, in the first instance, a re-creation of the securities of 'home' – housing, jobs, education for their children, social networks – which had come under threat and for many had been destroyed.[30]

The persistence and renewal of 'home'

It is when migrants talked of their new lives upon arrival in the Russian Federation that a distinction could be seen more clearly between 'homeland' and being 'at home'. As shown above, the narratives of life in the former republics demonstrate the close association of *rodina* and *doma*, and their roots in the continuity and security of the past. In the present, this close association is severed, as *rodina* continued to be rooted in the past for the majority of returnees. It was not just attached to the physical space where they were born, but also to their memories of that place, the roots in that locality, the identity and security that both the time and place had provided, which could not in that form be re-lived or re-created. For many, an association of Russia as their homeland had never been consciously made; their *rodina* would always remain in the former republic, or in other cases in the wider space of the Soviet Union:

> I consider that Uzbekistan remains and will always be my *rodina* (homeland). I never considered Russia, there is only one *rodina*, and for me it is Uzbekistan.
>
> *53, Samara, 1999*

Thus, on arrival in the Russian Federation many migrants had a sense of having 'no homeland'. Nevertheless, although 'home' was also located in the former republic and in memories of the past, these memories could be used in the reconstruction of 'home' in the present place of residence. This demonstrates the persistence of 'home' for the displaced over time and space, despite its disruption in a physical sense. Papastergiadis rightly queries, on what grounds do stories and images of the self rest when the 'I' has been dislocated from home?[31] Perhaps it is through these continuing memories and expressions of 'home'.[32] Jansen notes that individuals may use narratives of everyday life in an attempt to preserve a certain continuity, a sense of spatial and temporal orientation, so that war (and displacement) are not seen as immediate when they are kept out of the places, networks and meanings that constitute 'home'.[33] For those respondents in the present study, past memories of 'homeland' and 'home' in the former republic were constantly retold to hold on to and maintain a connection with the security of the past, and a sense of self.[34] Nevertheless, they acknowledged the very real and necessary process of reconstructing 'home' on Russian territory as the present task.[35] The process would be one of 'becoming' or 'rooting', of finding 'their own place'. The following quotes display these intentions:

> I lived all my life there, of course the nostalgia torments me. I remember all the good days there, but I have faced up to the fact that I have to live here. Do you understand? I was born there, I studied there, I have many friends, many memories, all that was good, my youth, was spent there. But I have set myself the task that I will live here, but of course there is nostalgia.
>
> *27, Saratov, 1999*

> I plan to find permanent work here, to find my 'nook' and to live, to work further, to make friends.
>
> *22, Saratov, 1999*

When will it be home? Probably when I already have a place of my own, you know, when I've found myself a niche.

70, Novosibirsk, 2002

The possibility of a future 'homeland'

The narratives above describe a process of 're-creation' and transferral. There was a clear acceptance that the period of *rodina* being 'there' was over in a physical, lived sense. Respondents rarely envisaged return as a real possibility, although the memory of the 'homeland' remained potent. The goal upon arrival in the Russian Federation was to attempt to rebuild their 'home' – signifying the security of housing and employment, the establishment of family and friends and a future for their children. The first step was to re-create 'home' in Russia; if they managed this successfully, it might become 'homeland' for future generations. The quote below clearly demonstrates the way in which a female migrant from Kazakstan perceives Russia upon 'return'; it embodies her hopes for the future clearly centred on her children, and also demonstrates that what she sees will facilitate a 'sense of home' for her: in this case housing, acceptance and integration with the local community, forming new friendships:

> Well, I think I am better here. Of course, it is not my *rodina* (homeland). My *rodina* is there, where I was born, where my friends are. But I think Russia has to become my 'home' (*dom*). If there is housing, I will consider that Russia is my home. I am prepared to kiss the Russian earth. . . I think, yes definitely, our home is amongst the Russian nation. With time, they will understand us and we will understand them. Up to now we haven't had much close contact with the local population. They think that we, who have come here, are rich, but with time. . .it is very difficult to get to know people. . .you know at our age? How do you get to know people? How do you make new friends? You see, we have come here, and we generally just talk to our own people – migrants. To get to know them, the locals – they are not really open towards us. . . If we get housing then it will be easier for us. Then, Russia will become 'homeland' and 'home', because our children will be here. Our children will have children, and there will be grandchildren. And then we will have everything here. There is already no road back to Kazakstan – it would be very difficult. No, we put up with everything for the sake of our children. How can it not be difficult for us now, without friends, without close ones, without housing, but it is possible to put up with for the sake of our children. That's how I think. A future will be here for our children. We will try to ensure that there will be everything for them.

35, Saratov, 1999

The fact that Russia was envisaged as a future homeland for the children is significant.[36] Firstly, it again demonstrates the centrality of kin, and its re-rooting, to perceptions and possibilities of 'homeland'. Secondly, it suggests that the feelings of displacement and loss of 'homeland' that the returning migrants were experiencing would be transitory across generations. The relationship of the first generation to the place of migration is obviously different from that of subsequent generations. Reactions amongst initial returnees to the new 'home' is mediated by memories of what was recently left behind, and by the experiences of disruption and displacement as they try to reorientate, to form new social networks, and learn to negotiate new economic, political and cultural realities.[37] Migrants spoke of how some of their children had already grown up on Russian territory, for them the sense of displacement from their previous 'homeland' was not felt to such an extent. The children would go through the process of growing up and establishing their own 'roots' in the Russian Federation, the place where both their 'home' and 'homeland' would be located, as their parents had done in the former republics. However, for their parents their *rodina* was rooted 'there', and the dislocation from their *rodina* could not be overcome even with the re-creation of 'home':

> I cannot say that I exactly feel at home. But I feel calm, simply calm. It is already the children, grandchildren, this will be their *rodina* in time, when it has all settled down.
>
> *39, Saratov, 1999*

Thus, despite the displacement experienced, it is clear that migrants have a strong sense of what Russia 'will be' upon arrival – if not for them, then for their children. This immediately warns against assuming that a 'sense of place' either at the wider national or immediately located level is permanently lost with physical displacement. 'Home' and 'homeland' can be seen as situational, and therefore also mobile, as changes in both the immediate and wider environment challenge their stability and reality. Massey notes for example that the identities of places are unfixed, precisely because the social relations from which they are constructed are themselves dynamic and changing.[38] This allows for a place to be thought of as 'home', but also allows for the mobility of 'home' and its re-creation in a new location. The processes of 'return' and 'migration' would engender the negotiation of a relationship with the Russian Federation and its possible existence as a location for the creation of a new 'home', where it was hoped re-entry into the 'operating structures' of society, the re-creation of social networks and a sense of security within the surrounding environment would occur. From the insights of their lives in the former republics, it is clear that the process of transferral of 'home' and 'homeland' would occur in distinct stages and at different levels. Thus, the 'return' is best understood not as the immediate 'return' of ethnic Russians to their 'homeland' but as the migration of individuals to a new locality, where they face the challenges of recreating what constitutes 'home' in this new locality and where they hope to establish the connections, particularly for their children, for an eventual future 'homeland'.

CONCLUSION

> Where is my homeland (*rodina*)? Well, I was born in Ukraine. My father went there to open up the virgin lands, his relatives are still there. So, if you think of *rodina* as being by birth, then it is Ukraine, it is a moral perception, it is my *rodina*, where I was born – that is the main thing that occupies my consciousness. But then Kazakstan, probably it is my *rodina*, I spent the longest period of my life there, from when I was little to when I was 30 years old – I spent my youth there, and memories, happy times, youth, all those memories. And here, here is today's life. But, then for me *rodina* is something wider, it is probably the Soviet Union, it was the union of everything.
>
> *63, Novosibirsk, 2002*

This statement made by a female migrant from Kazakstan, who had arrived to Novosibirsk *oblast'* in 1993, reiterates the complexity of locating 'homeland' in a specific territory, or even within a distinct period of time. It also disputes the idea of Russia as naturally representing the 'homeland'. Although during the period of the Soviet Union it is likely that Russia was present in the consciousness and imaginations of the Russian communities resident in the former republics, the narratives of migrants involved in this study demonstrate that in contrast with other 'diasporas', the 'myth of homeland', a dream of going home[39], did not exist. Russia – though present as an 'imagined community'[40] to which they had been attached through the Soviet Union – only became relevant to everyday life with the collapse of the Soviet Union, when the reality of living in their physical 'homeland' (the former republic) significantly changed, and when this territory was suddenly cut off from the Russian core.

Therefore it was only upon the collapse of the USSR, when the normality and security of their previous lives were displaced and replaced by uncertainty and insecurity about the future, that Russia presented itself as a possible alternative place of residence. As the situational contexts within which the Russian communities were located radically changed, they were forced to renegotiate their relationship with the territory of the former republics.[41] Some members of the communities would successfully rebuild their sense of home and 'belonging' within that same territory.[42] Another outcome of the renegotiation was the migration and 'return' to the Russian Federation which respondents in this study 'chose' to do. In the case of the migrant respondents included in the present study, this 'choice' emerged out of a mixture of socio-economic and ethno-political factors, which transgress the voluntary/involuntary divide. Once the decision to 'return' was made, Russia had then to be imagined as a real possibility to provide a future 'home'. However, it is often when places imagined at a distance become 'lived spaces' that tensions arise.[43] The possibility of Russia, as a distant imagined community during the period of the Soviet Union and now imagined location for a 'lived home', would be put to the test upon 'return'. The contrast of the image of Russia constructed after the decision to migrate had been made, with what was experienced upon 'return', made it difficult for expectations to be realized as the economic, social and political realities of the new location were confronted. As will be shown in the following chapters, the migration experience and the experience of the 'homeland' when it is confronted upon return often results in 'misrecognition' of Russia on many levels. Furthermore, in some cases Russia is reconfigured as the 'other' against which some form of diasporic or 'other Russian' identity is forged *after* return, when the former republic, or Soviet Union, is reinforced as the genuine 'homeland'.[44] For many the actual process of migration would be one of leaving both their immediate 'home' and wider 'homeland' rather than returning to it.

4
'Return' and Resettlement: Recognition Within the Russian State

This chapter moves the focus of analysis to the territory of the 'home-land', and the sites of resettlement – the regions of Samara, Saratov and Novosibirsk – to which the migrants in the present study arrived. Initially providing an overview of the migration occurring to the three regions, and tracing the development and nature of the regional migration regimes, the main body of the chapter concentrates on migrant experiences of resettlement at the regional sites in a number of key areas including: acquisition of forced migrant status, registration at place of residence and negotiation of employment and housing. These are spheres that migrants prioritized when they spoke of their resettlement. The chapter explores both migrants' perception of and interaction with state structures (institutional, legislative, provisory) in these spheres. The narratives of 'confrontation' with state structures during the process of resettlement which emerge provide an insight into the nature and level of interaction between the state and migrants at the site of resettlement, and indicate that migrants' expectations are rarely met. In fact, the nature of the interaction often impedes resettlement and generates widespread disillusionment with, and dissociation from, the Russian state. This in turn impacts upon migrants' understanding and experience of Russia as both 'home' and 'homeland'. However, the chapter also suggests that migrants may choose to distance themselves from state structures not only *because of* their often negative experience. Subsequent chapters reveal the role of alternative structures that prove more fruitful in facilitating resettlement and in helping to re-create 'home', and which are positively utilized in the 'absence' of – but also in preference to – state provision.

MIGRATION FLOWS AND MIGRATION REGIMES IN SAMARA, SARATOV AND NOVOSIBIRSK *OBLASTI*

Migration flows and migrant resettlement

Table 4.1 provides a snapshot profile of the size and nature of the migration flows arriving in the three regions. All three *oblasti* have been popular in-migration areas and are situated within major regions for migrant settlement in the Russian Federation. The figures given here are primarily for the period 1991–2000, so they refer to the economic region of the Federation within which the *oblasti* were situated and for which in-migration flows were calculated by *Goskomstat* (the Russian State Statistics Committee), rather than to the current federal *okrug* (see note 1). Samara and Saratov were situated within the Volga economic region, which by 1 January 2000 had received the second highest number of forced migrants and refugees in the Russian Federation -- a total of 250,840. Samara and Saratov are ranked first and second respectively within the region in terms of receiving the highest numbers of migrants. Novosibirsk was situated within the Western Siberian economic region, which by 1 January 2000 had received the third highest number of forced migrants and refugees in the Federation – a total of 196, 971. Novosibirsk has received the second largest number of migrants within this economic region (see Map 4.1).[1] In all three *oblasti* the migrant population makes up approximately 2 per cent of the total population. However, the figures cited in the table represent only those arrivees who have received forced migrant or refugee status; numbers of migrants arriving from the other former republics of the Soviet Union are much higher. In 1998, for example, the number of registered forced migrants in Samara *oblast'* made up only a third of all migrants arriving from the republics of the former Soviet Union.[2] In Saratov *oblast'* it is estimated that since 1992 the actual number of migrants from the former republics could be as high as 200,000.[3] In Novosibirsk, it is estimated that only 30 per cent of those who arrive in the *oblast'* from the other former republics of the Soviet Union turn to the migration service to apply for official status.[4]

In all the regions, the numbers of registered forced migrants have decreased from the mid 1990s; the decrease is representative of in-migration flows to the Russian Federation as a whole (see Chapter 1). However, restrictions on settlement and reduction in resources available in the three regions may also have impacted upon the numbers of individuals being officially registered (see below). The urban concentration of migrant resettlement reflects the predominantly urban nature of the arriving migrant population and the personal preference of individual migrants, despite the restrictions that are placed on settlement in

TABLE 4.1 Key characteristics of migration flows and migrant resettlement in Samara, Saratov and Novosibirsk *oblasti*

Characteristic	Samara	Saratov	Novosibirsk
Total number of registered forced migrants and refugees (1 July 1992–1 January 2002)*	73,369	57,244	51,943
Main regions of departure of forced migrants and refugees (in order of intensity)**	Kazakstan Uzbekistan Tajikistan Azerbaijan	Kazakstan Uzbekistan Tajikistan Azerbaijan	Kazakstan Uzbekistan Tajikistan Kyrgyz Republic
Numbers of registered forced migrants from within Russia (1 July 1992–1 January 2000)***	138	4,709	438
Urban/rural settlement**	Urban: 68% Rural: 32%	Urban: 70% (45% in the city of Saratov) Rural: 30%	Urban: 52% (36% in the city of Novosibirsk) Rural: 48%
Ethnic composition of migrant population**	Russian: 77% Tatar: 7% Ukrainian: 6%	Russian: 78% Ukrainian: 6% Tatar: 5%	Russian: 90% German: 3% Ukrainian: 2.5%
Gender breakdown**	Male: 49% Female: 51%	Male: 48% Female: 52%	Male: 49% Female: 51%

* *Source*: Federal Migration Service 1998; *Goskomstat* 1998: 68; *Goskomstat* 2000: 115; *Goskomstat* 2002c. This number represents the total number of individuals that have arrived and have registered over the period. Some of them will have subsequently been taken off the list of those registered due to the cessation of their status, or failure to re-register.

** *Source*: Samara Migration Service 1998, 1999a; Saratov Migration Service 1999a; Novosibirsk Migration Service 2002a.

*** This figure is taken to represent the numbers of forced migrants from Chechnia, as only these internal migrants qualify for forced migrant status. The figures are from a *Goskomstat* statistical bulletin on migration (2000). However, the amounts contradict figures received from the Saratov territorial migration service, which put the number of registered forced migrants from Chechnia at 5,526 by 1 April 1998, and figures from *Goskomstat* in Samara *oblast'* which put the number of registered forced migrants for just the period 1997–8 at 221. Figures from Novosibirsk territorial migration service show the lower number of 219 (of which 159 individuals are from Chechnia, but the figure also includes those registered as forced migrants or refugees from Dagestan, Tuva, Ingushetia and North Ossetia). The much greater number of forced migrants from Chechnia on the territory of Saratov *oblast'* was due to the availability of emergency accommodation in the *oblast'* in the form of temporary resettlement centres and subsequent directives of the FMS.

Map 4.1: Distribution of forced migrants and refugees, Russian Federation, 1999

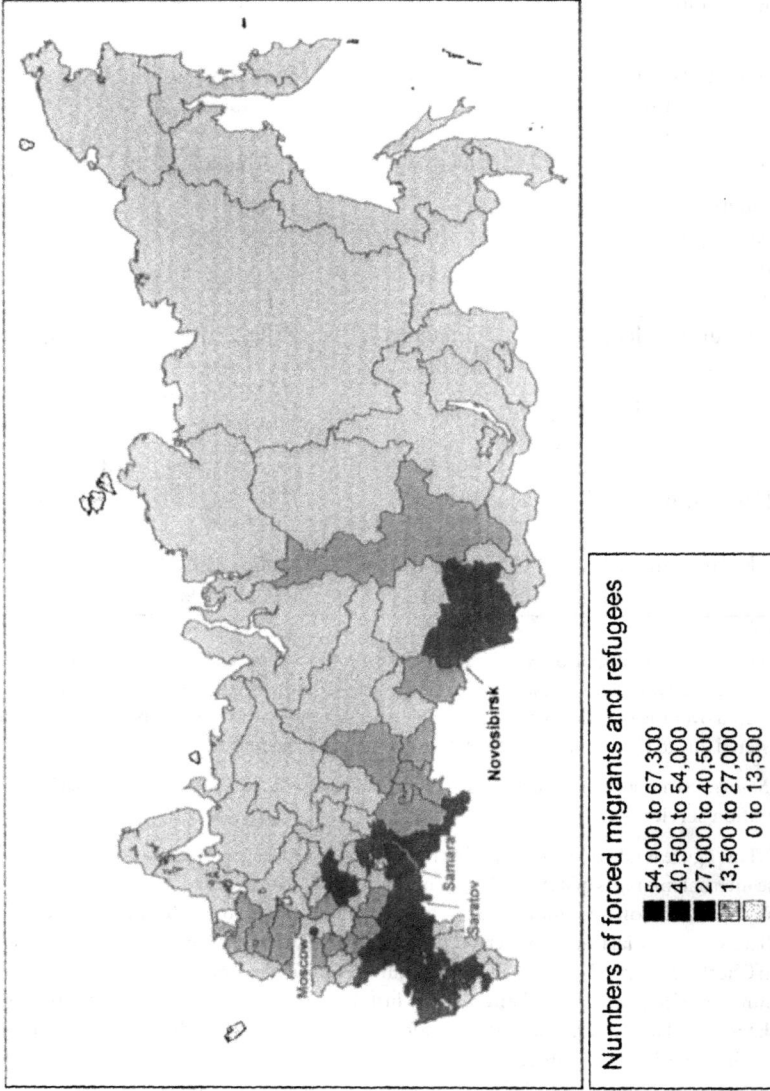

Numbers of forced migrants and refugees

- 54,000 to 67,300
- 40,500 to 54,000
- 27,000 to 40,500
- 13,500 to 27,000
- 0 to 13,500

Moscow

Samara

Saratov

Novosibirsk

Sources: Goskomstat 1998, 1999a

major cities and towns and the greater ease of acquiring accommodation in rural areas.[5] The relative stability and prosperity of the regions, particularly of Samara and Saratov, is one reason for the high levels of in-migration.[6] In addition, the geographical location of the three *oblasti*, the good communication and transportation networks existing across and out of the three territories, and the attractive climatic conditions in the regions, particularly Saratov and Samara *oblasti*, encourage in-migration. These external factors encouraging migration must be qualified by the more individual, personal motivations for choice of settlement, particularly the presence of family, friend and acquaintance connections which are explored in Chapter 6.

The development of regional migration regimes

Since the creation of the Federal Migration Service in 1992, parallel regional migration structures have been created across Russian territory. At its maximum size in 1997 there were 89 territorial migration services (TMS) spread across the subjects of the Russian Federation, and additional *raion* branches in some regions subordinate to the central *oblast'* service.[7] Following the abolition of the FMS in May 2000, the TMS came under the authority of local branches of the Ministry for Federal Affairs, National and Migration Policy. With the transfer of responsibility for migration affairs to the Ministry of Internal Affairs (MVD) in October 2001, local migration services were incorporated within the regional structures of this Ministry. Although the changes led to cuts in staff, resources and the number of *raion* level branches, and most recently the introduction of staff from the MVD (frequently, an MVD official is appointed as head of the service), many of the personnel and the everyday running of the services have not changed.

Although regional migration structures are connected to federal level structures, and are located within and directed by institutional and legislative frameworks created at the federal level, additional and conflicting forces operating at a regional level impact upon responses to in-migration and migrant resettlement. In particular, regional administrations have shown that they are able to establish their practices as dominant over migration service policy and practice, and it is often a combination of regional ethnic, socio-economic and political priorities that determine whether the region is more 'restrictive' or 'receptive' to the arrival of migrants.[8] Some administrations have shown that they are able to enforce practices in violation of both federal legislation and international norms and conventions to which Russia is signatory. This tendency has been particularly evident in Moscow city and Krasnodar *krai* and Stavropol *krai* in the Southern Federal *okrug* of Russia. The power regional administrations have had to determine policy lies partly in the ambiguity of federal migration legislation, and the lack of substantial connections – both financial and directive – between the federal and regional branches of the state migration service, which have allowed different 'types' of regional migration regime to develop. However, in many cases federal organs of power not only overlook the violation of federal and international law by regional authorities but also demonstrate solidarity with such approaches.[9]

The development of regional migration regimes therefore is not only influenced by federal directives and objective migration flows – the levels and types of migrants arriving in the region – but by the way in which migration issues are constructed according to the local socio-economic and ethno-political environment. As can be seen in Table 4.1, similar numbers and 'types' of migrants are arriving in Samara, Saratov and Novosibirsk *oblasti*. Yet the arrival of migrants has evoked different responses on the side of both the regional administrations and territorial migration services, which are summarized in detail in Table 4.2. To what extent this 'difference' is experienced at the individual level, and how it impacts upon the resettlement experience in a particular region, is a question which is explored below and in subsequent chapters.

Within Samara *oblast'* the dominant tendency has been to discourage in-migration, primarily due to concerns for the socio-economic stability and security of the region. The implementation of this policy approach may be demonstrated in a number of ways. In 1995 the Samara governor, Konstantin Titov, issued a decree stipulating that only those migrants who were able to register (obtain a *propiska*) with family or friends at their place of residence would be able to settle on the territory of the *oblast'* – in addition, to make an application for forced migrant status the possession of a permanent *propiska* was demanded.[10] Although the *propiska* or registration system is a legacy of the Soviet period and was officially abolished on 1 October 1993, in reality the permanent *propiska* was replaced by 'registration at a place of residence' (*zhitel'stvo*) and the temporary *propiska* by 'registration at a place of temporary abode' (*prebivanie*).[11] Without a *propiska*, individuals are denied access to employment, and to educational, medical and other state services.[12]

The decree therefore limited the possibilities for in-migration and, in effect, established the priorities of the Samara regional government over federal migration practice and violated the right to 'freedom of movement' guaranteed by the Russian constitution. This 'restrictive' attitude is accompanied in the *oblast'* by an overall lack of political interest in the issue of migration, and a corresponding absence of specific institutional or policy development or inter-departmental or inter-sector cooperation. Migration is not a central issue of debate or concern at the level of the Samara *oblast'* government, and any consideration of the

TABLE 4.2 Saratov, Samara and Novosibirsk regional migration regimes: a comparison

Variable	Saratov	Samara	Novosibirsk
Size and nature of flow	Consistently high levels of in-migration, predominantly ethnic Russian	Consistently high levels of in-migration, predominantly ethnic Russian	Consistently high levels of in-migration, predominantly ethnic Russian
Socio-economic priorities	In-migration seen as benefit, and possible way of attracting federal resources	High levels seen as possible danger to 'demographic' and socio-economic stability of regions	In-migration seen as benefit due to demographic crisis in *oblast'* and need for labour resources
Political priorities	Migration present within regional political discourse	Migration not present within regional political discourse	Migration present within regional political discourse
Operation of regional actors			
Federal-regional relations	Violation of federal migration legislation with the 'citizenship clause' Lack of allocation of federal resources	Violation of federal and international legislation with the use of the *propiska* Lack of allocation of federal resources	Violation of federal legislation with the use of the 'citizenship clause' Lack of allocation of federal resources
Regional administration	Move from 'receptive' to more 'restrictive' approach to in-migration High level of interest in resolving migration issues, development of regional migration programme and institutional bodies	'Restrictive' approach to in-migration Low level of interest in resolving migration issues, lack of institutional bodies and migration discourse	'Receptive' approach to in-migration High level of interest in resolving migration issues, development of regional migration programme, and cooperation with 'academic'/research community
Territorial migration services	Move from liberal to restrictive interpretation of forced migrant law Efficient use of resources for migrant provision Coordination with, and tolerance of, non-state bodies	'Restrictive' interpretation of forced migrant law Role to 'control' migration Lack of coordination with non-state bodies	Acceptance of need to attract migrants but 're-strictive' interpretation of forced migrant law and prioritisation of 'control' of migration Low levels of coordination with non-state bodies
Migrant activity	High levels of migrant activity, coordination with state structures and federal/international organisations	Low levels of migrant activity and lack of coordination with state structures	Medium levels of migrant activity Low levels of coordination with regional migration service, greater coordination with other regional state structures
Presence and activity of international actors	High levels of activity, cooperation with regional state structures and regional migrant structures	Low levels of activity, lack of cooperation with state structures and some levels of cooperation with regional migrant structures	Medium levels of activity and cooperation with regional state structures Limited cooperation with regional migrant structures

question seems confined to regional migration structures – although on a number of occasions this discussion has been extended out to regional migrant organizations (see Chapter 5). Discussion of a new regional migration programme for the period 2000–2002 took place, but no concrete strategy existed and there was a lack of inter-departmental cooperation to foster debate within the regional government. Statements made by the director of the migration service in 1998 reflected the wider regional administration priorities concerning in-migration. He acknowledged that migration was positive for the development of the *oblast'* economy and that the *oblast'* potential for receiving arriving migrants was high, yet he stressed that the *oblast'* capacity to absorb migration flows was limited by the minimal levels of available provision for forced migrants in terms of accommodation and work places. This necessitated state regulation of the flows to keep the overall 'socio-economic and demographic situation in the *oblast'* under control'.[13]

In Saratov *oblast'*, in contrast, the development of a more receptive policy towards in-migration was encouraged. In-migration was seen as beneficial for the region, although in part the policy was due to a wider regional attempt to attract external federal funds for arriving migrants.[14] The TMS adhered to federal directives concerning migration, and practised a fairly liberal and progressive approach to migrant resettlement. The level and nature of regional political debate was also reflective of this approach. Within the regional government there has been significant political interest towards developing regional migration programmes, and enthusiasm for the formation of institutional bodies to foster debate and cooperation between different government agencies and the non-governmental sector (see Chapter 5). The development of a regional migration policy in Saratov *oblast'* was prioritized by the governor Dmitrii Aiatskov who encouraged the development of a programme in 1998.[15] The interest and involvement of the regional government in migration affairs was felt within the migration service itself; in 1999, the director of the service identified a shift towards a deeper understanding of migrant issues within the regional government over recent years, and a greater willingness to work towards constructive solutions to the problems of migrant resettlement. He defined the attitude of the regional government to the migration issue as being 'informed, rational and constructive'.[16]

However, in 1999 there was a shift in approach, demonstrated by a change to the registration requirements for those seeking forced migrant status. The TMS began to demand that arriving migrants held Russian citizenship prior to arrival on the territory of Saratov *oblast'*; that is, the individual must have acquired citizenship in the former place of residence (former republic).[17] The introduction of the 'citizenship' clause represented a clear change in migration policy. Representatives of the migration service claimed that acquisition of Russian citizenship prior to arrival on Russian Federation territory had been a legal requirement since changes to the law on forced migrants in 1995, but this did not appear to be the practice before 1999 in the *oblast'*.[18] Although a regional government resolution was not issued, it is unlikely that this was a result of an independent migration service decision but rather a reflection of changing regional priorities. When federal resources were not forthcoming, a reassessment of the region's (and migration service's) capabilities to accept and provide for migrants resulted in the introduction of the 'restrictive' citizenship clause. Representatives of the migration service accepted that migrants arriving with citizenship required help, but claimed that those without citizenship did not require any assistance and could not be 'forced migrants'.[19] The practice aimed to reduce those numbers of migrants eligible for forced migrant status, and for whom the service was 'legally' responsible, thereby reducing the burden upon the *oblast'* administration to compensate for the absence of federal resources.

Socio-economic and demographic concerns were at the root of the development of the response to migration on the territory of Novosibirsk *oblast'*. The *oblast'* suffered from a serious economic crisis during the 1990s, accompanied by a worsening demographic situation due to an increase in mortality rates, decrease in birth rates and out-migration of the local population.[20] The demographic decline has been partially offset by the increasing numbers of migrants arriving in the *oblast'* from the former republics of the Soviet Union since 1991, and attempts have been made at the regional level to attract further migrants and facilitate their resettlement. The response reflected federal priorities as Western Siberia was listed as one of the areas for migrant resettlement in the Federal Migration Programme of 1994, and the 14 regions allocated as specific reception areas for the resettlement of forced migrants included Novosibirsk *oblast'*. In 1997, with the introduction of a differentiated loan system, migrants could receive an interest free loan for ten years of up to 70 per cent of the cost of housing on the territory of the *oblast'*.[21]

Cross governmental/non-governmental debate has been encouraged to further discussion about the role of migration for the *oblast'*. A regional migration programme prepared in 1995 involved the local administration, the regional migration service and local academics. A large amount of collaborative research has been carried out across the *oblast'* to address the problems of migrant resettlement over the last decade.[22] Public discussion of the issue has been consistently high; in 1995, a seminar involving the *oblast'* administration, the migration service and several migrant organizations took place as part of a series of regional conferences across the Russian Federation on migration issues in the CIS, sponsored by international actors and preceding a later international conference held in Geneva in 1996 (see Chapter 5). Such inter-sectoral debate has continued.[23] The practices of the migration service support the policy of encouraging migration to help the demographic situation in the region. Information is sent to embassies in other CIS countries about the possibilities of moving to the *oblast'*, and detailing the political and socio-economic situation and employment vacancies.[24] However, by 2002 the citizenship clause that is active in Saratov *oblast'* was also utilized on the territory of Novosibirsk. As in Saratov, its introduction coincides with a significant reduction in federal funding for migrant provision in the *oblast'*.

In all the regions, regardless of an apparently more 'restrictive' or 'receptive' approach, the possibilities of providing assistance to arriving migrants have been severely limited by a lack of resources from both federal and *oblast'* levels. In Saratov *oblast'* the federal resources received were only sufficient for the resettlement of 8–10 per cent of the migrants who had already settled in the region, or who were arriving during 1999. In Samara *oblast'*, as a result of federal directives issued in 1997, the migration services faced cutbacks in resources, and the numbers of both employees and *raion* branches of the service were reduced.[25] In 1998 only 11 per cent of the required resources were received from the federal budget, while nothing was received from the *oblast'* budget.[26] In both regions, the regional migration programmes remained largely unfulfilled due to a lack of both federal and regional resources.[27] In Novosibirsk the federal targeting of the *oblast'* as a region to receive migrants demanded a huge amount of resources to enable realistic resettlement; such demands have largely been unrealized.[28] Although approved, the Novosibirsk regional migration programme was never signed into law by the head of the regional administration, and thus never received funding. Finally, since the federal reorganization of the migration service, and its transfer to the Ministry of Internal Affairs in 2002, no federal resources have been received by the Novosibirsk migration service to fund its activity.[29]

The development of the regional migration regimes in Samara, Saratov and Novosibirsk reflects the interaction of migration flows, federal migration policy and socio-economic and political regional priorities in determining local responses to migration. Even in relatively stable socio-economic conditions, migration can be seen as a 'threat' and something that is not required (Samara). When expected federal resources are not forthcoming, priorities can change and restrictions are placed upon in-migration (Saratov and Novosibirsk). However, although there has been a move towards limiting in-migration through the 'citizenship' clause in Saratov and Novosibirsk, the nature of the regional migration regimes appears more receptive than in Samara. Yet, in all the regions the priorities of the region are held as paramount over the needs of the migrant.

Furthermore, the shift in discourse and policy at a federal level towards the securitization and control of migration can be seen in the gradual changes in approach that have taken place in the more receptive environments of Saratov and Novosibirsk. In Novosibirsk, for example, although migrants are identified as a positive labour force, they are increasingly represented as a force to be 'managed' and 'controlled'.[30] While there is support for the in-migration of 'compatriots' from the 'near abroad', a clear stand is being made by the migration service against other 'illegal' migrants, which are seen as a threat to the 'security' of the region.[31]

MIGRANT RESPONSES – NEGOTIATING RESETTLEMENT

To further interrogate the nature of the regional migration regimes, it is necessary to move to the level of the migrant and explore migrant interaction with and perception of state attitudes and structures (institutional, legislative, provisory) during the process of resettlement. The chapter now concentrates upon migrants' experience in a number of key spheres of resettlement: the process of negotiation for official status, registration at a place of residence, and the acquisition of employment and housing. Migrants' attempts to gain socio-economic and political 'recognition', which will allow inclusion in the receiving society, are focused upon. Such recognition and inclusion are found to be central to any initial re-creation of 'home'.

Recognition as a 'forced migrant'

As outlined in Chapter 2, forced migrant status is the official indication of the Russian state's acceptance of responsibility for those individuals eligible for Russian citizenship who have been 'forced' to leave their former place of residence, and have chosen to settle on Russian territory. However, the migrants in the present study expressed scepticism about what forced migrant status could provide, and furthermore about the operation of the migration service itself. Although all the migrant respondents, to a greater or lesser extent, defined their movement to the Russian Federation as 'forced', they did not automatically apply, or qualify, for official 'forced migrant' status. Out of the 72 respondents, 48 individuals received forced migrant status, four individuals received refugee status, and 20 individuals were in possession of neither.[32]

One reason for non-registration was a lack of information amongst respondents about the existence of the migration service and the possibility of gaining forced migrant status. A female migrant who had arrived in Saratov *oblast'* from Azerbaijan in 1992 stated:

> We did not turn anywhere. We did not know that we needed to go to someone. We only knew after two years, then we knew that there was a migration service, and that we needed to go there. We are considered 'forced migrants', we did not even know that. They said we could have received compensation, but we didn't go there, and we still haven't gone there.

30, Saratov, 1999

For a male migrant from Kazakstan, receiving official forced migrant status was not seen as a priority within the context of other issues of resettlement. In addition, it was important for him that he and his family did not identify themselves either as 'migrants' (*migranty*) or as 'refugees' (*bezhentsy*). For this migrant, the fact that he was a Russian citizen should have been enough to guarantee inclusion and acceptance by state and society:

> We didn't go (to the migration service). I am a Russian citizen (*rossiianin*), I am from Russia. We just found a place for ourselves, we found some solid ground. And we didn't turn to anyone with those claims that we are migrants or refugees. No one oppressed us, it simply became very difficult to live, difficult for the children. So I came to my people (*narod*) and everything is normal. We didn't have time to turn to anyone, maybe it would have been worth it to apply, but you understand we had to think about work, about how to feed the family.

31, Saratov, 1999[33]

Another migrant, who had returned from Uzbekistan, was also adamant that he should not be labelled as an 'immigrant'. He had been born in Russia, and had gone to Uzbekistan to work. For him, it was of great significance that he was coming to his homeland (*rodina*), to a place where he had grown up and where the language and culture were familiar. The label of 'immigrant', although he had obtained forced migrant status, was not appropriate:

> Do you understand? I don't feel like an immigrant, I simply don't feel like that, what am I? I have come to my *rodina*, and that is all. How can I be an immigrant? – if I had gone somewhere like Israel, or somewhere else, like America, then I would be an immigrant. But I have come home, it is my *rodina*, my culture is here, everything. I was born here. I lived here for 20 years. The culture, the language, everything, from childhood. What sort of immigrant am I?

67, Novosibirsk, 2002

A number of the migrant respondents who were interviewed were ineligible for official forced migrant status. This was due either to their having housing and employment, in which case the migration service concluded they were not 'in need', or because they lacked the necessary documentation: Russian citizenship or a *propiska* (registration at place of residence). A male migrant who had fled ethnic conflict in Tajikistan and who had arrived in Samara *oblast'* in 1998 described the difficulties he faced:

> We haven't got it (forced migrant status) still. It is difficult to get status, how can I explain, the actual process of receiving status is very difficult. You see to get status you need a *propiska*, it is very difficult to get a *propiska*, all of that and citizenship, they are all connected, it is very hard.
>
> *52, Samara, 1999*

The statement demonstrates the complex relationship that exists between forced migrant status, citizenship and the *propiska*, and how the absence of one can prevent the acquisition of one of the others. As shown above, in Samara *oblast'* it was essential to have a *propiska* prior to making an application for forced migrant status, while in Saratov and Novosibirsk *oblasti* Russian citizenship was required. The significance and difficulties of obtaining a *propiska* are explored in more detail below. With regard to Russian citizenship, many respondents spoke of the increasing difficulty of obtaining it in the former republic before departure. Large amounts of money were demanded and the process frequently took a long period of time. Migrants in Novosibirsk, in particular, spoke of the increasing difficulty of obtaining citizenship due to the changing situation in the former republics and the tightening up of the qualification procedures under the new law introduced in May 2002 (see Chapter 2). The greater awareness of the problems in receiving citizenship amongst these migrants is likely to be connected with their having been interviewed at a later date:

> When I came here I had already got citizenship through the consulate in Kazakstan. I got it without any problem, but now it is more difficult. My parents can't get it. Although they were born in Russia, there shouldn't be any problem. My mother is from Moscow *oblast'* and my father is from Voronezh *oblast'*, and they can't get citizenship.
>
> *68, Novosibirsk, 2002*

> Even if he [the father of the respondent] wanted to leave now, there is nowhere for him to go because they have tightened up with regard to citizenship, now it is much harder to get citizenship. If he came here, he wouldn't be able to get his pension.
>
> *70, Novosibirsk, 2002*

In addition to the difficulties in receiving forced migrant status, doubts were expressed about its relevance, particularly as it provided little concrete assistance in the process of resettlement. Opinions of what the status provided were similar for both migrants who had or had not received forced migrant status. The first statement comes from a migrant who had not received the status, while the

second shows that even for those who received the status, its practical significance was frequently disappointing and limited:

> I did not go. I do not hope for any kind of help, and to go there and waste time. Some
> people go but all the same they do not get any help. I did not take the status, nothing.
>
> *28, Saratov, 1999*

> We have forced migrant status, but it does not give us anything.
>
> *2, Saratov, 1999*

The dominant perception of forced migrant status amongst migrants, therefore, was negative. The majority of migrants had received no help, or just a one-
off emergency monetary payment which they considered as insignificant and
worthless:[34]

> For three of us – 245 roubles (the amount of emergency monetary help). That is all
> the help that there was. And what is 245 roubles. You most probably know what it is
> like here. What is it possible to get with that amount of money? That is all the help,
> nothing more.
>
> *34, Saratov, 1999*

> It was no help whatsoever. No one gave us anything, no sort of assistance, nothing.
> That status, principally, it does not give you anything, no privileges, nothing. The
> only thing people might hope for is a loan.
>
> *72, Novosibirsk, 2002*

The lack of concrete help the status provided, and the reception they met at the
migration service, shaped migrants' impressions about what the state was doing
to help in their 'return' and had a direct impact upon their resettlement. Forced
migrant status was something that had to be negotiated, acquisition was not
only restricted due to the requirements of the forced migrant law but by the operation of other barriers such as the *propiska*, citizenship or a lack of information. The majority of migrants also expressed a lack of faith in the state
institution that was meant to provide for their 'return' and resettlement. Despite
the apparently different approaches of the migration services in the three
oblasti, the perception amongst migrants of what the service provided was similar. The respondents' testimonies suggest a feeling of psychological distance
from the service, which was not seen as central to their resettlement. Migrants
sensed that the employees of the service could not, and did not want to, understand what had happened to them and were unwilling to help or provide information about what assistance might be available:[35]

> We received the status. It was absolutely no help. Absolutely nothing – if anything
> the opposite. If we had known about some laws we would have got settled quicker.
> They simply kept some laws from us. Not that they kept them from us, they just

didn't talk about them, they were silent. And when we asked 'why didn't you tell us that there was a queue or something, they said 'you didn't ask'. Nothing, no information, no help, in five years we have not received anything.

21, Saratov, 1999

You know, in the first few years there was the sort of attitude that we didn't ask you to come here, why have you left your three room apartment there, why have you come here, it wasn't necessary that you came. It is difficult for them [migration service workers] to understand, if they haven't experienced that nationalism on an everyday level, it is difficult to understand, what for, why we have come? Now the attitude is indifferent and cold, like with all bureaucrats maybe? We are all midges, who are not interesting. . .

69, Novosibirsk, 2002

Recognition through registration – the propiska

Despite the disillusionment with forced migrant status and the migration service, there was still a real desire and acceptance of the need to be 'recognized' via other state structures such as the *propiska*. The possession (or lack) of a *propiska* had both practical and symbolic significance for the returnees.[36] However, gaining permanent registration was something that required negotiation, it was not a 'right' granted upon arrival and its absence could prevent qualification for forced migrant status, eligibility for citizenship and receipt of benefits or access to essential social services including medical assistance. In addition, potential employers frequently demanded a *propiska*:

I want to get citizenship here, but that is a problem, you need a propiska. It is all a kind of bureaucracy. Why? I am Russian (*russkii*), why do I have to do this? They put a spoke in your wheels. It is possible to find work, but first you need a *propiska*, you need citizenship, it is a vicious circle. As yet I am not registered here, and I cannot find work anywhere.

38, Saratov, 1999

It was very difficult to get a job at the factory because I didn't have a *propiska*. It was impossible to get one. In Novosibirsk, they are very expensive, a permanent *propiska*. And without a *propiska*, without it, you can't do anything.

68, Novosibirsk, 2002

Those without somewhere to register upon arrival used other strategies. Often migrants registered at the housing of family or friends, or purchased a *propiska*, in effect obtaining it through illegal means:

We have paid a lot of money to get registered. We registered in a hostel but with no right to any living space. I did not even try. But, thank god we are registered, because, here without a *propiska* you cannot get work, without a *propiska* you cannot get anything, a loan, overall – nothing.

35, Saratov, 1999

In the newspaper, in any newspaper, you see adverts: *propiska* on offer, *propiska* for sale, *propiska* to buy. But it is very expensive, my [monthly] salary is 3,000 roubles, it costs 7,000 roubles. Or for one person, 4,000 roubles. It was almost impossible for my daughter and I to get one. And without a *propiska* it is impossible to do anything. I couldn't get child benefit during that time, for half a year I didn't get anything because I didn't have a *propiska*.

68, Novosibirsk, 2002[37]

The lack of permanent registration and the constant pressure to reregister temporarily, experienced particularly by migrants living in hostels, was a restriction of rights, a cause of uncertainty and a source of humiliation.[38] A female migrant who had left Uzbekistan and had been living in a hostel for five years since her arrival said:

We are not registered – we only have temporary registration according to place of temporary abode. We are restricted in our possibilities everywhere. I have lived here for five years in such a condition of suspense – in many ways our rights are restricted. I have had enough of these five years, my nerves have been so strained. You have to explain to everyone why you came, who you are, why you are here.

19, Saratov, 1999

The lack of a permanent *propiska* impeded the development of a sense of economic, political and social security, and underlined the fact – both to the individual migrants, and to those with whom they came into contact – that they were arrivees.[39] The respondents identified the possession of a *propiska* as their right, and related this to the fact that they were both Russian (*Russkii*) and Russian citizens (*Rossiianin*). Possession of a *propiska* (as it had done during the Soviet period) represented proof of identity and status, allowed participation within Russian society, and provided a 'legal' attachment to a fixed place. Without a *propiska*, migrants felt – and in practical terms were – 'on the outside' of the operating structures of society. Yet the host state, Russia, did not guarantee the acquisition of a *propiska*, and in fact used it to restrict acquisition of forced migrant status and resettlement possibilities. This comment of a migrant who had managed to acquire a permanent *propiska* demonstrates its centrality to feelings of security and stability:

I did not have any confidence when I did not have a *propiska*. I did not feel that I was a Russian citizen (*rossianka*). It was as if I was only living here temporarily when I did not have a *propiska*. It was only a month ago when it happened, we have lived here for four years. Only now have I calmed down. A *propiska*, I consider it the most important thing for a person.

21, Saratov, 1999

Recognition through employment and housing

We have a house, and we have work. That is most important for us. Yes, if a person has a house and work, then he already feels like a person. We will become like people again.

28, Saratov, 1999

The sentiments in this quote are echoed through other migrant narratives and reveal the centrality of housing and employment in the process of re-creating 'home' and establishing an attachment to the new locality. The possession of a secure job and an apartment in the former republic was frequently and logically expressed as a loss which migrants were finding hard to replace. Housing and employment were often spoken about in tandem; the attempted negotiation of both was closely related. For those migrants who had managed to secure some form of permanent accommodation and stable employment upon 'return', these represented the first signs of greater stability and attachment. However, their absence in the new place of residence prevented feelings of security and of being 'at home' developing. When understanding ideas of home, it is necessary to appreciate how this varies according to social, cultural and economic circumstances.[40] When 'home' has been challenged, this prevents over-sentimentalism about 'what is home'. For many of the migrant respondents, home was literally wherever they had a job or housing:

I would not say this is my home. I still do not feel that I am my own mistress here. I do not feel relaxed. There I am a stranger, and here I am still not myself. That is, I am between the sky and earth. I am not there, or here. . .if everything were settled, if there were housing and work, then I could say I would never leave here – it would be my 'home'.

43, Saratov, 1999

Securing employment
Upon arrival migrants consciously identified their labour potential, and that of their children, as something positive they were bringing to Russia. The migrants wanted the opportunity to invest in Russia for both the nation's and their own future:

We are Russian, we came to our Russian brother, we did not go elsewhere. Help us, and we may show our gratitude. After a year or two we will be of benefit to you, we will work. How many children will we have? All of them will work in Russia, our roots will remain here.

35, Saratov, 1999

We are the descendants of the virgin land workers, earlier it was Russians who raised the land, blazed the trail, we are the descendents of those who went to a new land, we are highly valued, specialists, workers, engineers, we are responsible, disciplined.

72, Novosibirsk, 2002

However, the difficulties migrants faced in gaining any employment or in finding suitable work in terms of their individual skills and professional status led to widespread feelings of discontent, redundancy, instability and insecurity.[41] Although the majority of the migrants were professionals or highly skilled workers, many were forced to change their profession and suffer a drop in professional status.[42] Of the migrants who were of working age and able to work, 17 individuals experienced professional downgrading, 12 made a sideways professional move and 15 managed to find employment according to their profession. 17 migrants were unable to find work.[43]

Problems were encountered in finding suitable employment in both urban and rural locations. In urban areas the scaling down and closure of industries, and lack of funding in state-financed sectors such as education and health care, meant that migrants found it difficult to secure employment commensurate with their skills and experience. A number of female migrants who were technicians and chemists by profession worked as market traders. The relocation of individuals in rural regions, often directed or encouraged by the regional migration service, had an even greater impact upon employment opportunities.[44] Enterprises had been set up at compact settlement sites in the rural areas of the *oblasti* where migrants were resident. However, when the enterprises failed migrants both lost their jobs and were hindered in finding other employment due to the location of the settlement.[45] Amongst the respondents resident in rural areas, a tendency was seen for 'skilled' workers (teachers, technicians) to become general farm labourers. A 40-year-old female migrant from Uzbekistan spoke of her experience: [46]

I went to work on the *kolkhoz*, four kilometres from here, of course they do not give me work according to my profession [a teacher] that is not needed there. On the whole they just need manual labour.

43, Saratov, 1999

Little help was provided by the state, either the regional migration services or employment service. Migrant experiences indicate that the migration service did not accept responsibility for this sphere of resettlement, and refute claims made by these services that alternative assistance was provided by the employment service. Instead respondents frequently expressed feelings of no longer being 'needed':

> When it turns out that we (migrants) are not needed it is a huge psychological trauma. It is not the problem of the actual movement, because that was thought out, we decided, we are not 'refugees' after all, it was the fruit of long thought. It is namely a problem of adaptation and a problem of employment, of course it would be easier if work places were created.
>
> *62, Samara, 1999*

The current state policy – or rather lack of one – ignores the labour potential the migrants represent and identify themselves as. This is despite the fact that Russia is facing a huge decline in its working-age population over the next 15 years. The potential of the migrant labour force is being destroyed due to a lack of state effort in integrating migrants into the existing labour force, and by unsuitable settlement which results in de-skilling and a drop in professional status.[47] The negative experience of de-skilling and professional downgrading has a wider impact upon the individuals' confidence and the likelihood of their successful integration into society.[48] Employment is central as a facilitator in other areas of resettlement, both in practical terms of material benefit and psychological terms in providing social interaction and a sense of purpose. Those migrants who had either managed to secure employment in the same profession, or who had made a 'sideways' professional move, expressed feelings of fulfilment and contentment with their employment, and a sense of being 'on an equal level' with the local population. For these individuals there is some sense of continuity with their previous life: a crucial symbol of security has been restored. The following quote is from a migrant who was the head of a regional migrant association. Although unable to find work as an engineer, she was content with her new occupation and felt that it provided her with a similar professional status:

> I looked everywhere, but they wouldn't take me, although I had a lot of experience. I'm not a young specialist, I have experience. Neither I, nor my husband, could find work according to our profession, but it doesn't matter. I found something good, the most important thing is to find something, to find some sort of niche.
>
> *72, Novosibirsk, 2002*

Securing housing[49]

The apartment or house where respondents had lived in the former republic was a central factor when they spoke of their lives 'there'; it was representative of the normal, secure life they had enjoyed, was the focus of an extension of 'home' within the wider locality and mentioned in conjunction with work, family, neighbours, summer houses and gardens. Possession of a house or apartment had formed part of the migrants' identity in the former republic, and was a symbol of attachment to the territory. The importance of housing was very apparent in conversations with migrants, especially if the interview occurred at their place of residence. Migrants apologized for the conditions in which they lived, stressed the contrast between the housing that they had possessed and their present housing situation, and frequently expressed a sense of loss concerning what they had 'left behind' in the former republic[50]:

> We left such an apartment there. We had a three-roomed apartment, we had only just decorated it. A beautiful apartment. Then we were put in this hostel, it is to be honest like a shed. All the same we have sorted it out, we have decorated, and tried to make everything as good as possible. We would like it to be bigger and better, but that is a dream.
>
> *21, Saratov, 1999*

The reality of the migrant respondents' housing conditions demonstrates why the issue caused distress. In the hostels, migrants lived in cramped conditions, the infrastructure was poor, they were often under the constant threat of eviction and held only a temporary *propiska*. Conditions at rural settlement sites were equally difficult. The location of the settlements and their distance from good transport facilities and urban centres proved problematic for the mainly urban migrants, especially with regard to accessing work, schools and medical services. There was a lack of adequate infrastructure at the sites, including absence of running water or communication links.[51] Many of the migrants had only chosen to settle in rural areas because of the guarantee of both housing and employment.[52] A female migrant from Tajikistan described why her family chose to settle at one of the rural sites:

> He (the director of the village) said that he would give us a house. It was something for us then, he gave us housing, he gave us work, so we work here, it is the countryside of course, and after the city? We lived in the city. . .
>
> *27, Saratov, 1999*

The lack or insecurity of property ownership caused concern. In a village in Saratov *oblast'*, migrants were involved in long-term, ten-year contracts which stipulated continued employment on the farm or village enterprise, and the .purchase of housing over this time. Although migrants were reassured with the security of employment and housing, many expressed concerns about the long-term commitment they were making. In effect, those involved were being denied the right to freedom of movement: if they chose to move they would lose any right to the housing they had invested in. At other compact settlement sites migrants invested a great deal in the construction of housing, but the legality of their residence was uncertain and they had no legal rights to ownership.[53]

The difficulties faced in buying or building property were due to both a lack of state help and an absence of personal means. Out of all the migrant respondents in urban and rural areas, only four had succeeded in buying their own apartment or house after arrival. State assistance was rarely forthcoming and was confined to a loan provided by the migration service. Seven of the migrant respondents had received the loan, and one individual was awaiting a decision on his application. However, for a number of respondents the loan only provided sufficient resources to build the foundations of the housing, or for housing in rural areas. If migrants wished to purchase accommodation in an urban area, then personal resources were needed. Thus, for the majority of the migrants in all three regions the loan system was not viewed as a realistic option:[54]

> I am in the queue for a loan. But it is only enough to buy something in the countryside and in the countryside there is no work. It cuts both ways, I don't know what to do.
>
> *69, Novosibirsk, 2002*

Furthermore, the employment gained by migrants was rarely sufficient to provide the extra resources that would enable improvement of their housing circumstances.[55] A 26-year-old female migrant from Tajikistan whose family had begun to build a house at a compact-type settlement spoke of the difficulties faced:

> It is very expensive to build a house. What can you do? You can build, gradually, to the extent which is possible. But it is a very long story. If everything were stable here, it would be different. But with delays in the payment of wages, and the level of wages compared to prices, it turns out that things don't work out, what you want doesn't happen.
>
> *19, Saratov, 1999*

Migrants' opportunities to regain what they had lost in the former republic, in terms both of housing and employment, were constrained by the economic environment they were operating within, the lack of personal resources they were able to draw upon and the absence of viable help from government structures. Although the long-term prospects of migrant resettlement would more likely be resolved in the urban areas of the *oblasti*, on the whole the migration services encouraged rural resettlement, the contradictions of which were clearly identified by migrants:

> They [the state] are so distant from us. In my opinion they cannot imagine what we do, how we live. All these discussions, they are discussions for them, not for us.

> Absolutely nothing is done on the federal level, not on the regional level, in order to improve our lives. The [migration service] suggested I move to an apartment in the town of Dorogino. It is not a town, it is a settlement – a small, dying settlement. There is absolutely no work.
>
> 69, Novosibirsk, 2002[56]

The majority of migrants wished to re-create the experience of urban living in the new place of residence. 'Home' had been located in an urban environment, where there was access to suitable employment, adequate social infrastructure and the wider social interaction which urban living may provide. Many had not been able to re-create this experience in the Russian Federation. The difficulties migrants faced in gaining employment, and in acquiring suitable accommodation instead, led to widespread feelings of discontent, redundancy, instability and insecurity, and clearly impeded the development of a sense of 'home':

> We do not feel at home here, it is a fairly difficult problem. It is a problem of housing and of interaction with other people, it is a problem of what your needs are. Therefore I cannot say that we feel 'at home' here yet. To feel more comfortable here, we need to organise everything here, to organise work, to feel needed.
>
> 62, Samara, 1999

Disillusionment with the 'homeland'

Migrants' narratives of 'return' and resettlement show how the 'reality' of the experience contributed to a sense of disillusionment with the Russian state, and consequently with Russia as 'homeland'. The first statement below, made by a female migrant who had fled Grozny, may reflect the particular response which she felt forced migrants and refugees from the conflict in Chechnia had received from the Russian government. However, the same sentiment is present in the second quote and has been seen in the earlier statements of other migrants who have arrived from outside the borders of the Russian Federation:

> I am insulted by our government, the state, for the way they have handled us.
>
> 2, Saratov, 1997

> Do they give us anything apart from a piece of paper? I don't know but I feel that the state could relate to us in a more humane way. After all, we haven't come here to drink; we have come here to offer our labour, our knowledge to this state. We haven't come to steal – we haven't done anything wrong. We are also Russians. If only they had helped us a little at the start, we wouldn't feel alienated, we could have carried on ourselves from there. We aren't asking for much, we don't want them to build us a three-storey mansion. We are not asking for that, just elementary things,

to have a roof over our heads, not to have to buy this *propiska*, to know that we weren't going to be evicted, that our rent wasn't put up, a place of our own.

68, Novosibirsk, 2002

Upon confrontation with the new 'homeland', through interaction with state structures during the process of negotiation for official status, registration, employment and housing, most returnees felt an overwhelming absence of state concern. This often generated a feeling of hurt amongst migrants, many of whom felt that while they had 'done their duty' for Russia (the Soviet Union) 'there', in the former republic, they were denied this role upon 'return' and the Russian state now considered them 'redundant' and was indifferent to their plight:

> We are also Russians even though we have come from Kazakstan. Where did the Russians in Kazakstan appear from? They came from Russia. Then it was in the interests of Russia to send them there – so they would open up a new land. . .But now, when we want to return, after three or four generations, because we are being driven out – they will not take us here. It turns out that we are redundant – do you understand? That question, I think, needs to be discussed at some sort of higher level.
>
> *36, Saratov, 1999*

The state indifference was encountered in the first instance through direct interaction with the migration service. It was also felt in relation to local (and federal) government administrations. The returnees did not see themselves as an issue of concern at the regional or equally the federal level:

> I have the feeling that they [the local administration] don't consider us at all. I don't know whether it is just this local administration [Samara] that has this attitude. I don't know if other migrants live better, maybe there is somewhere, where they live worse than us. But in principle you don't expect help from anyone, it is necessary to survive on your own. It is evident that in Moscow they have forgotten we exist. It has become almost insulting.
>
> *46, Samara, 1999*

> I think they relate to us in a slipshod manner, in any case they do not resolve the issue. I consider that at a high level, that is at the level of the president, they could resolve this issue.
>
> *40, Samara, 1999*

Nevertheless, as was seen in the sphere of employment, migrants frequently questioned the logic of this state indifference by instead categorizing themselves as a positive force needed by the Russian state. A female migrant, arriving from Kazakstan to Novosibirsk, identified her family as being of potential worth for Russia and its future:

. . .of course I listen to what they are talking about now, that in Russia, well generally in all of our countries, that there is practically no birth-rate. I say to them – here are three children, I am already thinking of writing to Putin, the president. Because I haven't brought drug addicts, not at all, but normal children, my third daughter already studies here at school, she is an excellent student. . .

64, Novosibirsk, 2002

This woman is responding to the perception amongst some members of the Russian government of the arriving migrant population as a source for demographic revival. However, although the majority of migrants identified themselves as a positive rather than needy sector of the population, and were keen to prove this is the case, they have not as yet detected any suitable action or response on the side of the Russian state. This perception, reinforced in a real sense through their 'confrontation' with the Russian state on an everyday level, limits an association with Russia as a present and 'future' homeland.

CONCLUSION

Upon 'return' to the Russian Federation, migrants prioritize recognition at the immediate locality of resettlement and the inclusion within socio-economic and political structures that had been assumed in the former place of residence. At this prior location migrants had often occupied a secure socio-economic and political position, they had possessed the relevant documentation, their identity had been legitimized by the state, and the resulting security had been enjoyed. Upon arrival in the Federation, migrants are 'outside' many of the structures that allow participation and involvement in the receiving society. Once secure in their Soviet citizenship, they now have no established identity and are no longer 'possessed' by any socio-economic or political framework.[57] As Humphrey suggests, there is a need for the 'dispossessed' (in this case the migrants) to establish their identity in the new place of residence if they are to be noticed.[58] In theory the acquisition of citizenship, forced migrant status and a *propiska* should reestablish their identity, facilitate subsequent political and socio-economic participation in society, and enable the securing of employment and housing. However, the re-acquisition of these constants upon return is not guaranteed. Furthermore, the process of 'reinclusion' is not facilitated by the Russian state through the operation of migration and other governmental structures, both institutional and legislative – instead, the process is often impeded.

The level and delivery of provision was so limited in all three regions that the 'receptive'/'restrictive' division and the different nature of the migration regimes in Samara, Saratov and Novosibirsk *oblasti* suggested in the first part of the chapter is rarely apparent in migrants' narratives. Rather, migrants related very similar experiences regardless of the region of settlement. Although some ex-pressed acknowledgement of the difficulty of the position that Russia is in, and recognized that the general socio-economic and political situation within the country was a factor in the lack of state attention to their plight, interaction with state structures did not foster feelings of inclusion within Russian society. The absence of concrete help; restrictive and bureaucratic mechanisms like the *propiska;* and frequent indifference and lack of understanding upon interaction with state officials all generate a practical dissociation from relevant state struc-tures and a more general disillusionment with the Russian state. Both in an im-mediate and a more abstract sense, the Russian state is not seen as relevant to solving the everyday problems of resettlement that will facilitate the re-creation of 'home', or foster a sense of 'return' to a wider 'homeland'. Instead, migrants both rely upon and choose other strategies to facilitate their 'return', resettle-ment and their re-creation of 'home'. These strategies, rooted in both formal organizational networks made up of other migrants and/or immediate net-works of families and friends, are considered in detail in the following chapters.

5

The Developing Non-governmental Sector

This chapter traces the development and activity of one sphere of the Russian migration regime – the non-governmental sector – within which actors have attempted to contest the official migration frameworks that have been created in the Russian Federation. It continues to challenge the dominance of these frameworks, which started to emerge through the migrant narratives presented in Chapters 3 and 4. The analysis is focused at three levels: international, federal and regional. The chapter firstly assesses the impact of international involvement upon the development of the migration regime in the Russian Federation. Secondly, it explores the origins and growth of domestic non-governmental organizations in Moscow, and demonstrates how these actors have attempted to reshape dominant migration discourse and practice to offer Russian migrants an alternative 'homeland' to that offered by the Russian state.

The chapter then moves to the regional level to explore the development of regional migrant associations in Saratov, Samara and Novosibirsk *oblasti*. There is insufficient room here to look at perceptions of the regional organizations amongst individual migrants who were not directly involved in their activity; these are explored in Chapter 6.[1] Rather this chapter focuses upon the regional migrant organizations themselves: their origins, constitution and activities, their interaction with regional governmental institutional and legislative structures, and their relationships with other non-governmental bodies. It explores how the organizations which have emerged from within the arriving migrant communities attempt to provide alternative means of resettlement to those provided by the Russian state – and demonstrates how, for the involved individuals, the organizations have become a strategy that has facilitated a sense of integration and inclusion at the regional site of settlement and beyond.

INTERNATIONAL ACTORS IN THE RUSSIAN
MIGRATION REGIME

Organizational development and activity

International organizations concerned with migration issues have become
significant actors within the Russian and post-Soviet migration regimes, providing one of the key links with the global migration regime of which Russia has
become a part. The activities of international organizations on Russian territory have influenced the development of the national and regional migration
regimes and individual migrant resettlement. As is the case for the Russian government and, as will be seen, for Russian non-state bodies, a number of different
economic, political and ideological priorities influence the activities of western
actors. Initial reactions of western governments to the collapse of the Soviet
Union and the 'threat' of possible large-scale migration flows from the east led to
the consolidation of a 'Fortress Europe' (see Chapter 1).[2] Western governments
were keen for institutional and legislative structures to develop on the territories of the former Soviet Union so that the migration flows would be managed
and controlled within the post-Soviet space. The concern was reflected in the
participation of western governments in the 1996 Geneva CIS Conference on
Refugees and Forced Migrants, and their support for the subsequent 'Programme of Action'. As fear of the 'threat' has decreased, however, the amounts of
money being allocated by donor countries for the solution of migration problems on the territory of the FSU have been reduced, which has impacted upon
the programmes, priorities and capabilities of international organizations.[3]

   The specifics of the post-Soviet migration space have influenced the action of
international organizations. As a representative of UNHCR stated, in 1992: Russia was unknown territory, it had not been part of the global migration regime
and there was very little information indicating the necessity of international
help, as the extent of population displacement was unknown to the world community.[4] The initial activity of international organizations was marked by uncertainty, a reluctance to become directly involved in the regulation of migration
issues and an often inefficient and patronizing level of assistance to local NGO
groups.[5] Greater understanding of the complexity of the problems of migration
flows in the post-Soviet space has developed since; there is more cooperation
between different international actors, and between international and domestic
NGOs and governments. Nevertheless, the activity of international organizations on Russian territory demands a critical approach in order to provide a
fuller picture of the impact of western organizations, funding and priorities
concerning migration issues in the Russian Federation and post-Soviet space.[6]

The two organizations that have been most active on Russian territory in the migration and refugee sphere are the United Nations High Commissioner for Refugees (UNHCR) and the International Organization for Migration (IOM). A regional branch of UNHCR opened in Moscow on 6 October 1992 following the signing of an agreement with the Russian government. The agreement was also followed by the accession of the Russian Federation to the 1951 UN Convention and 1967 Protocol Relating to the Status of Refugees. The creation of the FMS and the introduction of the laws on forced migrants and refugees were recognized by UNHCR as the first institutional and legislative steps for the fulfilment of the organization's aims, these being: to ensure the realization of laws in accordance with international standards; to uphold the principle of non-refoulement (the right not to be returned to a place where an individual may experience persecution); to ensure a correct and fair procedure for defining refugee status; and to assist in the elaboration of long-term solutions to the problems of refugees.[7] The UNHCR mandate establishes the organization's responsibility for 'refugees' as defined in UN legislation. Initially, this placed restrictions upon UNHCR's action in the Russian Federation, but the specifics of the Russian situation led to the widening of UNHCR activity to include internally displaced persons and forced migrants from the former republics of the Soviet Union.[8]

The work of UNHCR in the Russian Federation has been divided into support for the legislative and institutional development of migration structures, and the provision of direct assistance to different categories of migrants. During the 1990s, UNHCR was involved in the evaluation and formulation of national legislation on refugees and forced migrants in cooperation with the FMS, other federal departments and the State Duma. The organization has provided support and training for Russian structures working with refugees at both the federal and regional level, specifically regarding correct status determination of both forced migrants and asylum seekers from the 'far abroad'. UNHCR also played an important role in the provision of direct assistance to forced migrants; it implemented a series of regional micro-credit projects targeted at Russian forced migrants through the American NGO Opportunity International and, through the Danish Refugee Council, provided loans specifically for internally displaced persons. The organization ran a 'Capacity Building Programme' to facilitate the development of regional migrant associations, and provided grants for the implementation of larger scale projects to already established migrant associations (see below). At the end of 2000, UNHCR shifted its focus away from Russian forced migrants to concentrate primarily on providing assistance to – and helping the Russian authorities develop an efficient system for managing – asylum seekers and refugees from the 'far abroad' and the CIS in collaboration with its local implementing partner *Equilibre-Solidarity*. It has provided training for the re-formed migration service within the MVD at both federal and regional levels.[9]

IOM signed an agreement of cooperation with the government of the Russian Federation and opened a regional bureau in Moscow in March 1992. The original areas of IOM activity in Russia encompassed: institution building in the field of migration, informational activities and direct assistance to migrant groups. IOM organized training seminars and foreign exchange visits for representatives of the FMS, other government departments and NGOs, and provided equipment for the development of the infrastructure of the central and regional branches of the migration service and NGOs. Through its migrant-processing centre in Moscow, the organization worked to aid emigration from the Russian Federation, and to assist the return of stranded students from developing countries.[10] The IOM 'Direct Assistance Programme' (DAP), which began in 1993, provided the most immediate ground-level help to facilitate the resettlement of forced migrants on the territory of Russia by providing equipment to help migrant organizations form small private enterprises.[11]

The priorities and activities of IOM underwent a change from 1999, due to internal changes in the staffing of the organization and the reduction of resources available for funding the existing programmes. The latter was due to a decrease in contributions from donor countries, and the impact of humanitarian and refugee crises in other parts of the world – namely Kosovo, Macedonia, Albania and Bosnia. The main priorities were refocused and became: direct assistance to migrant enterprises in selected regions of the Russian Federation through the provision of grants or micro-credits; the improvement of health care services for displaced persons; and migration management and border control (in conjunction with the Russian government and relevant ministries). The head of the IOM mission in Moscow attributed the shift in focus, and narrowing of the scope of IOM programmes in the Federation, to a realization of the mass nature of the problems being faced and the need to target resources.[12] However, the organization continues its assistance to potential emigrants (primarily to Canada and the USA) and facilitates voluntary refugee repatriation (both back to, and from, Russia). In 2001 it initiated the Moscow Migration Research Programme, its aim being to strengthen the link between research, academic institutions and IOM programmatic activities across the Russian Federation and CIS.[13]

The 1996 CIS Conference on Refugees and Forced Migrants and the Programme of Action

UNHCR and IOM, together with the Organization for Security and Cooperation in Europe (OSCE) and the Open Society Institute (OSI), were the main organizers of the CIS Conference on Refugees and Forced Migrants held in Geneva in May 1996. The idea for this began with Russia's sponsorship of a 1993 UN General Assembly resolution calling for a world conference on migration. Despite a lack of international enthusiasm, in 1994 Russian Foreign Minister Andrei Kozyrev requested that UNHCR and IOM organize a conference on issues of migration in the Russian Federation.[14] This was attended by represent-atives of governments of 12 countries of the CIS, 70 other interested states, 30 international organizations and 100 NGOs.[15] A 'Programme of Action' (POA) was adopted and annual steering group committee meetings – involving repre-sentatives of governments, international and inter-governmental organizations and accredited NGOs – were held to review the progress of implementation of the programme. A final meeting was held in April 2001 to determine the future course of action.

A number of positive consequences resulted from the CIS Conference and POA, which impacted upon the development of the Russian migration regime. Key achievements were the stimulation of the activity of the non-governmental sphere across the post-Soviet space, the generation of communication between NGOs in the CIS and the facilitation of links between state bodies and non-governmental organizations. These advances are widely acknowledged both by external commentators and by representatives of NGOs at the federal and re-gional level.[16] The process also facilitated the development of relations between international organizations working in the CIS, and the collaborative action of IOM and UNHCR on a number of programmes was recognized by the Russian state as 'commendable'.[17] Despite these positive outcomes, criticism has also centred on the lack of both western and CIS government commitment, the nature of the POA (which had no obligatory force), the deficiency of internal and external resources and the absence of joint-governmental action.[18]

The reduction of donor support impacted directly upon the operations of international organizations. It is clear that both IOM and UNHCR no longer prioritize programmes for Russian forced migrants; with the many new chal-lenges and competing migration concerns within the Russian Federation, this is understandable. Nevertheless, criticism has also been made of the nature of the activity of international organizations, and their failure to fulfil their obliga-tions to Russia.[19] Specific complaints have been levelled at IOM: for misusing funds allocated by the Geneva conference; for acting in a political rather than neutral manner; for prioritizing donor over Russian interests; for violating the contractual agreement between the organization and the Russian government; and for bypassing the Russian state and dealing directly with regional NGOs.[20] The difficulties were attributed to a lack of understanding of the specifics of the Russian situation and operation of Russian culture and society; the hasty imposition of western priorities and practices;[21] the unrealistic expectations of the west concerning the transition of Russia to a 'democratic' and working 'civil society';[22] and the failure to develop 'equal' relationships of partnership with their Russian counterparts, both state and non-state.[23] These problems have been acknowledged by both Russian and western commentators as deserving of greater attention and resolution.[24]

The CIS Conference, the POA and the activity of international organizations reflect the positioning of Russia within the wider European and international migration regimes. The reduction in western governmental attention and funding to migration issues across the FSU reflects a tendency to see the former unitary territory as distinct and separate from the European and global migration systems. The Russian government has clearly articulated its disappointment concerning the input of international assistance since 1991, and has called it 'disproportionate to the migration problems being tackled'.[25] Concerns about the west's reluctance to be involved are not confined to the financial level but extend to the lack of understanding of Russia's migration problems at the level of international society, which will deepen if western interest subsides.[26] Russia places the solution of the migration problems on its territory within the wider European and global arena, but interprets current western governmental approaches as closing the door 'literally' on the migration processes going on beyond their eastern borders.[27]

Nevertheless, in the decade following the breakup of the Soviet Union, the material and practical assistance and knowledge provided through international organizations like UNHCR and IOM has been significant for the development of both the government and non-governmental structures of the Russian migration regime at a regional and federal level. The importance of establishing contacts with international bodies is particularly visible for regional migrant associations. This is not only due to the possible financial and material rewards; such connections also help regional migrant organizations to gain legitimacy in the eyes of regional government structures, and provide opportunities for inclusion in legislative and policy debate at the regional and federal levels (see below).

RUSSIAN NON-GOVERNMENTAL ORGANIZATIONS[28]

Organizational development

The development of federal level organizations directed at helping refugees and forced migrants mainly originated amongst activists from professional legal, journalistic and academic backgrounds. At the same time, self-initiated migrant associations began to develop at the regional level (see below). The origins, priorities and nature of the federal level NGOs and regional level migrant associations differed significantly. The federal level Moscow-based groups were NGOs in the more 'true' sense of the term, rooted in the circles of the liberal intelligentsia and former dissidents, and the experience of the informal groups of the perestroika period.[29] This background is reflected in the predominantly political nature of the federal organizations and their defence of 'human rights', alongside the provision of humanitarian assistance. In contrast the regional organizations, established primarily by groups of returning migrants, were initially more pragmatic and focused upon socio-economic concerns. They were not always 'strictly' NGOs, but could be informal self-help groups or commercial legal entities involved in commercial or industrial activities and/or attached to a compact settlement site.[30] However, they were still concerned with migrants' rights and have often developed into effective lobbying bodies at the regional level. Institutional links gradually developed to connect the federal and regional non-governmental migrant sectors.

The three main Moscow-based non-governmental organizations concerned with migrant and refugee issues are the Civic Assistance Committee (CAC), the Coordinating Council for Aid to Refugees and Forced Migrants (CCARFM) and the Forum of Migrant Associations. The development of these bodies is closely linked, although they have pursued their own priorities and individual approaches. Lidiia Grafova – the head of both CCARFM and the Forum, and member of the joint committee of CAC – described the three organizations as making up a set of Russian *matreshka* dolls,[31] a description which aptly represents the nature of their evolution. Following the outbreak of violence in Baku, Azerbaijan in 1989, and the arrival of the first refugees in Moscow, academic and legal expert Svetlana Gannushkina set up CAC in 1990. Up to this point there had been no informal, non-state associations concerned with migrant or refugee issues in the Russian Federation. CCARFM evolved from CAC, and was officially formed in March 1993 by the journalist Lidiia Grafova. The Forum of Migrant Associations, an umbrella organization for federal level migrant NGOs and the widespread network of migrant associations that exist in the Russian Federation, held its inaugural meeting in 1996 – the CCARFM operates as the permanently functioning working apparatus for the Forum.[32] Closely associated with CAC is the human rights organization *Memorial*, whose main focus is the defence of the legal and human rights of refugees and forced migrants. The creation and development of the three organizations received support from international bodies such as UNHCR, Helsinki Human Rights Watch and IOM.

Reframing the process of 'return'

The development of the Moscow-based organizations reflects the specific nature of the migration regime in post-Soviet Russia. These bodies have focused predominantly upon the issues of Russian forced migrants, rather than on refugees from the 'far abroad'. They have evolved completely independently of and in opposition to the state, and have developed a dual role: that of filling a 'gap' left by the ineffectiveness and inadequacy of state action through the provision of legal/practical information and material aid to refugees and forced migrants, and challenging and influencing state discourse and policy through lobbying, involvement in the formulation of legislation, and representation of migrant interests within official institutions. At the core of their activity and philosophy is the attempt to provide an alternative construction of the 'return' and resettlement of the Russian communities to that developed by the state; primarily one of welcoming the 'return' of 'repatriates' and prioritizing adequate provision and viable policies to foster successful resettlement.

Over the period of the 1990s, in the face of ineffective legislation, a lack of concrete state support for migrant resettlement, the infringement of the rights of refugees and forced migrants, and the shift in the role of the FMS from one of provision to control, the role of the organizations both widened and strengthened. Initially hostile relations with the FMS, and government and parliamentary bodies, improved as a result of the inclusion of the NGOs within joint-institutional structures that allowed limited participation of NGOs in legislative development.[33] In 1994 and 1995 when representatives of the organizations took part in discussions regarding amendments to the laws on 'forced migrants' and 'refugees', this was the first major involvement of the sphere in influencing the formulation of migration policy.[34] The organizations were also central actors in the earlier repatriation debate of the mid 1990s (see Chapter 2)[35] and have continued to be active in their support for the idea of and the need to develop a repatriation law.[36]

In addition to their involvement in legislative development, the organizations have been effective in challenging discriminatory government practice at the ground level. CAC, in particular, has made a large number of successful representations of migrants in court, particularly over the question of registration in the city of Moscow.[37] CAC and *Memorial* set up a network of legal consultation points for refugees and forced migrants across the territory of the Russian Federation in 1996; such points now exist in 40 regions of Russia. Yet despite their oppositional role and the conflict which arose with the FMS over questions of government migration policy, CAC in particular accepted that it was necessary to work with state structures and did not claim that NGOs should or could replace basic services offered by the state, or other professionals such as lawyers.[38] However, with the changes in migration policy at the end of the 1990s, relations deteriorated between the two spheres. The transfer of responsibility of migration affairs to the Ministry of Internal Affairs was met with outrage amongst the migrant NGO community. Svetlana Gannushkina said that the Ministry was 'incapable of dealing with the human side of migration', and relations between the Forum of Migrant Associations and MVD were described as 'hostile and without significant mutual understanding' – although subsequent efforts have been made to foster cooperation.[39] Legislative developments also met with opposition. The organizations spoke out against the new Russian Federation laws 'On Citizenship' and 'On the Legal Status of Foreign Citizens in the Russian Federation', which they viewed as discriminatory and restrictive towards all migrants, and as cutting off the path of 'return' to Russia for Russian communities in the 'near abroad'.

The development and activities of the three main organizations profiled here have been closely intertwined, and with the support of other concerned federal level non-governmental bodies such as *Memorial*, they have presented an often united front that has challenged government policy and practice. The Forum in particular is seen by some as a sign of the political strength of migrants and their ability to articulate their demands at the level of the Russian government.[40] However, the mass organizational nature of the Forum has been problematic; it has been accused of representing an NGO monopoly, which has created a 'battleground' between different migrant organizations vying for western grants and projects.[41] Those bodies which succeed in being included in the Forum, and getting the support of Lidiia Grafova, receive assistance; those who are excluded are left to survive alone.[42] By 2000, conflicts had developed within the Forum due to the 'politicization' of certain regional associations. The 'Council of Migrant Associations', formed under the speaker of the State Duma in 1999, was predominantly made up of migrant associations enlisted by the Communist Party who had broken away from the Forum.[43] However, relations between the two bodies subsequently improved.

In clear contrast to the CAC, CCARFM and Forum is the Compatriots Fund (Russian Fund for Aid to Refugees), which was set up as a semi-state organ and in the early 1990s worked in collaboration with the Federal Employment Service in the creation of housing and employment at compact settlement sites for forced migrants. However in 1994, due both to the increasingly critical stance of the Fund vis à vis the FMS[44] and to government accusations of misuse of allocated resources, state support ceased and the Fund assumed the role of an independent non-governmental organization. The relationship subsequently improved with a change of leadership at the FMS in 2000.[45] Today the Fund is the only 'non-governmental' body concerned with migrant provision that nominally receives state subsidies for its work at compact settlement sites.[46] Its emergence and operation as a semi-state structure set the organization apart from the other Moscow-based organizations; it clearly separates itself from the activity of the Forum, which a representative of the Compatriots Fund identified as mainly dealing with purely 'legal' questions.[47] Overall, the Fund has focused upon socio-economic provision and assistance for migrant resettlement, rather than prioritizing the political and human rights of migrants or the need to challenge government legislative or policy frameworks.

In contrast, both the CAC and the CCARFM/Forum have consistently sought to challenge the dominant state frameworks (discursive and legislative) established by the Russian state, and to reframe the 'return' migration of the Russian communities in their terms: principally as a right of 'repatriation' that 'compatriots' are entitled to, as economically, culturally and demographically beneficial for the Russian state, and as a movement that should be welcomed by the state. Their work, which has extended beyond the federal level, has provided essential practical and legal assistance to migrant associations and individual migrants, and has also created a wider space within which migrants' voices are heard. This has facilitated the challenge to state discourse and policy at both the regional and federal level. Furthermore, the influence of the organizations has extended beyond the borders of the Russian Federation. They were all involved in the initial CIS Conference in Geneva, and the subsequent follow up meetings and Programme of Action. They have successfully negotiated a position from which to advocate the positive reception of the Russian communities from the 'near abroad', and to challenge restrictive discursive and legislative practices. However, in discursive terms they perhaps tend to define the movement too holistically, as a natural 'post-imperial' repatriation that is beneficial both for the migrants themselves and for Russia. Such a definition, like others, fails to take into account the individual stories of 'return' told by migrants themselves.

THE DEVELOPMENT OF NON-GOVERNMENTAL ACTIVITY IN SAMARA, SARATOV AND NOVOSIBIRSK *OBLASTI*[48]

As the federal level non-governmental organizations emerged during the 1990s, regional migrant organizations began to spring up across the Russian Federation and, in some cases, in the other former Soviet republics amongst Russian communities prior to migration. In contrast to the federal level organizations, the initiative for these regional bodies lay with migrant communities themselves. However, the environment that was fostered by the actions of both international and federal level non-governmental structures often provided the space for this 'migrant' non-governmental voice to emerge. The chapter explores five regional migrant organizations that were present in the regions of study: *Saratovskii istochnik* (Saratov Spring), *Vozvrashchenie* (Return) and *Komitet bezhentsev iz Chechnii* (The Committee of Refugees from Chechnia) in Saratov *oblast'*, *Samarskii pereselenets* (the Samara migrant/resettler) in Samara *oblast'* and *Ruka pomoshchi* (Helping Hand) in Novosibirsk *oblast'*.[49] Chapter 4 demonstrated how migrants often felt disillusioned with and distanced from regional and federal state structures upon 'return' and resettlement. The regional migrant associations provide an alternative structure to which migrants can turn. However, despite the fact that they are migrant-led bodies, the levels of engagement of migrants who are not directly involved with these non-official structures cannot be assumed as automatic. As suggested above, this is explored in more detail in Chapter 6.

Organizational initiatives and actions[50]

> I received forced migrant status in 1993, but since then, despite all my efforts, I don't feel settled. Saratov hasn't become a place that I can call home. Maybe I haven't done something. Perhaps the state system provides some sort of support, but for me, it has not worked in the way that it should. And I needed assistance. So, I came to the conclusion that we [migrants] must help ourselves.
>
> *Saratov, 1999*

This quote demonstrates a sentiment that was apparent when individual migrants spoke of their resettlement experience (see Chapter 4), and was a central reason given by representatives of all the organizations for the formation of migrant initiatives at a regional level – the inadequacy of state assistance and the realization amongst migrants that they had to depend upon themselves. The profiles of the five migrant associations (see Appendix 4) show how these bodies attempt to fill the gap left by inadequate state provision. The central role of all five organizations was consultative: the provision of general information, that was either unavailable or difficult to access from state structures. In addition, all the organizations employed trained lawyers who provided free legal consultation and, when necessary, represented individual migrants in court.[51] Minimal material support was sometimes provided (small monetary payments, clothes, food vouchers). In some cases, the associations were able to extend the scope of their activities and provided limited 'direct' help to migrants regarding employment and housing. Representatives of the organizations identified employment as central to enabling migrants to sort out other aspects of their resettlement independently. A number of the organizations also sent information about resettlement opportunities in the *oblast'* to potential migrants in the former republics, and served as a resource centre for individuals coming on scouting missions to investigate possibilities for settlement in the *oblast'*.

In addition, the organizations perceived their role as providing a vital source of moral and psychological support. Their ability to perform this role was attributed by their leaders, and also by individuals who had visited the organizations (see Chapter 6), to the fact that they were run by migrants who could understand what their 'client group' were experiencing, whereas employees in state services were seen not to have the necessary skills or comprehension:

> The most important thing is that they [migrants] do not feel that they are alone here, they need to feel that they can talk to someone. State structures cannot help with this. Perhaps if a psychologist or sociologist worked there, then they could help – a person who would listen and give advice. Personal, family problems arise, not always just to do with migration. At the moment social organizations fulfil this role. A person comes to a social organization and knows that the same people as him/her are there, that they will listen, try to help, provide support. Sometimes, you cannot give them anything, you can only listen and sympathize, but they feel better. Because s/he understands, that there is support, that it actually exists. S/he can come at any time to be given support, to be listened to, advised on what to do.
>
> *Saratov, 1999*

> They know that I am a migrant, that attracts them, because I am a migrant I can understand and can help.
>
> *Samara, 2002*

The organizations also attempted to raise the level of awareness of migrant issues within state structures, to direct state attention to areas of concern, and to ultimately affect regional state policy and practice. Integral to their activity were efforts to reframe the migration movement as positive for Russia as a whole, and for the particular region in which they had arrived. These attempts aimed to make the hopes of being received as a positive force, as expressed by individual migrants, a reality:

> Russia must be ready to accept migrants. The future of Russia is linked very closely with migration, with migrants, because Russia has lost a lot of people – the infrastructure in depopulated regions can no longer be supported, there isn't a sufficiently large population. What we need to do is to change public opinion. It is necessary to pass a whole set of laws which will allow the reception and resettlement of migrants.
>
> *Saratov, 1999*

> Initially, refugees and forced migrants were perceived very negatively, as strangers, as people who were not needed. But now, because of the work of social organizations,

the opinions of these people have changed. We have shown that although we were people who have been forced to flee, we have come here prepared to work, to help, to offer our knowledge. If we are needed, that we will be useful. But for this to happen, they [the regional administration] need to know who has come, what specialities can they offer, what is their potential, how can they be used for the good of Saratov *oblast'*. We can provide this information to the heads of different state departments, it will be useful for them, they will then see us as a solution to their problems.

Saratov, 1999

Negotiating a voice within the regional migration regime

The statements from representatives of the regional migrant organizations demonstrate that they had a very clear idea about the role they wished to fulfil at the regional level, both in relation to the migrant communities and within the wider regional migration regime. However, they were often constrained precisely by the nature of the official regional migration regime in which they were operating. When understanding the activity of the organizations, and their ability to act, it is important to consider that they were operating in a sphere that was unknown and unfamiliar, both to them and to the societies in which they were located. Furthermore, it was not only the attitude of regional government structures that affected the development and work of the organizations, but also connections with regional, federal and international level non-governmental structures, and access to funding and other material resources. The experience of migrant non-governmental organizations in Russia is specific, not least because of the 'newness' of the issue. However, parallels can be drawn with other studies looking at the development of the wider non-governmental sector in post-Soviet Russia.[52]

Relations with regional migration services

The key government/non-governmental relationship that existed was between the organizations and the regional migration service, but this relationship differed significantly according to the region in question. In Saratov *oblast'*, the dominant impression gained from interviews conducted with representatives of the migrant organizations was a willingness to work 'with' – rather than in opposition to or in isolation from – the migration service. The initial development of *Saratovskii istochnik* had been closely linked with the central migration service and had established this tradition of cooperation. However, the levels of cooperation varied across the organizations, changed over time and depended upon individual personalities. For instance, in 1997 initial visits to the *oblast'* revealed a very strong working relationship between *Saratovskii istochnik* and the head of the migration service; whereas by 1999, *Saratovskii istochnik* had been displaced as the main organization with which the migration service cooperated by *Vozvrashchenie*, due to a change in leadership at the migration service.

Despite acceptance of the need to cooperate, migrant organizations in Saratov *oblast'* clearly saw their role as 'correcting' migration service practice. These bodies were particularly critical of the lack of understanding and professionalism of the service's employees; they disagreed with the service's practice concerning forced migrant registration, and court appeals were successfully made in a number of cases against the 'citizenship' clause.[53] Meanwhile the migration service occupied an ambiguous position in relation to the activity of the migrant groups. The director of the service recognized the need to work 'in a consolidated way' with the organizations, accepted that they provided additional help to specific categories of migrants for whom the migration service could not provide, and saw the possibility for the social organizations obtaining extra resources from external sponsors such as international bodies.[54] However, the service also perceived the organizations as supplementary, unprofessional and insufficiently informed, and as failing to offer concrete solutions to the housing and employment problems of forced migrants.[55]

The relationship between *Samarskii pereselenets* and the Samara TMS provided a stark contrast to that in Saratov. Relations with the first director of the migration service, who was replaced in June 1997 as part of the federal campaign to clamp down on corrupt practices at a regional level, were particularly difficult. Despite the change in directorship the situation did not improve. In 1998 although representatives of the migration service acknowledged that migrant social organizations might exist, they claimed they had no knowledge of their activity.[56] When interviewed in 1999, the organization identified the lack of cooperation and support from the migration service as one of the most serious problems they faced.[57] The service's attitude reduced the general legitimization of the organization's activity within the region, and restricted its access to the migrant community. The Samara TMS forbade the advertising of the migrant association at the service's premises, in contrast to Saratov and Novosibirsk migration services which allowed the posting of information. Nevertheless, by 2002 the organization appeared to have found a 'working compromise' with the migration service.[58] This may be partly attributed to the more secure and legitimate standing the organization itself had gained via its regional, federal and international contacts (see below).

The situation was similar in Novosibirsk *oblast'*. Although *Ruka pomoshchi* had made attempts to approach the migration service, they often felt their

efforts were met with hostility and that the migration service could not understand why the organization was duplicating its work, seeing migration as an area
of 'state concern'. One particular source of conflict was over both structures providing a computer data-base of job vacancies. However, as representatives of the
organization noted, the service knew that they worked with those migrants the
service itself did not recognize, i.e. migrants who may not have had a *propiska*,
or citizenship.[59] The vice-director of the migration service claimed that social
organizations did not offer 'real help' to migrants and that ultimately they were
only concerned with making money. In particular, she opposed migrant organizations offering any legal help, claiming that they were unqualified and often
misinterpreted the laws. Furthermore, she asserted that the migration service
provided such legal consultation and told migrants all they needed to know[60] –
a claim disputed both by the migrant organization and by migrants themselves.
The difficult nature of the relationship between *Ruka pomoshchi* and the migration service appeared to stem from their specific experience of cooperation, i.e.
the migration service's perception that *Ruka pomoshchi* was a competitor, and
that it was 'not qualified' to provide reliable advice or real support. This perception on the side of state structures was apparent in all the regions and stems
from a suspicion of, and reluctance to embrace, non-governmental actors as
viable partners in the solution of specific social issues.[61]

In addition to relations with the migration service, the opportunity to criti-
cize and contribute to regional migration debates varied between the regions.
Coordinating Councils, an initiative of the FMS, were set up across the Russian
Federation during 1999 to foster government/non-governmental debate, and
were also an important indication of the recognition of the role and importance
of migrant non-governmental organizations by the state. In Saratov *oblast'* the
setting up of a Coordinating Council under the regional State Duma in November 1998 actually preceded the federal initiative. All the migrant organizations
were invited to participate. However, *Saratovskii istochnik* and the *Komitet
bezhentsev iz Chechnii* excluded themselves from this state-led initiative, dis-
agreeing with the fact that the 'elected' head of the Coordinating Council was
the director of the migration service, i.e. a state representative. In contrast the
head of *Vozvrashchenie*, who was the vice head of the council, believed that having the director of the TMS as chairman of the council brought state and non-
state structures into close cooperation, and ensured migrants an influential
voice.[62]

In Samara *oblast'*, a Cooordinating Council was established in May 1999.
However, the body was created under the migration service rather than the
oblast' Duma, which limited its influence at the regional government level. Representatives of the migration service claimed the meetings had increased

'understanding' of their work amongst the migrant organizations, although a representative of *Samarskii pereselents* saw the meetings as just for 'men in suits'.[63] Nevertheless, one positive outcome of the council meetings was to bring together different organizations, groups and individual migrants from the districts of the *oblast'* who previously had no contact with one another. In both regions, the stance of *Saratovskii istochnik*, the *Komitet* and *Samarskii pereselenets* reveals that in some cases it is migrants (in this case as organizations) who choose *not to* engage directly with the state, preferring to retain a more independent position.

However, despite their misgivings about the coordinating council, all the migrant organizations in Saratov *oblast'* were able to participate in the development of the regional migration programme during 1999. *Vozvrashchenie* was the main migrant association involved in the development of the programme due to its close relations with the migration service and its position and willingness to work within the coordinating council. Lidiia Grafova has commented on the significant involvement of social organizations in the development of regional migration programmes in Saratov, which is not seen in many other regions.[64] In Novosibirsk, there was also a productive tradition of bringing together actors from different spheres (research, government and non-governmental) to debate the issue of migration in the *oblast'*.[65] Another institutional body where state and non-state actors could work in tandem was the Commission for Compensation for Forced Migrants and Refugees from Chechnia. In Saratov, it was made up of representatives of the regional migration service, the *oblast'* administration, *Vozvrashchenie* and the *Komitet bezhentsev iz Chechnii*. *Samarskii pereselenets*, however, was not included in the Samara Commission, nor in discussions for the development of a regional migration programme. The lack of effective joint-sector institutions and the exclusion from any government debate concerning migrant issues severely constrained the scope of the migrant association's activity, and restricted the representation of a wider migrant voice at this level.

Relations with individual government departments and regional deputies

The migrant organizations were also keen to develop connections with governmental structures apart from the regional migration services, especially where this relationship was hostile or uncooperative. Personal relations between the migrant associations and individuals within other governmental departments proved to be very significant for the organizations. A representative of one migrant organization stated:

. . .perhaps it is true everywhere in the world, but in Russia a great deal is achieved by individuals. Everything depends on personality, on the individual. . .Thank goodness there are people high up, who understand our problems and respond to them on an individual basis. . .

Saratov, 1999

All the organizations had developed similar positive relationships with individuals in different government departments who were seen to understand the problems of forced migrants. Such individual understanding was crucial to the migrants when often the response that they received from state structures was one of indifference and a lack of comprehension of their situation. Representatives of *Ruka pomoshchi* also felt that individuals within the Novosibirsk city administration 'welcome our work', and that they recognized the importance of the organization and the role it fulfilled. Nevertheless, in all regions a number of departments refused to deal with the associations and claimed they would only work with the 'official' state structures, i.e. the regional migration service.

By using the potential political and electoral significance of the migrant population, relations with individual Duma deputies were established. In Samara *oblast' Samarskii pereselenets* gained the support of the trade union movement in return for providing electoral support for the trade union's representatives. The organization approached a range of political actors, seeing them as a means by which to increase lobbying for forced migrants and to make the regional administration gradually aware of the problems migrants faced. During the elections for the *oblast'* Duma in 1998 *Saratovskii istochnik* supported four deputies for election, three of whom were elected. A representative of the organization saw the involvement as a way of ensuring that migrants had a voice in the *oblast'* Duma, and promoting understanding of the problems of migrants at this level:[66]

We must act in the political arena, we must participate in elections. . .as a result, the situation alters, people's opinions change. It is essential that we show them that we are important.

Saratov, 1999

Contacts with individual government departments and deputies were important for migrant associations as they provided an alternative way of representing migrants' interests if the migration service was hostile. Nevertheless, the main state actor influencing non-governmental migrant activity in the *oblasti* was the regional migration service. In Samara and Novosibirsk *oblasti* the more hostile nature of the relationship impeded the development of migrant non-state structures, and constrained their opportunity to participate and effectively act at the regional level. The difficult relationship in Novosibirsk *oblast'* was rooted in the migration service's determination to maintain state control over migration affairs and migrant provision, and its interpretation of the (relatively new) migrant organization as unqualified and unprofessional. In Samara *oblast'* the relationship reflected the 'restrictive' approach to migration of the wider regional migration regime. In contrast, the tolerant and sometimes cooperative nature of the relationship between the migrant organizations and migration service in Saratov *oblast'* facilitated the development of organizations and provided them with a voice at the level of the regional regime. This gave them the potential to represent the interests of the wider migrant community within regional migration debate, and allowed them limited influence over regional migration discourse and policy. A migrant leader in Saratov was positive about the progress they had made:

> Five years ago, the [regional] governor said to us we have so many of our own problems, we don't need any more, especially migrants. But, we showed him that we could work, in the social, industrial, political spheres, now they [the regional administration] already recognize that it is very important to work with migrants, with migrant associations, they realize that they must also support their 'compatriots'.
>
> *Saratov, 1999*

The regional non-governmental sphere

In addition to relations with regional government structures, connections within the NGO sector – at the regional, federal and international level – were vital for the development, visibility and legitimization of the migrant associations.[67] However, inclusion within the wider non-governmental sector could not be assumed. In Samara *oblast'*, *Samarskii pereselenets* had developed productive links with the western funded NGO resource centre/association *Povol'zhe*, which provided a means of strengthening the organization's position within the non-state regional sector.[68] However, difficult relations with state structures again constrained the wider involvement of *Samarskii pereselenets* in government/non-governmental debate. In the *oblast'* generally, cooperation between the state and non-state sphere was a frequent subject for discussion between representatives of different government and non-governmental bodies, although representatives of the NGO sector claimed that cooperation often remained at the abstract theoretical level, and that any real cooperation depended upon individuals within the government departments.[69] However, *Samarskii pereselenets* was excluded from these discussions, and from the network of 'official' social organizations in the *oblast'* who received support and some funding from the administration.[70] Furthermore, the organization was prevented from attending the All-Russian Civic Forum, held in November 2001 in Moscow (a government organized meeting to facilitate state/non-state partnerships), as it did not receive the necessary recommendation from the Samara city adminis-tration. The organization attributed their exclusion in this case, and more gen-erally, to the fact that they were an association representing forced migrants – in an *oblast'* where the regional administration did not acknowledge the issue of forced migration or wish to deal with it.

In contrast, *Ruka pomoshchi* was an active member of the *oblast'* 'Association of Social Organizations' and, due to a recommendation by the regional admin-istration, was able to attend the same Civic Forum meeting in Moscow in No-vember 2001, a visit which allowed the organization to establish crucial federal connections. In Saratov *oblast'*, the head of *Vozvrashchenie* was also a committed member of the Regional Committee of Social Organizations there, although the involvement of the other organizations within the Committee and the general non-governmental sphere was limited. Rather than being excluded, interviews with the leaders of *Saratovskii istochnik* and the *Komitet bezhentsev iz Chechnii* suggest that the organizations tended to exclude themselves, preferring to con-centrate on their own particular issues and to maintain a sense of distance and independence. The different levels of inclusion of the five bodies in the wider non-governmental sphere across the three *oblasti* indicates the involvement and influence of the state, but also demonstrates how the organizations might find alternative means to gain a voice within the sphere, or may choose to distance themselves from the sphere to independently pursue their own priorities.

International and Federal connections

. . .The first push we received towards the possibility of independent development was from the grant we managed to get from UNHCR. It was to strengthen the po-tential of the organization. Now we have our own computers, our own equipment. That first grant, it played a very significant role, it gave us some authority. We could attract the attention of a wider circle of people. It gave us the chance for an inde-pendent life.

Saratov, 1999

This quote demonstrates the central importance of a UNHCR grant for the de-velopment of the organization in question, an importance that was echoed by other associations. The start-up grant was seen as the key that had provided the organization with the opportunity to become independent and to develop its own work and programmes.[71] Representatives of all the migrant associations noted that although gaining recognition by federal and international structures was difficult and time consuming, and could detract from addressing the more immediate problems of arriving migrants, it was essential in two principal ways: both as a source of funding to enable the actual running of the organizations, and in terms of information, experience and legitimization.

Financing for the basic running costs of the migrant organizations was found to be a sufficiently problematic issue.[72] No resources were available from the state at the regional level.[73] Alternative sources of funding were local commercial or business enterprises, although the possibilities were limited.[74] The primary source of funding was therefore identified as western bodies. To varying extents, all the organizations had been successful in securing grants and material assistance, and they all admitted that their continued existence would be impossible without further international grants. Kay notes in her study of grassroots women's organizations that western grants are seen as a quick and easy solution to an organization's financial problems, that securing such a grant becomes an absolute imperative and grant-application writing an art.[75] Writing grant applications seemed to dominate the everyday activity of some of the migrant organizations and to detract from their other activities. However, in the climate that existed, there appeared to be no other option to ensure the association's survival. For example, when asked about the future of the organization, a migrant representative stated:

> Well, carry on with what we are doing at the moment, and of course, write grant applications, sit and write grant applications. Every organization must find its own niche, and the ability to pay its way.
>
> *Novosibirsk, 2002*

However, the 'competition for grants' sometimes led to conflict. Kay shows how a dependence upon western grants as the only source of available funding has generated intense direct competition for grants between local organizations. As a result, opportunities for potentially significant and fruitful cooperation between organizations are prevented, fostering resentment and division amongst them.[76] The hostile and competitive relationship that developed in Saratov *oblast'* between the three migrant organizations is indicative of these wider tendencies. A joint proposal to develop a medical rehabilitation centre for forced migrants and refugees, made to a funding body in Moscow, was prevented due to hostile relations between the three applicant bodies. Individual projects were submitted but subsequently rejected.

The connections with international organizations were not just seen as a way of securing material resources, however; they also provided a source of recognition and legitimization. In Saratov *oblast'* the assistance received, and long-term presence of, international-level connections had furthered recognition of the associations by the regional state sector. In contrast, *Samarskii pereselenets* was the first migrant initiative in the *oblast'* to have been targeted by UNHCR. It was noticeable that since the organization had established productive relationships with international and federal level non-governmental actors, there had been some improvement in their relationship with regional state structures.[77] The earlier limited international involvement in Samara *oblast'* may be rooted in the nature of the regional migration regime, the 'restrictive' attitudes of the Samara regional migration service, and a lack of migrant initiatives. However, it impeded the development of more positive relations between the state sector and migrant non-governmental structures in the region, due to the absence of 'legitimization' which international support and approval seemed to bring, and also the practical factor of initial start-up funding which enabled an organization to prove it had a role to play. Because of the relative newness of *Ruka pomoshchi*, it is difficult to make a judgement in this case.

In its criticism, this study acknowledges that resources for international assistance are not limitless. However, the Samara and Saratov cases reflect the preferred practice of international organizations in the migration field when choosing the regions in which to focus their activities, and are informative for what they indicate about post-Soviet NGO development and western involvement. The presence of cooperative and receptive local government structures were preferred, their absence discouraged international interest.[78] In turn, international organizations favoured NGOs which had productive links with these 'cooperative' local government structures. This reflects the wider dominance of 'multi-agency working', where western bodies prefer to work in regions where well-established and effective state/non-state relationships have been developed.[79] Although a successful state/non-state relationship may generate productive results, the evidence of the present study suggests that in some cases there is a need for international organizations funding NGO activity to look beyond the 'state' structures in a region, and equally beyond the 'same' regularly funded regions, to the efforts of alternative and independent group initiatives that are not as yet included within the wider system.

The activity of the federal level Russian organizations reflected such an approach. Evidence from this study suggests that they have been willing to establish contact with regional bodies not necessarily favoured by local government structures, which may be due to the indirect nature of the working relationship these organizations have had with the Russian state, and their frequent criticism of and opposition to state migration institutions. Links with Russian federal organizations provided essential information and direct access to the wider federal and international migration regimes. In addition, through setting up programmes (which often receive international support) such as *Migratsiia i Pravo*, the federal level organizations have created a working institutional framework of which regional associations can become a part. Representatives of the regional migrant organizations particularly stressed the value of establishing contact and exchanging knowledge and information with the Civic Assistance Committee and Forum, and the importance of individual support from Svetlana Gannushkina and Lidiia Grafova.[80] The migrant organizations often positioned themselves as regional branches within the Forum's vertical structure, and stressed the importance of connections to and unity at the federal level, both for their own development and for the wider advancement of migrant influence at the regional and federal levels:

> I have been a member of the executive committee of the Forum for a year already. Being able to turn to people there, to visit, to be involved in joint projects and programmes, it has widened our horizons, and has meant that we are included in activities not only at the regional, but also at the federal level. Because of that we have grown.
>
> *Saratov, 1999*

> When they (the Russian government) see that social organizations are coming together at a federal level, solving their own problems – then we gain more power. When we are discussing things, working out solutions – the state structures are forced to listen, because they see our strength, it is very significant.
>
> *Saratov, 1999*

CONCLUSION

The non-governmental sphere is an essential part of the emerging Russian migration regime, analysis of which shifts the focus away from official government frameworks and reveals the 'alternative' frameworks within which individual migrants are moving. Although the practical help offered by regional migrant associations is limited, they – along with the federal level migrant NGOs – represent an important voice. Their development, and their influence on institutional and legislative structures, has been constrained by the frequently restrictive nature of the surrounding migration regime; nevertheless they have created a space from which they can act, and in many cases they have had an impact. The connections that have developed, which often transcend the borders of either the regional or federal to the international, have been essential in fostering the growth of migrant NGOs across Russia. These organizations are surely sites of further potential.

Particularly at the regional level – where the migrant associations have emerged from and are primarily made up of migrants – they directly represent the interests and concerns of *some* of the migrants arriving from the former republics, and demonstrate one strategy that they are using to negotiate for inclusion within the Russian 'homeland'. The 'receptive'/'restrictive' nature of the official migration regimes of Samara, Saratov and Novosibirsk became more visible through the experiences of the regional migrant organizations, in comparison to the more homogenous experience that emerged from individual migrant narratives (see Chapter 4). This may be due to the persistent attempts by the migrant organizations to engage with state structures, despite initial hostility or rejection. Such engagement ensured more immediate levels of contact.

For the involved migrants the organizations have become an important site of resistance and identity as they, as individuals, adapt to new roles, learn new skills and engage with actors and issues that extend well beyond the borders of the region in which they have arrived. However, the organizations do not represent all of the arriving migrants; the vertical links extending down into the migrant community are limited and many migrants choose not to engage with NGO structures. To understand further the levels of engagement between the individual and state and non-state structures within the Russian migration regime, it is necessary to return to the level of individual migrant agency. The following chapter reveals the central importance of informal family and friendship networks for individual migrants in the migration and resettlement process and the re-creation of 'home'. These kinship and friendship ties frequently enable some 'distance' to be maintained from state structures, and also from wider migrant networks including regional migrant organizations, at the site of settlement.

6

Depending on 'Selves': Family, Friendship and Migrant Networks

This chapter analyses in greater depth the levels of migrant networks that have emerged through the book. It explores the importance of 'alternative' migration and resettlement strategies for migrants based around immediate/primary networks of family and friends and wider networks located at migrant organizations and rural compact settlement sites. The chapter continues the analysis of regional migrant non-governmental organizations that began in Chapter 6, but shifts the focus away from the organizational role and activity of the networks in order to explore how they are perceived by the individual migrant.

Initially, the role of migrant networks is discussed with reference to the wider 'network' society that is suggested to exist in post-Soviet Russia. By drawing directly on individual migrant narratives, the chapter proceeds to demonstrate the centrality of different levels of networks at all stages of the migration process in question – in the decision to move, during the actual movement and at the site of resettlement. The experiences of migrant respondents enable the practical and psychological significance of levels of networks for individual migrants to be portrayed. They also further illuminate the place of networks within the wider context of the migration and resettlement process, and their relationship to official state discourse and practice. Although individual/collective activity can mean disengagement from official state structures, the activity of the different levels of migrant network, independently from state influence, can shape the nature of the migration movement and the type of resettlement taking place. Thus the chapter continues to debate the gap between state discourse and practice and migrant reality, and from a migrant-centered perspective, furthers understandings of 'home' and 'homeland'. An important component of the chapter is to explore how migrants relate to the different levels of networks that exist. It is shown how returnees are often unaware of or choose to distance themselves from wider migrant networks such as migrant organizations and compact settlements, preferring to focus in the short term upon immediate circles of family and friends.

POST-SOVIET RUSSIA – A SOCIETY OF NETWORKS?

A significant body of recent research has pointed to the importance of personal/social networks in post-Soviet Russian society.[1] The focus and approach of the research reiterates the call that is being made to go to the level of 'the micro world of day to day life'[2], to more adequately understand and assess the process of 'transformation' taking place across post-socialist countries (see Chapter 1).[3] Instead of dismissing practices – such as a dependence upon personal networks – as outdated legacies of the communist past, the authors of the research suggest that attention should be paid to the ways in which these practices are both surviving and being adapted to new environments. In the face of much macro-level collapse, a space for change at the micro level has been created; it is at this level that individuals both negotiate strategies for coping and, in addition, renegotiate their relationship to existing and emerging macro-level/ state structures. Individual/collective activity in fact influences the nature of these macro-level structures and the type of economic, social and political 'transformation' under way.[4]

The presence and centrality of personal/social networks in Russia is not confined to the post-Soviet period. Ledeneva demonstrates how the study of *blat*[5] helped to better understand the operation of Soviet society, and how these 'informal' relations were not confined to the economic sphere.[6] Within her study Ledeneva also considers post-Soviet Russian society and suggests that although the practice of *blat* has changed, it is beneficial to analyse its usage in contemporary conditions so as to precisely understand the 'sources, limitations and consequences of post-Soviet reformation'.[7] Other studies of post-Soviet Russian society confirm the continuing role of networks.[8] They stress that many of the present-day practices have Soviet antecedents, but at the same time they reiterate their contemporary relevance[9]; they propose that in a wider environment of turmoil and scarcity, people are inclined to turn to existing networks, often based around particular structures such as the workplace.[10] These studies concur with Ledeneva's claim that during the Soviet and post-Soviet period, the formation and operation of networks has been a valuable medium for alternative understandings of the way in which Russian society is evolving.[11]

The above research highlights the need for rigorous empirical analysis of the development and role of networks in post-Soviet Russia, rather than the mere metaphorical usage of the term 'a society of networks'.[12] Factors to consider include the levels of network (family, friends, acquaintances, wider social connections), the types of ties that exist between members of the network,[13] the location of these individual ties within larger configurations of social relations, the purpose for the formation of the network and its subsequent operation.[14] An understanding of a network's constitution, formation and subsequent function can help to elicit how the involved individuals interact with – or equally disengage from – the state and the wider environment of political, social and economic transformation.[15] This empirical challenge is addressed here by shifting the debate to the specific case of the communities of returning Russians, and the role of personal/social networks in their migration and resettlement.

FURTHERING THE DEBATE – THE CASE OF RUSSIAN RETURNEES

The experience of migration and resettlement amongst Russian returnees provides an alternative and informative view of the role of personal/social networks in post-Soviet Russia. The operation of migrant networks takes place within the context of the suggested wider 'society of networks', but their role and usage is particular. The research mentioned above primarily focuses upon individuals and communities who, although experiencing the effects of social, economic and political upheaval, are static. In the case of the displaced, traditional, longstanding and 'rooted' networks have been disrupted or destroyed. During the process of migration and resettlement, attempts are made either to sustain existing networks in some form, to adapt existing networks to radically novel conditions, to draw upon distant resources to develop networks, or to develop completely new networks in the region of settlement. The specific nature of migrant networks is precisely that they are 'in flux' and in a state of re-formation sometimes transcending, in this case, newly formed national boundaries.

In the field of migration studies, 'household' or 'social network' approaches to migration have focused attention on the widespread usage of personal networks to facilitate the migration and resettlement process.[16] As kinship ties are major sources of personal networks, this has often served to direct attention to the role of families and households in migration.[17] However, as Gurak and Caces suggest, social arrangements may well extend beyond the family or friendship unit.[18] These approaches therefore use a particular level of migrant network to identify a connection between the individual and surrounding structural environment and to provide a method for analysing migrant action and interaction

with other parts of the migration system.[19] Migrant networks, whether based
upon immediate kinship or wider social ties, may act as important conduits of
information about the destination site to potential migrants, and about sources
of assistance to newly arrived returnees. They often provide initial help in the
provision of housing, employment, food or other requirements. As Van Hear
states 'they are the vehicle for the transmission of migratory cultural capital'.[20] In
this case migration is the organizational foci for the network; that is, migration
and later resettlement invoke the formation of networks when people are drawn
upon for their usefulness according to the particular requirements of the situation.[21] Through their operation, migrant networks may support and encourage
additional migration.[22] In some instances, wider migrant networks – often
based upon kinship and friendship ties – develop into more formal associations
to address particular needs, for example the absence of concrete government
provision.[23]

The call for empirical analysis to increase understanding of the role of networks in post-Soviet Russian society is reiterated in approaches to understanding the operation of migrant networks. Gurak and Caces suggest that adopting
ideas from social network research would add to the clarity of conceptualizing
migrant networks including addressing the concept of strong and weak ties, the
non-territorial conceptualization of communities and the organizing foci of
networks.[24] Factors to consider, therefore, are the nature of relations within the
migrant networks,[25] the individual perceptions of the role of the household/
social network in the resettlement process and the feelings of inclusion or exclusion from the level of network in question. It should not be assumed that in all
cases networks encourage or facilitate integration; instead they can be prescriptive and prevent the wider participation of migrants in the receiving society.[26]

The use of personal/social networks by Russian returnee communities is
arguably distinct from their usage by 'resident' Russian communities. The returnees have been displaced from their place of residence where many traditional networks were located (e.g the work-place, local neighbourhood). During
the Soviet period, the territorial stratification of society meant that the position
of an individual, their standards of living and life chances, were closely linked to
the place where they were located, and mobility was strictly regulated through
the use of the internal passport and the *propiska* system.[27] The rigidity of the
system generated a 'dread of being outside' that reinforced a sense of 'rootedness' amongst the population.[28] However, as demonstrated in Chapters 3 and 4,
with the collapse of the Soviet Union and the existing political and economic
system, those Russians who migrated from the former republics to the Russian
Federation lost this deep and long-standing 'rootedness' which in turn had
supported and engendered 'rooted' networks, both professional and personal.

Nevertheless, narratives of migrant experiences show that despite this loss, and the experience of displacement, both existing and newly created networks still play a vital role in the migration and resettlement processes. These networks are both invoked by the needs of migration and resettlement, and are embedded in the legacies of the Soviet past and the needs of the post-Soviet present. They not only facilitate the migration and resettlement on a practical and psychological level; they also shape the actual nature of the movement and the type of settlement according to individual migrant priorities. This occurs both in relation and in opposition to (and even in some cases independently from) state migration discourse and practice and the wider receiving environment of the Russian Federation. The interaction between individual/collective activity, macro-level structures and the shaping of the nature of 'transformation', as suggested by Burawoy and Verdery[29], is therefore demonstrated through the case of migration and resettlement in contemporary Russia.

MIGRANT EXPERIENCE AND RESPONSE — THE REFRAMING OF THE MIGRATION AND RESETTLEMENT PROCESS

As has been suggested throughout the book, the dominant state construction of the migration and resettlement of Russian returnees, at both a federal and regional level, has occurred through a restrictive and increasingly securitized migration discourse. The 'returnee' is positioned as a 'forced migrant', rather than a welcomed 'repatriate' in Russian society, and neither through state migration discourse nor state resettlement practice is Russia constructed as a welcoming 'homeland'. State provision at the regional site of resettlement is limited, and in some cases completely absent. Yet, as has already been revealed via migrant narratives, the individual migrant is not passive in the migration and resettlement process. Instead migrants are independent and rational actors who act within the official state migration 'regime' to locate themselves at the new place of residence. Due to the constraining aspects of state structures and the lack of suitable or adequate state provision and concern, migrants frequently distance themselves from the remit of the state. They negotiate their own resettlement and re-creation of home, with the help of alternative structures: immediate family and friendship networks or, in some cases, the wider migrant networks located around migrant organizations and compact settlements. However, migrants' narratives demonstrate that the reliance upon networks is not only due to state inaction. Rather, the picture which emerges shows that the networks best meet migrants' practical needs and facilitate the re-creation of what is required for an immediate sense of 'home' at the site of settlement: feelings of continuity, belonging and inclusion.

An absence of state concern

Migrants' accounts of their experiences of the migration movement indicated that the Russian state did not play a role in either the decision of migrants to move or their actual journey from the former republics to the Russian Federation. Amongst the 72 respondents included in the present study there was only one case where institutional help had been received in organizing the move. As related by a husband and wife who had moved to Samara *oblast'* [61/61, Samara, 1999] this help was received from the Russian embassy and military in Tajikistan, and an ethnic Russian social organization based in Tajikistan. Equally, as migrant narratives have shown, at the regional site of settlement state involvement was peripheral rather than central for the majority of migrants. In the face of state indifference to their plight, and/or its incapability to help, many of the individuals recognized that they must depend upon themselves and no longer look elsewhere for help. This attitude of independence is rooted in the lack of state assistance migrants have had since 'return'; in addition it can be seen as a reflection of the secure position the majority of the migrants had previously occupied in society, and their reliance on 'other ways' of doing things. Faced with finding themselves in a previously unknown condition of dependency they were keen not to be a burden to anyone, were reluctant to turn to any structure for help, and were ready to rely upon themselves:

> We do not ask the state for anything, we try our own path, everyone for themselves, if we waited we would die, like mammoths, we would become extinct.
>
> *51, Samara, 1999*

> I have got forced migrant status, but I did not got anywhere for help, I did not want to be importunate. We have always lived basically for ourselves, and we are not used to wait for, or to ask for, help.
>
> *6, Saratov, 1997*

> Up to now I haven't turned to anyone for help. I didn't want to consider myself a victim or ask for help, with an outstretched hand.
>
> *63, Novosibirsk, 2002*

Family and friendship networks

For the majority of migrants it was family and friendship networks that were central to every stage of the migration movement: in the decision to move; as the structure that 'moved'; as an important factor in influencing the choice of settlement region;[30] and in providing initial support upon 'return'. Although homes and employment had been lost, networks of family and friends could be more easily sustained. Migrants usually moved from the former place of residence either as a group (made up of family and friends/acquaintances), as a family group, or as an individual. The movement was most often made with other family members – husbands, wives, children, parents and grandparents.[31] In making the choice of the place of settlement, the main reason given by respondents was the presence of family and friends in the chosen region.[32] Equally, although many of the migrants requested state recognition upon 'return' and received forced migrant status, during the ongoing process of resettlement they depended primarily upon the support of informal networks of family and friends.

Family networks
The family ties that existed in the regions took varying forms: ancestral roots in the *oblast'*, family members who were permanently resident in the *oblast'*, prior residence and personal contacts in the *oblast'*,[33] and family members who had migrated to the *oblast'* at an earlier date. The presence of relatives resident in the region of arrival made the area attractive for resettlement as they provided one way of solving some of its immediate problems; especially practical help in the initial process of registration (gaining a *propiska*), finding accommodation or employment.[34] A young female migrant who made the movement individually and was able to register at her grandmother's apartment stated:

> I came here because I have relatives here. My grandmother lives here. That solves a lot of problems. . .I didn't go anywhere to register, because, simply, I have somewhere to live here. My grandmother has an apartment. We have such an institution called the *propiska*. I have the possibility to receive a *propiska* because I have relatives here. Therefore I didn't turn to the migration service.
>
> *20, Saratov, 1999*

In migrants' narratives, family connections were often seen as the only way out of a desperate situation: they both influenced the decision to leave and provided a practical and psychological basis for resettlement to begin. A female migrant from Uzbekistan spoke of the importance of these links:

> I have a cousin here. She helped me at the beginning, she often used to come to see my parents. My parents died there, I was alone, she is older than me, she rang and said that I have the possibility to help you to resettle, I am very grateful; it is thanks to her I am not on the street with my family.
>
> *53, Samara, 1999*

In some cases migrants used family networks to allow a form of 'staggered' migration to take place. Respondents often moved to family members who were recent migrants themselves, having been resident in the same city or town in the former republic prior to migration, and who had established themselves in the new place of residence. Family structures were identified as a source of essential support by a female migrant who had arrived in Samara *oblast'* from Kazakstan in 1998:

> I have a sister here. She left a year earlier than me and I came to her because other than her we do not have anyone. Our parents died a long time ago. And in order to somehow support one another, we came here together. She came a year ago. I came a little later. She managed to buy a little house with the money we had. Her daughter helped.
>
> *46, Samara, 1999*

In other cases members of the family acted as scouts (*razvedchiki*) and conducted 'scouting' missions to Russia to explore the possibilities for resettlement, particularly regarding accommodation and employment, after which they returned to the former place of residence to collect the rest of the family. The migration of different members of the same family might continue for a number of years. Migrants spoke of family members, often elderly parents, whom they hoped to bring to Russia when it was financially and practically viable.[35]

Another important role played by the presence of family connections in the region of arrival was to facilitate the creation of feelings of familiarity, security and belonging. As demonstrated in Chapter 3, when migrants spoke of their previous lives in the former republics they stressed the importance of establishing the continuity and security of a family over generations. This 'rootedness' had been lost with displacement; however, upon 'return' migrant statements suggested that the presence of family re-created a sense of something that they had temporarily lost, and allowed the continuation of familiar habits, customs and traditions:

> We had some distant roots here, links. When we came here it was a familiar place, familiar people.
>
> *22, Saratov, 1999*

> He [her brother] lives in Novosibirsk, he doesn't live in this region, he lives on Karl Marx street. As you see, I live here, so we mostly talk on the telephone. But we get together for all celebrations, New Year, birthdays, 8th March, always together. He helps so much morally. . .
>
> *69, Novosibirsk, 2002*

Even in the absence of family upon arrival, migrants envisaged that through the establishment of family roots and ties in the new territory Russia might become 'home' and ultimately, for their children, 'homeland':

> My homeland (*rodina*) is there, where I was born, where my friends are. But I think Russia has to become my 'home'. . .Russia will become homeland and home,

because our children will be here. Our children will have children, and there will be grandchildren. Therefore I will consider that Russia is my home.

35, Saratov, 1999

Friendship networks

Who helped most of all? Of course, close ones, our friends, with whom we moved . . .the locals, those who live here, it's all the same to them who is living nearby, they don't understand how hard it is for us. . .

64, Novosibirsk, 2002

The presence of friends or acquaintances was another key factor in the choice of the region of settlement, and as a source of assistance in the initial stages of re-settlement.[36] The contact was seen as a possible support structure, *in the absence of* family networks and state assistance. Friends or acquaintances provided an address where migrants could register (acquire a *propiska*), even if only temporarily. This was particularly important in Samara *oblast'* where, as shown earlier, initial resettlement was impossible if migrants did not have somewhere to register. Often friends and acquaintances were themselves migrants and provided information about possibilities of employment and accommodation in the region which was essential in the absence of official information:

We moved here because we have one acquaintance who allowed us to come and register, not live, just register temporarily. In Russia we have no relatives or acquaintances. There was simply nowhere for us to go, therefore this was our only chance, and we decided to use it.

21, Saratov, 1999

We came to some acquaintances of ours. They are not friends, but simply acquaintances. We used to live across the hallway in a block of flats. They moved here, he works for the railway, she stays at home with the children. Yes, Lena rang me herself. She said, 'It's boring, it's awful here, we are alone, why don't you come?' So I came. We had a very good relationship there, and here we've kept it up. Everyone who we have come across from our old town, we all pass on things to one another by phone, we all support one another. Yes, if someone finds something out, they phone someone else straight away and tells them, it reassures you, gives you hope.

68, Novosibirsk, 2002

Migrants frequently moved to friends or acquaintances who originated from the same region in the former republic and had moved at an earlier date – which, like the presence of close family members, created a sense of something 'familiar' being returned to:

> We are both from Samarkand. We are fellow countrywomen (*zemliachki*). We grew
> up on one street as friends. We grew up together. I lived with her for two weeks, then
> we were given the neighbouring room (in a hostel).
>
> *41, Saratov, 1999*

Similarly, new friendships with 'other' migrants, or relationships with old acquaintances that had become closer due to the experience of migration, also
helped to foster feelings of familiarity and security:

> Of course we are closer to those who have also moved. Those friends, who have
> moved, we can turn to each other for help. We met some of them here. Even when
> you hear a familiar word, you want to go up to someone and ask them 'where have
> you come from?' And straight away we will understand one another, we have the
> same problems.
>
> *63, Novosibirsk, 2002*

> There are not many of us here. If we lose contact here as well, that will be it. On the
> contrary, we have got to keep together. We are already united here. There we were
> just acquaintances, and here, we have already grown closer.
>
> *68, Novosibirsk, 2002*

In some cases migration and resettlement were undertaken as a group, consisting
of family members, friends and acquaintances, who had lived in the same region
in the former place of residence. The actual migration movement was staggered;
an individual or a number of migrants (usually male) acted as scouts and came to
the chosen region to explore possibilities for resettlement, after which the whole
group made the move. This was the case for a group of migrants from Uzbekistan
who formed a compact settlement in Saratov *oblast'*.[37] Here the wider migrant
group was formed out of smaller networks of family and friends precisely for
the purpose of migration. However, the reality of 'return' and resettlement, and
the difficult experience of construction of a compact settlement, led to difficulties which caused the wider group to break down. Nevertheless, the core of the
original group provided the basis for the formation of the migrant organization
Saratovskii istochnik (see Chapter 5). This case was the only such instance among
respondents in the present study of formal group migration. A more informal example of staggered, group migration occurred to a village in Saratov *oblast'* where
the presence of friends or acquaintances in the region of settlement generated a
type of larger scale, chain migration. The initial migration of certain individuals
and their sending back of information about possibilities for resettlement to the
previous place of residence in Uralskii region, Kazakstan, led to the migration of
other families and individuals from the region to the Saratov village.

In Novosibirsk *oblast'* there was evidence of more extensive networks that
were developing and being consolidated between the place of settlement and

the previous place of residence in the former republic, in particular in Kazakstan. The visibility of these networks amongst migrants in Novosibirsk may be due to the later date of the empirical work in this region, by which time it had become increasingly difficult for people to manage the move to Russia, particularly due to financial reasons. A number of migrants mentioned that children of friends were living with them in Novosibirsk. This occurred, for example, in instances where friends were unable or did not wish to move, but wanted their children to gain an education in Russia. They therefore sent them to live with close friends who had made the move:

> Their daughter is staying with us – she is studying here. The fact is the husband did not want to leave Kazakstan, because his parents are there, and there is no point in pensioners moving. But their daughter will get a Russian education here, and will live here in the future. Most young people who come here, they like it here, they don't want to go back.
>
> *Novosibirsk, 72, 2002*

> Someone I worked with there, she rang me and asked me to take her daughter. Of course I took her, because I know how necessary it is to send children somewhere. We understand the problems, and how it is difficult without any help. Her daughter has been living with us for half a year – she has just gone to visit her mother for the holidays.
>
> *Novosibirsk, 63, 2003*

Barriers to re-creating networks
Despite evidence of existing friendship networks that were essential to both the migration and resettlement process, many migrants had lost a very close network of friends rooted in the locality of their previous residence, and the social support that this network had provided. When they spoke of their previous lives, they frequently mentioned the importance of the 'network' of friends of which they had been part:

> It was wonderful there. We had a lot of friends. There was naturally respect and calm. That circle of friends helped you with everything. They enriched your soul and made you feel good.
>
> *21, Saratov, 1999*

> At first it was terrible. To lose friends. . .Russians, we are very sociable, and to lose all of that, childhood friends, and to come to a new place completely 'bare', it is very difficult.
>
> *49, Samara, 1999*

The loss was exacerbated by the fact that the re-creation of such a network upon arrival was problematic due to the inherent longstanding attachment of networks – 'social circles' – to a specific location:

> . . .those who live here permanently they have an established social circle, they have
> a system of cooperation with some sort of structures. Those people who arrive,
> they have nothing and to have to re-create everything from scratch. It is particularly
> difficult to create a 'social circle [*krug obshcheniia*] due to the situation at the mo-
> ment – everyone is occupied with their own problems.
>
> *62, Samara, 1999*

The process of 'making new friends' and building social networks was made
more difficult due to the sense of difference many migrants felt upon return to
the Russian Federation, grounded in experiences of life in the former republics
and in the shared experiences of migration and resettlement.[38] As seen in Chapter 4, migrants were clear about the potential they felt they represented for Russia
and the region to which they had moved. However, in the present socio-
economic conditions of the areas to which they had come, returnees claimed
that the local population saw them as a threat and that general economic problems were blamed on increased competition generated by their arrival:

> . . .it seems to them that we take their work, their money. When a country 'fills up',
> there are soon difficulties, therefore people already look at you in a different way.
> We are like competitors for life.
>
> *36, Saratov, 1999*

The lack of opportunities to fulfil their potential, and to regain the standards of
housing and employment they had lost by leaving the former republics, led to a
tendency amongst the migrants to contrast the superiority of their former lives,
living conditions and personal levels of education and culture with that of the
local Russian population and the locality in which they now lived:[39]

> The cultural level in Russia is very low, relationships between people are completely
> different. . .those who have arrived, they are highly educated and highly special-
> ized. They are very hardworking, and come with the desire to work. . .it is highly
> qualified, cultured, intellectual, well brought up people who have arrived. They
> want to bring their culture and strong labour potential to the economy and culture
> of Russia, there is a great potential amongst these people – their cultural level is
> high.
>
> *53, Samara, 1999*

The migrants directly compared the specific attributes of their 'community' in
the former republic with the one in which they were now resident in the Russian
Federation. In terms of the customs, traditions and conditions of life which represented their lives before and had made that place 'home': both the nature of
the physical environment (cleanliness, order, quality of buildings, the countryside) and of social relationships (the nature of social interaction, characteristics

of people), were compared with what was faced upon 'return', where such attributes were seen to impede understanding, rather than facilitate efforts to establish links with the local population:

> Russian people there and here – they are completely different nations, completely different people. For Uzbeks it is customary to help one another, we have an Eastern upbringing. If something happens to someone then everyone helps. For Russians this is not customary, here it is everyone for themselves. Everyone survives on their own. No one helps.
>
> *21, Saratov, 1999*

> In Asia people are brought up according to two faiths, two cultures, it gave us something of its own, children respect elders, our girls are more modest than those here. Our men drink but not to such an extent, everything is done for the home, cleanliness around the home, they do not understand here, it is difficult for us to get used to it here. It is bad, all of Russia drinks. It is her misfortune. There are a lot of drunkards, and do people pay any attention to around their home? I also do not like the unpaved roads, the dirt. We had everything, our roads were paved, our gardens well kept, everyone tried to make things tidy, comfortable, and here they do not understand that, it is difficult.
>
> *50, Samara, 1999*

> People here are rude, uncultured, they swear and shout. There, where we lived, amongst those people, my mother would not even talk loudly. Husbands never got drunk. And here, well women swear and shout. They didn't do that there. We were gentle, good people.
>
> *65, Novosibirsk, 2002*[40]

Although migrants of common ethnicity with the host nation may assume easier acceptance in a community where origins, culture and heritage are similar, the past lives of individuals, and the development of cultural and linguistic differences, can impede inclusion.[41] This was demonstrated amongst the migrant respondents. For some the hope that a return to Russia would dispel the 'ethnic discomfort' recently experienced in the former republic was problematized when they felt their Russian-ness, and what they had imagined as Russia, to be challenged by the local population and local environment:

> It is us who are strangers, we who have arrived. Yes, we are Russians (*russkie*), but we are not perceived as Russians. We are strangers, and I think that our children, who have come with us, they will also be strangers.
>
> *45, Saratov, 1999*

> I am Russian (*russkaia*), my husband is Russian (*russkii*), but everyone treats me as a Kazak (*Kazashka*) at work, if you are from Kazakstan [to them] it means you are a Kazak.
>
> *49, Samara, 1999*

This sense of difference, which was heightened by the often unsuccessful re-settlement experience and the difficulties of the socio-economic environment, impeded the creation of initial positive connections with members of the re-ceiving community and prevented a sense of social belonging. Yet, despite the perceived sense of difference and separation, empathy was also felt with mem-bers of the local community due to the shared experience of the difficult socio-economic situation in Russia and a sense of common state indifference towards them. A number of migrants mentioned that in place of initially difficult rela-tions with the local community there was growing understanding and toler-ance, and some of the early barriers were breaking down. Individual references were made to receiving help and support from local Russians, and of building up friendship networks within the local community that reflected the begin-nings of the re-creation of the social networks that had been lost. In addition, some migrants expressed a feeling of a wider sense of 'security' in the surround-ing environment. Even in the absence of employment or housing, the sense of personal security represented the first feelings of 'home' and belonging, and hope for a future, in the new place of residence – forming new localized net-works was key to this sense of security. It suggests that over time the intensity of feelings of cultural difference may lessen as communication and stability are ensured:

> You know, it depends on what you understand as home. If you consider your home as just four walls and that is all. . .well, of course, it is there, we haven't sold our apartment yet. But, if you consider your home as the surrounding environment, the atmosphere, all of that, then it is here, because I feel much better that I did there. I feel equal, a normal person, no one is going to try to 'knock you about' because you don't speak Uzbek for example.
>
> *23, Saratov, 1999*

> I feel better here. . .even though I live in a hostel, how can I explain. I have more confidence, I feel equal, here you can do something, you can show something, you can compete for something.
>
> *41, Saratov, 1999*

> You know I don't feel at home yet here, but I simply feel at ease here. I can calmly let my child go out into the street, and not worry that something will happen to her. 69,
> *Novosibirsk, 2002*[42]

The use of friendship and family networks reveals a desire amongst migrants to maintain or restore the framework of security that has been destroyed. Their importance points to how in conditions of displacement and uncertainty lives may become 'highly localized'.[43] Even in cases where sufficient government provision exists, studies of 'return' migration have demonstrated a tendency to depend upon immediate and familiar networks of friends and family.[44] The use of such networks may represent a psychological strategy to maintain a connection with the past and to immediately create the beginnings of family or friendship networks that had been lost with displacement. Individuals, responding to the loss of place and people, often accentuate the importance of those family and close relationships that remain.[45] In some instances distant or lost family members are contacted, perhaps in an attempt to establish an essential 'connection' with the new territory. Yet the use of family and friendship networks also represents a basic survival strategy where, in the absence of any state assistance, personal information and assistance channels are crucial to facilitate migration and to begin the reconstruction of a new life at the site of resettlement.[46] The dependence upon family and friendship networks demonstrated by migrant respondents strongly reflects the uncertainties of the wider environment, the position in which migrants are placed by the Russian state upon 'return', and how they negotiate that position and use these networks to initiate the recreation of a 'home' within an often unwelcoming and hostile 'homeland'.

Wider migrant networks: compact settlements and organizations

A sense of state indifference, together with feelings of difference and exclusion from the local Russian community, led some migrants to come together in groups that were more formally organized than the family and friendship networks discussed above. The ease of developing these migrant networks, and of becoming included within them, was due to a shared experience of life in the former republic and the common experience of displacement and resettlement. Two primary sites existed where migrants attempted to improve their possibilities of employment and housing, and where they were able to re-create the social support networks and friendships that had been lost. These were at compact settlement sites and within regional migrant organizations. However, automatic inclusion by, or the desire to be included within, these levels of migrant networks cannot be assumed.[47] Equally, the successful operation of these wider networks was not guaranteed.

Compact settlements
The idea for the creation of compact settlements first appeared in the newspaper *Literaturnaia gazeta* in July 1990, proposed by the federal level migrant NGO the 'Civic Assistance Committee' (see Chapter 5), and subsequently gained popularity amongst potential migrants in the former republics who had started to gather into collectives prior to return. Compact settlements seemed to offer a 'realistic solution' to the key problems of resettlement – housing,

employment and cultural adaptation faced upon return – which were an even greater obstacle for the individual migrant.[48] Government opinion on compact settlements has varied over time; initial government opposition was replaced by acceptance, possibly linked to pressure from non-governmental circles and migrant organizations, and the realization that it was more profitable for the FMS to allocate resources for group settlement and construction than to direct help individually. Yet although the Federal Migration Programme (1998–2000) included plans for investment and the creation of work places at compact settlements, budgetary constraints meant that these plans were not always realized.[49] Attitudes towards compact settlements underwent another shift in the late 1990s. State and non-state commentators reached a consensus which recognized that the majority of compact settlements had failed, and that they impeded long-term social and economic integration.[50] The only successful settlements were those located close to urban centres with an existing infrastructure.[51]

The impetus for the creation of two of the three compact settlements focused upon in the present research came from migrants themselves.[52] At one settlement in Saratov *oblast'*, prior to departure the migrants formed a group made up of family members, friends and acquaintances. Upon arrival the group acquired land from the local administration for the construction of a 'compact type' settlement. Another settlement in Saratov *oblast'* was the initiative of a female migrant from the north of Russia. Individual migrant families then arrived there from different republics, after finding out about the possibilities of employment and accommodation at the site upon arrival. In the third case, a settlement in Samara *oblast'*, the regional migration service acquired the land and directed migrants arriving in the region to construct a compact settlement at the site. However, following the initial involvement of the migration service, the migrants were left to manage themselves and the settlement very much became a migrant-led initiative.[53] The living conditions at all the compact settlements were very difficult, which placed the long-term future of the settlements in doubt and caused internal divisions within the migrant groups.[54] Amongst the problems faced were a lack of adequate infrastructure (water, electricity, roads); the failure of enterprises set up at the settlements; a subsequent and related absence of employment opportunities; a lack of assistance from the regional migration services; an absence of resources for the construction of adequate housing; and the location of settlements in isolated, inaccessible rural areas unfamiliar for the predominantly urban migrants.

Despite these difficult conditions, the sense of community that the settlements generated was obviously important to the migrant respondents. They were perceived by migrants as not only helping in the reality of resettlement, providing employment and housing on site, but also as a space where feelings of security and belonging might be re-created amongst 'similar' people – that is, other migrants. A female migrant resident in Saratov *oblast'* stated:

> . . .here we are all newcomers (*priezhie*). We are all close to each other in spirit. Everyone is from Central Asia here. We have our own way of life, although I am Russian (*russkaia*), my way of life is more similar to an Eastern woman's. Therefore we have found a common language. Newcomers, no one loves them anywhere. Here, we are all together, we are all a group. . .we can communicate, we have a great deal in common, our way of life, for example. We even have the same dishes. We prepare dishes in the same way. It means a great deal. And to have left there, to have lost everything, left everything. . .such little things give you joy. We have common recollections, a common outlook. It is something important for us.
>
> *27, Saratov, 1999*

Regardless of their unfamiliar rural location, the settlements immediately provided some of the basic networks, and the normality of life, which had been lost with displacement. Even with the uncertain future of the settlements, migrants had already invested a great deal of physical and emotional energy into them, and a sense of community and attachment to the physical space had developed which was strong enough to deter them from abandoning hope in its eventual success. A female migrant from Kazakstan, who lived at the settlement in Samara *oblast'* initiated by the migration service, stated:

> The place here is not bad, it is beautiful; we hope to achieve something here. The children like it, and we have already become accustomed, we know the place, it already seems a shame to leave. And here living on the hillside, we have our clan, we are all newcomers (*priezhie*), we have our community (*obshchina*), we have our own outlook and views, a lot of us do not want to leave the hillside, we already want to build our settlement here.
>
> *59, Samara, 1999*

Other migrants, however, viewed the idea of compact settlements as impeding the process of relocation. Firstly, the rural location of the settlements lessened the likelihood of acquiring professional employment, and secondly, they were seen as hindering integration with the local community, which could generate exclusion from wider Russian society and thus inhibit adaptation:

> I think it is better to live together with the local population. . .it is impossible to be separate, we must integrate faster. In order to integrate it is absolutely necessary to live with the Russians (*rossiiane*). If we acquire citizenship, we want to take part in the affairs of Russia. We will also feel ourselves to be *rossiiane*. Therefore we must mix with them. Compact settlements – I do not consider they are that good an idea.
>
> *21, Saratov, 1999*[55]

Migrant organizations

Migrant organizations provided another form of network that individuals could immediately draw upon for social interaction and support. As described in Chapter 5, all the organizations focused on in the study had been established by migrants themselves. New arrivees learnt about the existence of the associations via information sent by the groups to Russian communities still resident in the former republics, information passed by word of mouth upon arrival in the region, or from advertisements placed at the migration service:

> There are not many Russians left in Dushanbe. We pass on everything to one another, where to go, to what organisation, to which person, how to get there, etc., that is how I knew.
>
> *69, Novosibirsk, 2002*

Although the number and activity of migrant organizations was greater in Saratov than in both Samara and Novosibirsk *oblasti,* the opinions of their role amongst migrants were very similar. The perception of such organizations differed amongst those migrants who had made contact with them, or were actually involved in their operation, and those who had not made, or did not wish to have, such contact. Out of the 72 migrants interviewed in the two *oblasti,* 42 had not received any help from a migrant organization, a number of these had never heard of the existence of any migrant association. The help that had been received was predominantly legal and other general resettlement consultation, moral support, and material help (clothes, food). In addition, five migrants had received help with finding accommodation, and two with obtaining employment.

The migrants who had been involved in the activity of the organizations, or who had received assistance, saw them as an essential response to state indifference and lack of assistance, and as a source of real potential help:

> . . .if the government does not care, then we must come together in a group, what other way is there?
>
> *37, Saratov, 1999*

In the face of the confusing array of state structures and legislation concerned with migrant resettlement, the organizations were identified as a mediating structure between the individual and the state, which could make any interaction with official departments easier. They provided assistance regardless of whether migrants had citizenship or forced migrant status. In other words they were an information resource and source of help unavailable elsewhere:

> I think that they [migrant organization] are very important. Because, after all people are coming from different places. They do not know the laws, they do not

know who to turn to, they do not know how to get jobs or find housing. Many do not know because they have not had to do this before, they do not know their rights, and the laws are unclear. Here [at the migrant organization] they are given everything, full information, therefore, I think they are very important. If a person knows what is going on, he is able to get him/herself sorted out more quickly. We received valuable advice from the organization – after which we started to demand things from the migration service.

21, Saratov, 1999

Although often identified as a formal structure, migrant organizations were considered – unlike official government structures – to approach migrants with understanding and empathy. The reason for this was precisely that it was migrants who ran the organizations; they had experienced similar displacement, and might have come from the individual's previous 'homeland'. This reflects how representatives of the organizations themselves perceived the role and approach of the non-governmental migrant structures (see Chapter 5):

She [the head of one organization] always listens to you when you go there, she will always give you advice. She is our fellow countrywoman (*zemliachka*), also from Uzbekistan. She knows what it is like, she has gone through it herself, so it is easier for her to understand.

41, Saratov, 1999

If people have gone through it themselves, they understand that it is very difficult. All the people try to support you with warm words, to provide help in some way, to do something. In the migration service it is more difficult, you go there and it is like a 'deaf wall', a wall that doesn't understand, and people who do not understand – that a person has come with nothing, has to start again, and that adaptation is very difficult. Here [in the migrant organization] it is easier, you can always run to the organization with any question.

50, Samara, 1999

However, migrant organizations were sometimes identified as not beneficial to facilitating resettlement. Many migrants, after experiencing government indifference, identified them as yet another 'official' structure in which one should have little faith as a source of help. Often migrants refused to distinguish between official state bodies and unofficial non-governmental bodies, claiming that the migrant organizations had to be either 'commercial' or linked to state structures:[56]

I do not believe in any of these associations, or in this [migration] service, I have no faith in them.

54, Samara, 1999

> You know, I have no faith in anyone anymore, so we don't turn to anyone, and don't
> get anything from anyone. We are afraid to talk. Everywhere money is wanted, and
> we do not have the possibility to give any money.
>
> *40, Saratov, 1999*

In other instances, migrants saw the value of migrant organizations only for those who lacked other networks such as family or friendship ties. If migrants possessed these 'other' ties, they did not recognize the associations as relevant for them:

> I did not turn to it [the association] because I had other possibilities. I only found
> out about its existence recently. I think that it is important for people who do not
> have any other connections, no sort of acquaintances here at all. It is important for
> them.
>
> *20, Saratov, 1999*

For some of those migrants who were involved in the activity of the migrant associations or resident at compact settlement sites, networks were created where social interaction, facilitated by feelings of common identity and experience, could take place. The organizations and compact settlements fostered the re-creation of friendships and community networks that helped with the practicalities of resettlement, and in developing an immediate sense of the previous life that had been lost.[57] The actual site of the compact settlements provided an environment that was valued for the sense of security and familiarity it generated. Although many of the migrant respondents had an urban background and would have preferred settlement in the regional centre, they had clearly developed a sense of attachment to the location of the compact settlements, and were keen to point out the beauty of the surroundings and how they had adapted to (and had made the most of) living in a rural environment. Even if significant material help had not been received, the premises of the migrant organization created a focus for migrants, an environment they could enter where they knew they would be able to receive information and understanding, a space to which they could come and simply chat. In addition, the organizations created a link to other structures in the wider regional migration regime, and facilitated communication with and understanding of the operation of these structures which was often not achievable on an individual level.

Nevertheless, there was great diversity of interest and identity amongst the migrant community, and many returnees did not consider larger migrant networks as integral to their process of resettlement. In some cases, the compact settlement experience actually engendered the disruption and dissolution of the evolving migrant network. Knowledge of the activity of the migrant organizations amongst the wider migrant community in the regions was not widespread or uniform; access was often confined to those who already had existing personal links to members of the associations. The experience of the resettlement process, state indifference, and the characteristics of migrants themselves, often led to a strong sense of independence from outside structures, causing individuals to depend upon themselves and their immediate network of family and friends. In many cases resettlement and the reconstruction of 'home' remained an individual or family-centred process:

> You see, it was easier for me, I came to my parents – they supported me. When people come to a new place, of course it is hard. I can't imagine what they experience. But for me it was easier, I had my parents near, my relatives, they supported me here. I already feel that I am at home, I feel calm now, I know when I leave work, that I am going home.
>
> *27, Saratov, 1999*

CONCLUSION

By focusing analysis at the micro-level/s of the migrant network, the gap that exists between migrants' own interpretations and needs concerning migration and resettlement, as distinct from official Russian state migration discourse and practice, is further demonstrated. Equally the importance of the different types of migrant network is exposed. At the level of state discourse, the process of migration is constructed as 'forced', and the created 'homeland' environment of resettlement is indifferent and sometimes hostile. One way in which migrants reinterpret the migration and resettlement experience is via 'networks'. By providing the means for registration, accommodation and sometimes employment, networks facilitate the process of practical resettlement. By providing some continuity with the past and a sense of security and familiarity as a base for the future, networks ease the sense of personal displacement and dislocation. The networks that migrants utilize are primarily centred on the family unit; this often extends out to encompass friends and/or immediate acquaintances, and is characterized by the existence of relatively strong personal ties between its members. In a number of cases, wider networks emerge at the site of migrant organizations and compact settlement sites, which provide a safe environment for migrants who often lack other attachments and offer the opportunity for social interaction and practical assistance. The connections that develop between the members of these wider networks are based on the existence of common interests, needs and priorities, they are rooted in both past experiences and present realities, and they help to reinforce migrants' own sense of personal socio-economic and cultural identity, which has often been displaced with migration and the arrival at the site of resettlement.

It is clear from migrant narratives that the importance of family and friendship networks is rooted in a strong tradition of self-help inherited from the Soviet era. The continued importance of these networks during migration and resettlement is therefore not only a result of a present lack of state concern concerning migrant resettlement. Their centrality demonstrates how individuals previously negotiated, and are now *choosing* to negotiate, the 'everyday'. The experience of the returnees reflects how personal/social networks are being adapted, and in some instances re-formed, to meet current needs, i.e. those of migration and resettlement. The importance of the different networks that has appeared through the narratives of migrants in the present study points to the necessity for further in-depth empirical study at this level. At present it is immediate family and friendship networks that are dominant. Yet the existence of migrant organizations and compact settlements demonstrates the new forms of connections which it is likely many migrants will continue to develop in order to cope both with the aftermath of displacement and the needs of resettlement, and with the uncertainties of the post-Soviet Russian environment.

7

Conclusion: Reconstructing Immediate 'Homes' and Future 'Homelands'

IMMEDIATE 'HOMES' AND FUTURE 'HOMELANDS'

Overall, everything was better in Uzbekistan. At the moment, things are difficult here in Russia. There are problems. Maybe after five years, maybe after ten. . .to say that Russia is my *rodina*, no, I won't delude myself. I was born in Kazakstan so I should consider that Kazakstan is my *rodina*. But, I lived for most of my life in Uzbekistan, so I will say that it was my *rodina*, after all everything was better there. Please God, may Russia become a *rodina* for my children. That they don't have to live through the difficulties that we have had to live through.

70, Novosibirsk, 2002

This statement by a migrant from Kazakstan, who had arrived at Novosibirsk *oblast'* in 1994, demonstrates what has emerged through the book: the unfixed nature of 'homeland' and also of 'home' that exists amongst those individuals and communities who have been displaced within and have migrated from a previous 'homeland' (the Soviet Union, former Soviet republic) that no longer exists in space or time, to what many observers perceive to be their 'historical homeland' – the present-day Russian Federation. Upon migration a re-negotiation of 'home' is envisaged; however, Russia is seldom identified as an unproblematic territorial 'homeland'. The re-creation of both 'home' and 'homeland' is constrained by the fact that migrants are often located on the 'borderlands' of society, where their once secure economic, political, social and cultural identities, disrupted by stationary and physical displacement, are still challenged.

Through migrant narratives the book has shown how processes of displacement and migration throw attachments to place into doubt and yet at the same time can serve to highlight their basic premises. For many of the migrants, a secure identity and life rooted both in the Soviet system, in the locale of the republic and in immediate communities of friends and family, made that time and space both 'homeland' and 'home'. At this point, *rodina* (homeland) and *doma* (at home) could be understood as mutual and closely related concepts. Yet, with displacement and migration, the two concepts became separated and sometimes came into conflict with one another. This separation indicates that the extent to which a person may feel 'at home' within a space is not fixed. Rather, it is dependent upon how they are positioned and perceive they are positioned within the space, and can vary from the level of a 'house', a 'neighbourhood', a 'country' or a wider 'territory'.[1] It shows how people can be bound to 'geographical units' that are both larger and smaller than nation-states. These connections question the 'naturalness' of belonging to, or the dominance of, the nation-state.[2] Yet, although migrant narratives of displacement and resettlement demonstrate how 'home' and 'homeland' within different spaces and at different levels may be disrupted, they equally show how they can be reimagined, relocated and re-created.

To access these levels of home/land, and see how they are shaped and experienced through the migration process and subsequent resettlement, attention had to be given simultaneously to how migration and resettlement are constructed by key actors in the surrounding migration regime, and to the way in which the same process is perceived and experienced by the individual migrant. The theoretical and empirical approach of the study enabled the different levels of analysis to be revealed and addressed. The processes of movement and resettlement were located within the context of a wider migration system, which was in a state of constant transformation. Analysis of the space of the migration system demonstrated how, in particular, migrants' lives and identities cannot be contained within a bounded national territory but must be located within a 'wider field of action'.[3] At the point of departure, individual reasons for migration revealed the presence of personal socio-economic motivations that were rooted in a wider context of decolonization, political change, new nation building and ethnic upheaval. The migration movement and choice of place of settlement were influenced by the prior existence and present formation of personal and institutional connections between the former republics of the Soviet Union and the Russian Federation. Responses to migration and resettlement, at both state and individual level, were rooted in both the historical and contemporary context.

The significance of the sites of departure and arrival, the evolution of migration regimes, the nature and responses of the migrant populations and the wider historical and contemporary environments – all these factors reinforce the need to further resolve 'structure' and 'agency', and to combine (and give sufficient individual attention to) micro and macro levels of analysis, in any study of migration. Through attention to the 'micro' and 'macro', the discrepancy between the way in which dominant state actors read and construct the migration process at the federal and regional levels, as compared with the perception and experience of that same process at the individual migrant level, is revealed. The discrepancy is visible in real terms in the negative experience of government migration and resettlement policy amongst returning migrants, and in the frequent withdrawal of individual migrants from the surrounding migration regime.

The re-reading of the migration process and resettlement experience through the narratives of migrants reveals the distance of their lives from the dominant and contested state discourses of 'forced migration', 'repatriation' and 'diaspora'. This does not dispute the relevance of exploring the origins and development of such discourses to achieve an understanding of Russian migration policy. Equally, it does not detract from the significant power of the state, via discourse and policy, to frame migration and shape migrant resettlement. However, although migrants are positioned within and influenced by these discourses and resultant policy, they use alternative discourses to articulate both their personal identities and their experiences of migration and resettlement. Firstly, migrants' narratives concerning the migration movement reveal that political causes rarely stood alone or separate from the socio-economic realities of their lives. This problematizes the voluntary/involuntary dichotomy contained in migration legislation. Secondly, the narrative of home/land allows alternative understandings apart from the migration representing either a forced or voluntary 'return' to an ethnic 'homeland' to be gained. Via the uncoupling of this narrative, more grounded understandings of the migration and resettlement processes emerge, i.e. the prioritization of a 'return' to what is required for the re-creation of 'home'.

The images of home, that emerged through the narratives of both displacement and hoped for and attempted relocation, reveal how the re-creation of 'home' is a gradual and multi-levelled process. Based initially upon the sense that future hopes may be realized at the new site of settlement, it gains substance as feelings of personal security are regained and becomes more firmly rooted as employment, housing and social networks are established. The individual is an active participant in this process of re-creation. 'Home' is something in which individuals are ready to invest effort, it is a product that, unlike 'homeland', is seen as being within the capabilities of people to re-create. This was apparent in the hopes and plans which migrants expressed upon 'return' to Russian territory. Although in the short term the realization of these hopes and plans was problematic, the vivid memories of what 'home' had been allowed a sense of continuity and reality to be maintained. The immediate practical and emotional needs of 'everyday life', which are frequently forgotten in understandings of migration movements at both the theoretical and practical/policy level, were the priority. Although previous connections were central to the present identities and lives of the migrants, the strength of 'home' as a present and future narrative contributes to other studies which have warned of prioritizing external (transnational) ties when studying migrant resettlement, and of ignoring the reality of living at the new site of residence.[4]

Securing a place that could be called 'home' was an immediate priority for migrants, and its transfer and spatial repositioning within the new territory (Russia) was envisaged. Yet this does not mean that the 'return' to Russia was imagined as a movement to a natural 'ethnic' homeland. A longing for such a 'homeland' was not apparent in migrants' narratives of their previous lives, and for many the relocation and re-creation of 'homeland' and its rooting in Russian territory was either an impossibility or was positioned well into the future. Their 'homeland' remained in a past time and place, but the memories and inherited experiences of it remained potent. A future homeland would come about through the rooting of 'home', which meant the security of their family, job, house, social networks, present memories and future imaginings. By understanding what was envisaged, via migration, for the re-creation of an immediate 'home' and a possible future 'homeland', deeper insight was also gained into the changing relationship between these people and their places of habitation over time. Individual, and state, identities were formed and shaped by the existence of Russian settler communities being resident in the non-Russian republics of the Soviet Union, and were reshaped by the experience of separation and, in some instances, 'return'. Recognition of the fluid and changing nature of both nation-state and individual identities is important: although identities are rooted in the past, they are undergoing constant transformation. For both the returnee communities and the Russian nation, the evolution of identity is a process of 'becoming' as well as 'being'; it belongs to the present and future as well as to the past.[5] The return movement of the Russian communities, the response of the Russian state, migrants' own perception of the Russian 'homeland' and their memories and longing for their past 'homeland', throw light upon the fluid nature of the emerging post-Soviet, Russian national identity and reflect the longevity of its future development.

THE OPERATION OF THE RUSSIAN MIGRATION REGIME: AN ASSESSMENT

Analysis of the emerging migration regime of the Russian Federation demonstrates the extent to which contemporary migration politics are a contested arena where the differing ideological, political and socio-economic priorities of both state and non-state actors are played out. The constitution of migration regimes at an international, federal and regional level is under constant negotiation by these competing actors. At the federal level, the question of Russian nationhood, international and geo-political considerations, domestic socio-economic concerns and humanitarian issues are prioritized to varying degrees by the different political and non-political institutions vying for control over the formulation of policy. As Chapter 4 demonstrated, at the regional level federal directives are confronted by the political and socio-economic priorities of regional authorities, which shape their migration policy accordingly.

If the almost complete absence of structures and legislation in the Russian Federation in 1992 to deal with any type of migration flow is compared with what exists in 2002, then over the course of the ten years significant headway has been made in the development of an operating migration regime at the international, federal and regional level. The newly independent Russian Federation lacked both the knowledge and expertise and the legislative and institutional frameworks to cope with, for example, the arrival of forced migrants, refugees and 'repatriates', or the management of international labour migration, freedom of movement and permanent migration to or from abroad.[6] Some commentators have suggested that given the lack of complete control over its external borders, and the chaotic situation in some FSU states, it was premature of Russia to accede to the UN refugee convention in 1992.[7] Yet it may also be argued that greater assistance and comprehension were required from the international community to support Russia's attempts to cope with its new responsibilities.

Russian government structures have been clearly working within a difficult socio-economic environment where the resources available for any realm of social provision are limited. In reality, the created institutions and policy directives of the migration regime demanded levels of investment that were beyond the capabilities of the Russian federal and regional level budgets to meet. This study has been critical of the lack of a comprehensive programme of resettlement for the returning migrants, and a corresponding absence of concrete provision at the federal and regional levels of the government migration regimes. Such criticism is largely based upon the experiences that emerged from interviews with migrants who had encountered these regimes. The socio-economic difficulties, and the scarcity of available resources, must be taken into account. However, the criticism of government policy is not only directed at the lack of an allocation of funds and absence of provision. Government discourse over the period 1992–2002 moved to one that prioritized securitization and restriction, and relegated provision and assistance to second place. This discourse is partly rooted in socio-economic concerns; but with respect to the ethnic Russian and Russian-speaking communities and their potential migration, it also reflected Russia's nation-building priorities and geo-political and foreign policy interests that preferred the continued residence of the Russian communities in the former republics.

By providing an insight into the reality of resettlement experience at the individual migrant level, the study revealed some of the contradictions in current federal and regional migration policy. Positive policies that enable integration are needed, including: the removal or greater transparency of barriers to legalization of status, movement and resettlement (e.g. the registration system); the operation of an effective loan system that would allow the acquisition of housing in a suitable location; the identification of regions and labour market spheres that require and are suited to the specific professional, educational and employment skills of the migrant population; the adequate provision of information concerning employment, housing and any other social provision. The recommendations appear obvious, and some require an input of scarce resources. However, they would facilitate the immediate inclusion of migrants within the structures of society and would provide a more positive space of 'return' within which they could act more effectively. For the majority of migrants in the current case of 'return' migration, emergency humanitarian assistance is not required. Instead, migrants often identify themselves as a positive force that can be of use to Russia, rather than a needy community of 'forced migrants'. The gap between individual experience and perception and state policy reinforces the need to 'bring the migrant voice in' to ensure more suitable and viable policies.

One sector that has attempted to challenge dominant state discourse, and to redress the lack of state assistance, is the non-governmental migrant sector in the Russian Federation. In Chapter 5, the book traced the emergence of this alternative non-state migrant sector that has become a significant actor within the migration regimes at the federal and regional levels. The low levels of material assistance that these non-state structures have been able to provide is due to a lack of resources and their limited powers to act effectively. Nevertheless, both primary and secondary empirical evidence points to the real difference that they have made to the lives of individuals and groups of migrants. Furthermore, the non-state sphere at both federal and regional levels has served another role: it has provided an alternative discourse that attempts to positively reframe the 'return' of the Russian populations.

The book has demonstrated how non-state frameworks reach across the regional, federal and international levels and allow migrant group actors – e.g. regional migrant organizations, who are constrained by the limits of the immediate environment – to access structures and resources beyond that locale. The increased power the interaction provides improves the capacity of these local initiatives to act at the regional level. The existence of these frameworks is one result of the inclusion of the Russian Federation within the operation of a wider global migration regime made up of transnational government and non-governmental structures that transgress the borders of the nation state. At a national level, the stories of federal and regional migrant organizations reveal the intricacies of emerging state/non-state relations in post-Soviet Russia. The development of these organizations requires further research. However, the evolution of the sphere in itself, and the achievements of the associations focused upon in the present study, suggest a need for greater temporal and cultural sensitivity in studies of Russian 'civil society' that too easily decry its existence, or the viability of its future.

At an individual level, some migrants act within the immediate migration regime and draw upon state and non-state resources to facilitate their resettlement. For the majority, however, the capacity or desire to draw upon state resources within the regime are limited. It is specifically at the individual level of resettlement that the real implications of a lack of effective government policy and paucity of state assistance are revealed. Migrants are aware of the structures through which they are forced to act; they frequently position themselves within wider state discourses concerning their 'return'; and they may draw on certain of the state resources that are available. However, they also distance themselves from these discursive and institutional/legislative frameworks; on a practical and psychological level they withdraw to immediate networks of family and friends and, in some cases, the wider networks located in migrant organizations and at compact settlements sites.

The centrality of family and friendship networks in particular demonstrates how the migration and resettlement process is going on outside the frameworks set by the state. However, this 'network' strategy does not represent what, in a wider post-Soviet context, is sometimes seen as a reactionary return to dependence upon 'anti-modern' Soviet networks, but often indicates a positive continued reliance, further adaptation and utilization of these networks in the post-socialist present.[8] The narratives of migrant respondents indicate that their dependence on or use of networks takes place not only *because of* a lack of state concern, but is also due to the fact that only these 'known' and trusted networks provide what migrants prioritize and wish to re-create after displacement and upon 'return' – an immediate sense of belonging, familiarity and security, a sense of 'home'. Whatever strategies they adopt, migrants are still acting within the wider migration system, and through these strategies they shape experiences of migration and resettlement. An understanding of the relevance of personal networks provides one way to reread the operation of the migration system, and the nature of the migration process under way. As Burawoy and Verdery suggest, while the reconstruction of macro worlds is certainly going on in the post-socialist space, individuals, families and communities are working both within (thus affecting) and around these worlds.[9] If the workings and strategies of these alternative micro-worlds are ignored, many of the different and 'lived' stories, in this case of migration, will be lost.[10]

'REPRESENTING' THE MIGRANT

Both at the empirical stage of the research and in the writing of the book, a conscious attempt was made to allow the micro-worlds and 'different stories' of migrants to come through. The prioritization within the research of the individual/collective migrant and their 'lived realities' made apparent the absences in both theoretical and policy-oriented debates pertaining to migration and displacement. Theories of 'decolonization', 'repatriation', 'forced migration', or the often related discursive and policy frameworks created by the Russian state, fail to capture the complexity and personal histories of the individuals involved, or to react to or encompass their expectations and needs. Migrants in this and other contexts must be recognized as actors who, although restricted by the environment they are operating within, use their own strategies to migrate, resettle and make sense of the displacement and change that they are experiencing 'beyond' the boundaries of the theories and policies that position and label them.

This example can be broadened out to other environments of change occurring in post-socialist spaces where perceptions and narratives which emerge from within communities' experience – grounded in 'the familiar', 'normality', the everyday – are often found to be in opposition to superimposed theoretical/conceptual understandings. The 'home' narrative, for example, reflects Stark's questioning of the idea of a sudden break or change in peoples' lives in 1989–91. He suggests that social change might well have been taking place before the more easily observable wider political developments – in other words, ordinary citizens were already experiencing and trying to renegotiate a changing world where previously 'secure' domains (for the migrant their socio-cultural, political and economic position often guaranteed by their location within the Soviet system) were no longer integrated coherently.[11] In addition, the spatial and temporal importance of the 'home' narrative reflects what Burawoy and Verdery suggest is essential in studies of post-socialism: ethnographic attention to 'ephemeral moments' where, due to the environment of constant change, actors tend to strategize within time horizons that are short.[12] The 'realness' of the home narrative, and its attempted continuity, perhaps reflect the intricate and problematic course of migration and resettlement more closely than do more removed descriptions of the same process.

THE RUSSIAN MIGRATION REGIME: POSSIBLE FUTURES

The book covered a specific period of time in the life of the post-Soviet Russian migration regime. In 1992, the regime developed primarily to focus on the needs of certain of the arriving migrant populations, i.e. the ethnic Russian and Russian-speaking forced migrants and refugees from the Soviet successor states, the internally displaced from the Chechen conflict (many of whom from the first Chechen war of 1994–6 were ethnic Russians), and to a lesser degree the increasing numbers of asylum seekers from the far abroad. The immediate concerns of the initial decade of 'transition' – domestic socio-economic upheaval, the renegotiation of relations with the other post-Soviet republics, the forging of a post-Soviet Russian identity – were integral to the original formation of migration institutions and policy frameworks. Over the decade of the 1990s the priorities of the Russian government in relation to migration shifted, and different challenges arose. Although – still a crucial issue for many – the late 1990s saw a reduction in the numbers of ethnic Russian and Russian-speaking migrants arriving, the protection of the Russian diaspora within political discourse appeared to decline in urgency[13] and the significance of 'irregular' and undocumented migration increased.[14] The following paragraphs provide a brief review of the state of the Russian migration regime in 2003, taking note of the particular global context in which it is now set, and suggest possible future directions for Russian migration policy. However, the continued uncertainties of the post-Soviet migration space make any predictions difficult.

By the end of the 1990s, through state migration discourse, legislative frameworks and policy implementation, post-Soviet Russia had moved towards prioritizing the protection of the borders of the nation/state and individual regions over the rights and securities of the individual migrant. This development reflects the interplay between shifting migration discourse (e.g. migration as a 'threat' or resource) and the introduction of related institutional/legislative practice (which then further endorses the existing discourse) that is apparent beyond the borders of the Russian Federation.[15] The take-over of responsibility for migration by the Ministry of Internal Affairs – which undeniably represents the transferral of migration to within a 'system of control' – and the introduction of a stricter citizenship law mirrors similar legislative and institutional developments that have taken place within the EU.[16] In addition, the identification of migrant populations through discourse and practice as (a) homogenous group/s, is familiar. For example in the case of the returning Russians: a removed 'diaspora', a welcome 'repatriate community', a 'controlled' forced migrant community, or with respect to other migrant groups: 'illegal' migrants, 'criminal/terrorist threats'. It is likely that western governments will support efforts of the Russian government to securitize the field of migration and citizenship. In fact, Russian government officials often justify their actions in the field of migration with the argument that they are 'normalizing' procedures to come into line with frameworks that exist elsewhere. This justification was used both in the case of the new citizenship law, and in the incorporation of the migration service into the MVD.[17]

Approaches towards migration in post-Soviet Russia are still under debate and in a state of flux, however. Since President Putin took office in 2000, he has demonstrated a greater awareness of the country's migration problems and has proposed or instituted policies to deal with them.[18] This was seen in the significant upheaval in the institutional structures, i.e. the abolition of the FMS and Ministry of Federation Affairs, National and Migration Policy and the transferral of migration affairs to the MVD, and also in the legislative changes embodied in the law 'On Citizenship' and the law 'On the Legal Status of Foreign Citizens in the Russian Federation'. In addition, during the period of the Putin presidency a much clearer connection has been made between the apparent 'demographic crisis' and migration. Different political and non-political actors argue that in-migration is needed and look to the ethnic Russian and Russian-speaking communities as a solution for demographic decline and a force for economic revival.[19] President Putin's rhetoric consistently reflects this viewpoint and suggests that he views the arrival, primarily of the Russian-speaking populations, as the answer to population decline.[20] Although repatriation was present in migration discourse through the 1990s, the explicit connection to the demographic crisis and to socio-economic development has increased in recent years, and implies that it could become central to domestic migration debates.

However, as suggested in Chapter 2, Putin's hope for a regulated influx of legal Russian migrants, which may be compared with other countries' efforts to encourage the legal migration of certain groups while discouraging others, is problematic and contradictory. Firstly, the new Russian law 'On Citizenship', rather than making the in-migration of the ethnic Russian and Russian-speaking communities easier, removed the majority of privileges of former Soviet citizens in receiving citizenship. Secondly, domestic funding for a Federal Migration Programme was removed in 2001,[21] although a new concept for the 'regulation' of migration processes in the Russian Federation, approved by the Russian government in March 2003, mentions the voluntary migration of 'compatriots'. Thirdly, such a policy of 'return' assumes a common desire to move on the side of the Russian communities. Despite the large-scale migration of Russians to Russia, approximately 18–22 million individuals remain in the other former Soviet republics. The reasons for their continued residence are debatable – i.e. whether they wish to stay, or whether they are restricted by the unfavourable conditions for migration.[22] However, even assuming a greater degree of potential migration than is reflected in current migration figures, it is unlikely that the numbers required to have an impact upon population figures will arrive.[23] Fourthly, the policy raises serious concerns for the reception and rights of 'non-Russian' migrants, and would clearly evoke concerns amongst human rights and migrant groups. Finally, alternative answers or approaches to the demographic 'crisis' in Russia need to be found. Other issues, in the sphere of health and relating to the general socio-economic conditions of peoples' lives, also require to be addressed. In addition, the need for (and rationality and long-term socio-economic viability of) continued settlement of some areas of Russian territory requires examination.

Alongside the support that exists for the in-migration of particular types of migrants, there is a consistently strong and often dominant anti-immigration voice in post-Soviet Russia. 'Illegal' migration is increasingly being targeted as a major threat to Russian security and social cohesion.[24] Once on Russian territory the situation for any arrivee, including asylum seekers, is made difficult due to the inadequacy and ambiguity of institutional and legislative procedure that allow them to make their residence or temporary status legal. However, by giving migration regulation to the Ministry of the Interior, which was welcomed by the anti-immigration lobby, it appears that force will increasingly be relied upon to manage 'undocumented' migration flows – including asylum seekers and refugees. The anti-immigration lobby was also central to the development and introduction of the more restrictive citizenship law which, as noted, is already affecting the in-migration of the Russian communities. However, if the demographic and labour demands of the country – and equally the concerns of human rights groups and the requirements of the international conventions to which Russia is signatory – are to be met, the government must not just vocally express support for the in-migration of 'known' and 'desirable' migrants but also needs to acknowledge and respond to its existing migrants, including the 'undocumented' population.

This book, however, focused on one migrant population – the ethnic Russian and Russian speaking communities who were previously resident in the borderlands of the Soviet Union and who, in the aftermath of its collapse, moved to Russian territory. Although in official discourse (and in media and academic texts) the significance of this migration may have lessened, the process is continuing to be lived out by millions of individuals across Russia. While acknowledging the very real emotional and physical displacement experienced by the individuals involved, the book has sought to understand migration not only as a process of dislocation but equally as one of relocation. The importance of the narrative of 'home' emerged from the research project itself in the dialogues of migrants. Despite its perhaps unexceptional nature and logical presence, the contribution of this narrative to understanding both this and other processes of migration and resettlement is significant. It is a narrative that is too often ignored, and one that requires further empirical and theoretical interrogation. Through their 'home' narratives, migrants articulate the practical and emotional priorities that they feel need to be fulfilled for successful resettlement, which reiterates the need for migrants' dialogues to be listened to in policy development. Migrants across the Russian Federation have made their voices heard through regional and federal level migrant organizations, and have achieved positive change. Nevertheless, the present study suggested that more often migrants remain silent, disengage from the state and retreat into personal networks of family and friends that allow an immediate sense of 'home' and security to be maintained. It is hoped that, in the coming years, the energies and resources that were invested in migrants' decisions to move could be unleashed and engaged in a constructive way for post-Soviet Russian society. For this to happen the Russian government needs to prioritize the genuine needs of real citizens over the abstract, imaginary requirements of constructing or protecting a new Russian 'homeland'.

Appendix 1

Limitations of Statistics Concerning Forced Migrants and Refugees

Although official statistics show that between July 1992 and 1 January 2002 there were 1,576,100 ethnic Russian and Russian-speaking forced migrants and refugees registered in the Russian Federation,[1] these figures include only those who 'officially' registered with the federal/regional migration services. Due to ambiguous legislation and 'flawed' registration practices, official statistics do not necessarily reflect the magnitude of forced migration flows.[2] However, at the same time other figures that are proposed (such as the 8–10 million 'returnees' from the former republics of the Soviet Union, which is the current figure being offered both by government officials and in the media) may be exaggerated. There are a number of factors that problematize the validity and use of statistics concerning forced migrants and refugees on the territory of the Russian Federation. The present study acknowledges the likely inconsistency and unreliability of the acquired statistical data.

INCONSISTENCY OF DATA COLLECTION

The 'gathering' of data concerning numbers of forced migrants and refugees has been the responsibility of a number of different government agencies, and dependent upon different criteria, over the period 1991–2002. Initially in 1991, both the Ministry of the Interior and the Committee on Migration within the Ministry of Labour gathered data. The Ministry of the Interior based its figures upon applications made for a *propiska* (registration), while the Committee on Migration relied upon figures from local employment services who registered 'forced migrants'. During this period the definition of 'forced migrants' or 'refugees' was random, and varied between the two agencies. From July 1992, the FMS began to gather migration statistics concerning forced migrants and refugees, again together with the Ministry of the Interior. From 1 January 1994, the FMS adopted total responsibility; it received statistical information from its regional branches, and the system of data collection improved over the period of the service's existence. However, the FMS's statistics from July 1992 did not include migrants who had arrived since 1989; efforts made to correct this by encouraging migrants to re-register proved largely unsuccessful. The Ministry of the Interior recorded numbers of 'arrivees' who did not apply for forced migrant status, but registered with the local branch of the ministry for a *propiska*. With the incorporation of the migration service within the Ministry of the Interior, its federal and regional branches are now the source for records of all types of migrant registration.

DETERMINING BETWEEN 'FORCED MIGRANTS' AND 'REFUGEES' IN DATA SOURCES

A second difficulty is that although the laws on refugees and forced migrants were introduced in February 1993, statistics continued to be collected without distinguishing between the two categories. This remained as FMS practice until 1996, and the State Committee on Statistics (*Goskomstat*) continued to publish 'joint' data until 1998.

In addition, the distinction between 'forced migrant' and 'refugee' status, and to whom either status is awarded, has been highly ambiguous. Initially both 'categories' were available to those entitled to Russian citizenship. Particularly in the first half of the 1990s, persons who had arrived in the Russian Federation without Russian citizenship often acquired 'refugee' status. Up to October 1994 the law on citizenship required individuals who had arrived in the Federation prior to February 1992 to return to their former place of residence to obtain Russian citizenship. However, if they gained 'refugee' status they could establish their place of residence and then apply for Russian citizenship 'by registration' on Russian territory.[3] Once they had acquired this citizenship, they could apply for 'forced migrant' status and the slightly higher level of benefits it offered. According to the amendments to the law on forced migrants in December 1995, this had to be done within a month of gaining Russian citizenship, a fact of which many 'refugees' were unaware. With the introduction of the amendments to the law on refugees in June 1997, refugee status became much more difficult to acquire and in practice was no longer awarded to arrivees from the former republics who did not possess but were entitled to Russian citizenship. Therefore, the exact numbers of later 'Russian citizens' within the category of registered 'refugees', and who may have moved into the category of 'forced migrants', is difficult to predict over the period 1991–7.

REGIONAL DISCREPANCIES

The regional use of the *propiska* also problematizes standardized data collection across the Russian Federation. In regions where the *propiska* and other measures are used as a way of restricting migrant settlement, the discrepancy between the number of registered migrants and their actual number is very high, and the greater the numbers of arrivees who do not possess either forced migrant status or even a *propiska*. Neither the migration service nor the Ministry of Internal Affairs records the arrival of such migrants. Regions themselves distort migration statistics; it is suggested that some regions overstate the numbers of registered migrants in an attempt to attract increased funding, as the level of funding received by the local administration is dependent upon the numbers of registered migrants.[4]

INDIVIDUAL INCONSISTENCIES

Large numbers of migrants fail to register due to the lack of actual benefit they receive from the process, although they may be entitled to forced migrant status. Particularly in areas where there are restrictions on settlement, the meagre assistance but high risk of registering as a forced migrant or refugee has led many migrants to avoid approaching any official agencies.[5] However, there are cases where migrants may register more than once in order to get benefits several times, or in response to specific legislative initiatives. In December 1992, for example, when interest-free loans were first introduced the numbers of persons registering rose sharply.[6] Another group of migrants which are not accounted for are those who return to their country of origin; there is no special registration procedure for these people.[7]

Appendix 2

Migrant Settlement Sites in Saratov, Samara and Novosibirsk *Oblasti*

The sites of settlement described below are the locations where migrant re-spondents were interviewed. The descriptions provide a broad overview of the different types of migrant resettlement that are occurring in the three regions of study although they cannot claim to be representative of all the locations of migrants or types of settlement present on the territory of the three *oblasti*.

URBAN/SEMI-URBAN INDIVIDUAL SETTLEMENT

Migrant respondents in urban areas of the *oblasti* were located in the cities of Saratov, in urban settlements on the outskirts of the main urban centre, and in other *raion* centres of the *oblasti*. All the *raion* centres were situated in the central regions of the three *oblasti*. The majority of migrants lived in rented apartments/ small houses and in hostels. Four migrant respondents owned their own apart-ments. The hostels in this case had not been specifically allocated for migrant resettlement, and only individual migrant families resided there. The hostel ac-commodation was acquired through work or family contacts, while the apart-ment accommodation was acquired with the help of the migration service, through work or family contacts, or purchased using personal resources. The settlements outside the main urban centre tended to be semi-urban/rural dis-tricts, where the infrastructure (transport, water, electricity and other amenities) was less developed than in the more central urban districts of the *oblast'* cities.

URBAN/GROUP SETTLEMENT

Hostels

A number of respondents lived in hostels, where a part of the hostel had been al-located specifically for forced migrants. In one case the group of migrants had arrived together, in the other two cases the settlement of the migrants in the hostel took place at different times.

Hostel No. 1, city of Saratov
The hostel was situated in a *raion* on the periphery of Saratov city, was attached to a PTU (*Professional'no-tekhnicheskoe uchilishche*) and housed approximately 23 families of migrants who lived on one floor of the building. The group of migrants had arrived from Uzbekistan in autumn 1994 and had acquired the hostel accommodation through the PTU. However, since 1994 a number of the migrant families had acquired alternative, private accommodation. For the first three years, the hostel was free of charge, since the end of 1997 the migrants were required to pay rent. The hostel accommodation was intended as a temporary measure while the group of migrants constructed a compact settlement site on land acquired from the local *raion* administration. However, this venture was largely unsuccessful (see below). Conditions in the hostel were adequate but basic. Migrants had been resident there for a number of years and had made their own rooms as comfortable as possible. Initially there was overcrowding; however, over the years additional rooms were acquired which improved the situation. The majority of migrants at the hostel did not have a permanent *propiska* and had been threatened with eviction by the PTU administration. This had led to the formation of a migrant initiative made up of five of the resident families to specifically address the issue of obtaining permanent residence permits at the hostel.

Hostel No. 2, city of Saratov
The hostel was situated in a central *raion* in the city of Saratov. The migrants occupied one floor of the building, but they had arrived individually and at different times. Accommodation was acquired there through work, family/friend connections or the local administration. Conditions were very basic. The length of time the migrants had been resident in the hostel, or whether they viewed the accommodation as permanent or temporary, had influenced the extent to which they had made their accommodation attractive and personal. Some of the more recent arrivees were still living out of suitcases. The families of migrants who were interviewed lived in fairly cramped conditions, with two to three adults and up to two children living in one small room. Problems had been faced with acquiring a permanent *propiska*, as the hostel director refused to allow permanent registration. A group of migrants at the hostel came together to fight the issue in court, which resulted in those involved obtaining a permanent *propiska*.

Hostel No. 1, city of Samara

23 migrant families were resident in the hostel which was situated in a central region of Samara city. The living conditions were very difficult. During the period of fieldwork the non-payment of gas bills and the need for essential repairs meant that there had been no gas for three months and families were using small electric cookers for all cooking purposes. Nothing was being done to improve this situation. The water supply to the hostel was frequently switched off. The migrants lived in very overcrowded conditions. In some cases up to three adults and two children lived in one small room, and due to the large number of residents unsuitable rooms were being used which were damp and had no natural light. Individual families, depending upon their opportunities and the time they had spent in the hostel, had made their rooms as habitable as possible.

The hostel was owned by a construction firm which was itself bankrupt, therefore there were no resources to spend on repairs or renovation. Migrants had acquired accommodation there via the local administration or personal contacts. The settlement of the initial group of migrants occurred due to an agreement made between the local state committee for family and children and the construction company in 1993. At this point the local administration paid the migrants' rent, which continued for two years. The migrants then paid the rent themselves. During the period of fieldwork, discussions were being held with the firm about the possibility of some of the migrant families acquiring rooms on another floor. There was no coordination between the construction company and the migration service concerning the issue. The majority of the migrants at the hostel held a temporary *propiska.*

Hostel No. 1, city of Novosibirsk

The hostel was situated in a *raion,* on the opposite side of the river Ob to the city of Novosibirsk. It was located approximately 45 minutes by public transport from the city centre. The migrants (approximately 13 families) occupied two floors of one side of the hostel; students occupied the other rooms there. The building was technically a hostel for a local college. The resident migrants had arrived individually and at different times; they had been directed to the hostel either directly by the *raion* administration, or had received help from their workplace in securing a room. Although there was no formal migrant organization there was a great sense of community amongst the migrants, and obviously a strong support network existed in the hostel. The conditions within the hostel were very basic and the communal areas were not very clean. Migrants related that there were continuous problems with gas and electricity supplies; electricity had been cut off on a number of occasions for up to two weeks. However migrant families, who usually occupied one or two rooms, had made great efforts to make their immediate surroundings comfortable and home-like, with bookshelves, sideboards, fridges, sofas and tables brought from their previous apartments.

Temporary resettlement centre, Saratov oblast'

The temporary resettlement centre was located near a town approximately 200 kilometres from the city of Saratov. The town was small, with just a few shops and a market. The centre, situated in an isolated area seven kilometres outside the town, comprised two buildings which could house up to 440 migrants. Surrounding the centre were small plots of cultivated land on which migrants grew vegetables and fruit. Conditions inside the centre were very basic and migrants shared communal kitchen and bathroom facilities.

At the time of the initial visit in 1997 the hostel housed 311 migrants, 252 of them from Chechnia. Over the period 1997–9 the numbers of forced migrants and refugees in the centre decreased, mainly due to forced migrants and refugees from Chechnia receiving compensation payments and being able to obtain their own accommodation. Links had been established between the migrant community at the centre and the local town. Migrants visited the town to sell their grown produce and to purchase other goods, and the migrant children attended the school in the town. Despite this contact, however, the migrants were isolated and spent a great deal of time either in their hostel rooms or in their gardens.

The temporary resettlement centre was situated in a region with high levels of unemployment and a lack of housing. Opportunities for movement out of the centre were limited, especially for the socially disadvantaged migrants who formed the majority of the resident migrant community. The official period a migrant could stay in the centre was for three months, although most had been there for one to two years. Plans to implement micro-credit programmes to develop individual employment at the centre were not realized due to the poor business possibilities in the surrounding area and a lack of interest on the part of the migrants.

RURAL SETTLEMENTS

It is difficult to define the sites visited during the periods of fieldwork strictly as compact settlements. However, they were inhabited by groups of migrants where the original plan was to create a form of self-sufficient settlement through the provision of on-site housing and employment. There had been varying

levels of involvement by state structures, specifically the migration service. Two
of the settlements visited during the periods of fieldwork were located in Saratov *oblast'* and one in Samara *oblast'*. A further rural settlement in Saratov
oblast' was a village where a large proportion of migrants from different former
republics settled together with local migrants; however, it is not defined here as
a compact settlement. No rural compact settlements were visited in Novosibirsk
oblast', but migrants interviewed in a *raion* centre in the *oblast'* often resided in
rural-type conditions (usually in small wooden houses) on the outskirts of the
small town. However, the migrants were dispersed amongst the local town community.

Compact type settlements

Settlement No. 1, Saratov oblast'

The planned settlement of 20 houses was situated on the edge of a village approximately 7 kilometres from the outskirts of the city of Saratov. The group of
migrants from Uzbekistan, resident in Hostel No. 1 in the city of Saratov, had acquired a plot of land free of charge from the *raion* administration. The TMS
helped to finance the installation of gas and electricity. However, due to the lack
of resources after the initial investment, only the foundations for the 20 houses
had been completed. Work was continuing on seven of the houses, four of
which have roofs. There was no water supply to the settlement.

At the time of the fieldwork all the migrant families still lived in the hostel.
The settlement was not attached to the development of any specific enterprise.
Links had been established with the local community where there was individual migrant resettlement. In the village school, the director and a number of the
teachers were migrants, and migrant children made up approximately forty
percent of the students. The compact settlement had received continued support from the head of the local administration, but in the absence of either personal resources or assistance from state structures, the future of the settlement
was uncertain.

Settlement No. 2, Saratov oblast'

The settlement was situated approximately 12 kilometres from the outskirts of
Saratov city and 4 kilometres from the nearest village. It was made up of individual families of migrants from different republics who upon arrival had
found out about the possibility of work and accommodation at the settlement
established by a migrant from the North of Russia in 1992. Initially the enterprise attached to the settlement had been successful; the individual migrants

received loans from the TMS and together with the investment of their own money converted existing large farm sheds into houses. However, the situation had greatly deteriorated. The original director, unable to repay initial bank loans, faced bankruptcy; the enterprise and houses became the property of the bank, and responsibility for the settlement had been completely transferred to the local administration.

The migrants had received little help apart from the constant support of the migrant association *Vozvrashchenie*. They had no legal claim to the housing, despite the fact that they had been involved in its construction and had invested personal resources. Conditions at the site were very difficult, as there was no gas or water and all production had come to a halt. The local administration saw no future in the settlement and was encouraging all the migrants to leave. Although the migrants wished to remain, the uncertainty of a secure future at the settlement was forcing them to look for housing and work elsewhere.

Settlement No. 1, Samara oblast'
The settlement was situated on the outskirts of a village, located 73 kilometres from Samara city. The initiative for it originated with the migration service. In 1993 a plan was developed to construct 'American style' cottages for forced migrants on the piece of land, and to build a sawmill to provide both construction materials and future employment. Migrants arriving in the area were directed to the site, and were employed to renovate and build barracks which were intended as temporary accommodation prior to the building of the 'cottages'. However, the resources for further construction ran out and the sawmill ceased to operate. There were three barrack buildings, two completed and one under construction.

Conditions in the barracks were very poor. Although there was a cold water supply, gas and electricity, there were no showers in one of the buildings and all toilet facilities were outside. All the migrant families had their own plot of land surrounding the barracks where they grew vegetables and fruit. The settlement was situated on a hill approximately 20 minutes' walk from the main settlement. In winter the path became inaccessible; the road to the settlement was in bad repair and there was no permanent bus although one was provided on a temporary basis by the local administration or the local spirits factory. Access to the settlement for old people, and for children who attended school in the village, was very difficult. The migration service was planning to settle more migrants in the third barrack building. Those selected would likely have been on the priority-housing list, and thus in the category of socially disadvantaged migrants. Therefore such accommodation would have been highly unsuitable.

The village administration had been very helpful towards the migrants, some of whom were employed in the local spirits factory, and there was a good relationship with the local community as a whole. However, very limited help had been received from the migration service. Although the migrants held a permanent *propiska*, the legality of this was uncertain as there was no documentation concerning the registration of the barracks as permanent accommodation. Migrants were trying to negotiate for the division of the land to enable them to build their own houses. In the area as a whole there were few employment opportunities beyond the spirits factory and seasonal work on a nearby *sovkhoz* (state farm). On a return visit to Samara in 2002, the situation at the compact settlement had greatly deteriorated, as had personal relations between the migrants. Representatives of the regional migrant organization attributed this to the complete lack of employment possibilities at the site and the absence of any outside help, especially from the regional migration service.

Village settlement

Village No. 1, Saratov oblast'

The settlement was located in a village 126 kilometres from the city of Saratov. The initiative for it came from a local businessman who had been born and had grown up in the village. In 1994 he made the decision to invest in the restoration of the village that had been deserted in the 1970s. It was not the intention to specifically attract migrants; but the majority of the inhabitants were arrivees from the former republics, along with a number of migrants from neighbouring villages. There were 35 houses in the village and 180 residents.

Migrants from the former republics had found out about the possibilities of settlement either from the media (a television programme was made by the central Russian television channel 'ORT' about the settlement and shown in the former republics), or through personal contacts. The director of the village assessed the migrants upon arrival, but did not demand that they had either forced migrant status or Russian citizenship. Employment was provided in the village on the farm, in the dairy, shop or garage. Migrants concluded an agreement with the director of the village, which stipulated the purchase of a house at a reduced rate as dependent upon continued employment in the village for a period of ten years. All the migrants had their own plots of land where they grew vegetables and fruit, and the majority kept their own pigs, chickens and goats.

Problems had arisen on the settlement, as the urban migrants often saw residence there as a temporary step before trying to move to a more urban area. Due to a lack of construction materials some of the migrants were living in unfinished houses. None of the houses had running water. The director of the settlement originally had no dealings at all with the migration service, and although there was a district service in the *raion* he denied any knowledge of its existence. Contact had increased during 1999 due to the work of *Vozvrashchenie*, and efforts were being made to encourage new arrivees to register at the migration service.

Appendix 3

Table of Migrant Socio-demographic Data*

(See table on opposite page)

* The information presented in the table represents the socio-demographic data given by migrants at the time of the interviews. Abbreviations used in the table are: Sec./Spec. = Secondary Specialist Education; Un./Higher = Unfinished Higher Education; C.S. = Compact Settlement, MS = Territorial Migration Service; TRS = Temporary Resettlement Centre; N/A/ = not applicable. Any gaps in the table indicate that this data is missing, i.e. was not filled in on the form.

APPENDIX 3: Table of migrant socio-demographic data*

Code of migrant/ Gender	Date of birth	Nationality	Citizenship	Place of birth position	Family position	Education	Date of arrival in Russia	Republic of departure	Work position in Russia	Profession/ Employment before move
1 Female	1959	Russian	None	Tajikistan	Married	Sec./Spec.	1996	Tajikistan	None	Teacher
2 Female	1951	Russian	Russian	—	Married	Sec./Spec.	1995	Chechnia	Cleaner	Engineer
3 Female	1959	Russian	Russian	Uzbekistan	Married	Sec./Spec.	1995	Uzbekistan	Journalist	Journalist
4 Female	1957	Russian	Russian	Turkmenistan	Divorced	Sec./Spec.	1997	Turkmenistan	Teacher	Teacher
5 Female	1978	Russian	Russian	Uzbekistan	Married	Un./Higher	1994	Uzbekistan	Student	Student
6 Female	1956	Russian	Russian	Kazakstan	Divorced	Sec./Spec.	1995	Kazakstan	Secretary	Secretary
7 Female	1953	Russian	Russian	Tajikistan	Married	10–11 class	1992	Tajikistan	Builder	Builder
8 Female	1924	Russian	Russian	Azerbaijan	Widowed	Sec./Spec.	1993	Azerbaijan	Pensioner	Technician
9 Female	1931	Russian	Russian	Georgia	Widowed	10–11 class	1996	Georgia	Pensioner	
10 Female	1949	Russian	Russian	Azerbaijan	Divorced	10–11 class	1996	Azerbaijan	Mechanic	Mechanic
11 Male	1939	Russian	Russian	Tajikistan	Widowed	Sec./Spec.	1996	Tajikistan	Pensioner	
12 Male	1954	Russian	Russian	Tajikistan	Married	Sec./Spec.	1996	Tajikistan	Pensioner	Teacher
13 Female	1954	Russian	Russian	Georgia	Divorced	Sec./Spec.	1991	Georgia	Factory work	Engineer
14 Female	1939	Russian	Armenian	Azerbaijan	—	Sec./Spec.	1994	Azerbaijan	Pensioner	Technician
15 Female	1968	Russian	Russian	Tajikistan	Married	Sec./Spec.	1995	Tajikistan	Teacher	Teacher
16 Female	1938	Russian	Russian	Turkmenistan	Widowed	Sec./Spec	1997	Turkmenistan	Teacher	Teacher
17 Male	1974	Russian	Russian	Uzbekistan	Single	Higher	1995	Uzbekistan	Teacher	Teacher
18 Male	1973	Russian	Russian	Uzbekistan	Married	Sec./Spec.	1995	Uzbekistan	Policeman	Policeman
19 Female	1973	Russian	Russian	Uzbekistan	Separated	Higher	1994	Uzbekistan	Doctor	Student
20 Female	1974	Russian	Russian	Uzbekistan	Divorced	Higher	1999	Uzbekistan	Journalist	Journalist
21 Female	1959	Russian	Russian	Tajikistan	Divorced	Sec./Spec.	1995	Tajikistan	Volunteer	Teacher
22 Male	1971	Chechen	Russian	Chechnia	Single	Sec./Spec.	1996	Chechnia	None	Driver
23 Male	1948	Ukrainian	Russian	Russia	Married	Higher.	1996	Uzbekistan	Factory work	Engineer
24 Female	1957	Russian	Russian	Tajikistan	Married	Sec./Spec.	1992	Tajikistan	None	Technologist
25 Female	1957	Russian	None	Tajikistan	Widowed	Higher	1992	Tajikistan	Milkmaid	Teacher
26 Female	1954	German	Russian	Kazakstan	Married	10–11 class	1997	Kazakstan	Farm work	Teacher

Appendix 3: (Cont.)

Code of migrant/ Gender	Date of birth	Nationality	Citizenship	Place of birth	Family position	Education	Date of arrival in Russia	Republic of departure	Work position in Russia	Profession/ Employment before move
27 Female	1954	Russian	Russian	Tajikistan	Married	Un./Higher	1997	Tajikistan	Accountant	Inspector-factory
28 Female	1952	Russian	Russian	Kazakstan	Married	Sec./Spec.	1997	Kazakstan	Farm work	Midwife
29 Female	1961	Russian	Russian	Kazakstan	Divorced	Sec./Spec.	1998	Kazakstan	Shop work	Inspector-cashier
30 Female	1956	Russian	Russian	Russia	Married	Higher	1992	Azerbaijan	Farm work	Livestock manager
31 Male	1952	Russian	Russian	Russia	Married	10–11 class	1997	Kazakstan	Foreman	Driver
32 Male	1965	Russian	Russian	Kazakstan	Single	Sec./Spec.	1998	Kazakstan	Mechanic	Engineer
33 Female	1954	Russian	Russian	Russia	Married	Sec./Spec.	1997	Kazakstan	Farm work	Technician
34 Female	1956	Russian	Russian	Kazakstan	Married	Sec./Spec.	1998	Kazakstan		Technician
35 Female	1964	Russian	Russian	Kazakstan	Married	Un./Higher	1998	Kazakstan	None	Bookkeeper
36 Male	1969	Russian	None	Kazakstan	Married	Sec./Spec.	1999	Kazakstan	Welder	Technician
37 Male	1968	Russian	None	Kazakstan	Single	Sec./Spec.	1999	Kazakstan	None	Driver
38 Male	1971	Russian	Kazak	Russia	Married	Sec./Spec.	1999	Kazakstan	None	Mechanic
39 Female	1939	Moldovan	Russian	Russia	Divorced	Higher	1990	Tajikistan	Pensioner	Teacher
40 Female	1975	Russian	Tajik	Tajikistan	Married	Sec./Spec.	1995	Tajikistan	Maternity leave	Museum worker
41 Female	1970	Russian	Russian	Uzbekistan	Single	Sec./Spec.	1994	Uzbekistan	None	Secretary
42 Female	1972	Russian	Russian	Uzbekistan	Married	Sec./Spec.	1993	Uzbekistan	Nursery work	Dressmaker
43 Female	1966	Uzbek	Russian	Uzbekistan	Divorced	Sec./Spec.	1995	Uzbekistan	Farm work	Teacher
44 Male	1936	Russian	Russian	Uzbekistan	Married	Sec./Spec.	1994	Uzbekistan	Pensioner	Builder
45 Female	1967	Russian	Russian	Uzbekistan	Married	Sec./Spec.	1994	Uzbekistan	Shop work	Hairdresser
46 Female	1958	Russian	Russian	Russia	Widowed	Un./Higher	1998	Kazakstan	None	Technologist
47 Female	1973	Tajik	Russian	Tajikistan	Married	Un./Higher	1995	Tajikistan	Nursery work	Teacher
48 Female	1938	Russian	Russian	Russia	Widowed	Sec./Spec.	1994	Uzbekistan	Pensioner	
49 Female	1946	Russian	Russian	Russia	Widowed	Sec./Spec.	1994	Kazakstan	None	Technician

Appendix 3: (Cont.)

Code of migrant/ Gender	Date of birth	Nationality	Citizenship	Place of birth	Family position	Education	Date of arrival in Russia	Republic of departure	Work position in Russia	Profession/ Employment before move
50 Female	1958	Russian	Russian	Turkmenistan	Married	Sec./Spec.	1996	Turkmenistan	Policewoman	Policewoman
51 Male	1963	Tajik	Tajik	Tajikistan	Married	Higher	1998	Tajikistan	None	Teacher
52 Male	1960	Tajik	Tajik	Tajikistan	Single	Higher	1998	Tajikistan	None	Nursery nurse
53 Female	1954	Tatar	Russian	Uzbekistan	Married	Higher	1994	Uzbekistan	Statistician	
54 Male	1936	Chuvash	Russian	Tatarstan	Married	Sec./Spec.	1998	Uzbekistan	Pensioner	Military
55 Female	1962	Russian	Russian	Uzbekistan	Married	Sec./Spec.	1997	Uzbekistan	Bookkeeper	Bookkeeper
56 Female	1955	Russian	Kazak	Kazakstan	Married	Higher	1999	Kazakstan	None	Engineer
57 Female	1968	Russian	Russian	Kazakstan	Single	Sec./Spec.	1998	Kazakstan	Market trader	Bookkeeper
58 Female	1962	Russian	Russian	Kazakstan	Married	Sec./Spec.	1995	Uzbekistan	None	Technician
59 Female	1959	Russian	Russian	Kazakstan	Married	Sec./Spec.	1994	Kazakstan	Factory work	Nursery nurse
60 Male	1955	Ukrainian	Russian	Kazakstan	Married	Sec./Spec.	1994	Kazakstan	None	Technician
61 Male	1946	Russian	Russian	Russia	Married	Higher	1998	Tajikistan	Lecturer	Archaeologist
62 Female	1959	Russian	Russian	Tajikistan	Married	Higher	1998	Tajikistan	Editor	Historian
63 Female	1957	Russian	Russian	Ukraine	Married	Higher	1993	Kazakstan	Accountant	Economist
64 Female	1958	Russian	Russian	Kazakstan	Married	Higher	2001	Kazakstan	Unemployed	Doctor
65 Female	1948	Russian	Russian	Kazakstan	Widow	Sec./Spec.	1998	Kazakstan	Pharmacist	Head pharmacist
66 Male	1970	Russian	Russian	Kazakstan	Married	Sec./Spec.	2000	Kazakstan	Electrician	
67 Male	1950	Russian	Russian	Tatarstan (RSFSR)	Widower	Higher	1998	Uzbekistan	Electrician	Engineer
68 Female	1973	Russian	Russian	Kazakstan	Married	Sec./Spec.	2000	Kazakstan	Crane operator	Sales assistant
69 Female	1945	Russian	Russian	Ukraine	Divorced	Higher	1994	Tajikistan	Teacher	Teacher
70 Female	1961	Ukrainian	Russian	Kazakstan	Married	Sec./Spec.	1994	Uzbekistan	Invalid 3rd category	Nursery teacher
71 Female	1962	Russian	Russian	Uzbekistan	Divorced	Sec./Spec.	1998	Uzbekistan	Engineer	Crane operator
72 Female	1962	Russian	Russian	Kazakstan	Married	Higher	1998	Kazakstan	Head of migrant NGO	Engineer

Appendix 3: (Cont.)

Code of Migrant	Registration at migration service	Status	Emergency monetary assistance	Loan	Other help from migration service	Help from migrant association	Present living conditions	Propiska
1	Yes	Refugee	No	No	Accommodation	Advice	TRC	Temporary
2	Yes	Forced Migrant	No	No	No	Yes	Room in hostel	Temporary
3	Yes	Forced Migrant	No	No	No	Yes	Private house	Permanent
4	No	None	N/A	N/A	N/A	No	Room in hostel	None
5	Yes	Forced Migrant	No	No	Accommodation	Yes	MS apartment	Permanent
6	Yes	Forced Migrant	No	No	Accommodation	Yes	MS apartment	Permanent
7	Yes	Forced Migrant	No	No	Accommodation	No	TRC	Temporary
8	Yes	Forced Migrant	No	No	Accommodation	Yes	TRC	Temporary
9	Yes	Forced Migrant	No	No	Accommodation	Yes	TRC	Temporary
10	Yes	Forced Migrant	No	No	Accommodation	Yes	TRC	Temporary
11	Yes	Forced Migrant	No	No	Accommodation	Advice	TRC	Temporary
12	Yes	Forced Migrant	No	No	No	Yes	MS apartment	Permanent
13	Yes	Forced Migrant	No	No	Accommodation	Yes	MS apartment	Permanent
14	Yes	Refugee	No	No	Accommodation	No	MS apartment	Permanent
15	No	None	N/A	N/A	N/A	No	Barracks	Temporary
16	No	None	N/A	N/A	N/A	No	Room in hostel	None
17	Yes	Forced Migrant	No	Yes	No	Accommodation	Room in hostel	Temporary
18	Yes	Forced Migrant	No	Yes	No	No	Private house	Temporary
19	Yes	Forced Migrant	No	Yes	Accommodation	No	Room in hostel	Temporary
20	No	None	N/A	N/A	N/A	No	Family apartment	Temporary
21	Yes	Forced Migrant	No	No	No	Yes	Room in hostel	Permanent
22	Yes	Forced Migrant	Yes	No	Material help	No	Private house	Permanent
23	Yes	Forced Migrant	No	No	Accommodation	Accommodation	Room in hostel	Permanent
24	Yes	Forced Migrant	Yes	Yes	Material help	Material help	Rented house/C.S.	Permanent

Appendix 3: (Cont.)

Code of Migrant	Registration at migration service	Status	Emergency monetary assistance	Loan	Other help from migration service	Help from migrant association	Present living conditions	Propiska
25	Yes	Refugee	Yes	No	No	No	Buying house/C.S.	Permanent
26	Yes	Forced Migrant	Yes	No	No	No	Buying house/C.S.	Permanent
27	Yes	Forced Migrant	No	No	No	No	Buying house/C.S.	Permanent
28	No	None	N/A	N/A	N/A	No	Buying house/C.S.	Permanent
29	Yes	Forced Migrant	Yes	No	No	No	Buying house/C.S.	Permanent
30	No	None	N/A	N/A	N/A	No	Buying house/C.S.	Permanent
31	No	None	N/A	N/A	N/A	No	Buying house/C.S.	Permanent
32	Yes	Forced Migrant	Yes	No	No	No	Buying house/C.S.	Permanent
33	Yes	Awaiting decision	N/A	N/A	N/A	No	Buying house/C.S.	Permanent
34	Yes	Forced Migrant	Yes	No	Material help	No	Rented apartment	Permanent
35	Yes	Forced Migrant	Yes	No	Material help	Accommodation	Room in hostel	Permanent
36	Yes	Awaiting decision	N/A	N/A	N/A	Yes	Rented apartment	Temporary
37	No	None	N/A	N/A	N/A	No	Room in hostel	None
38	No	None	N/A	N/A	N/A	No	Room in hostel	None
39	No	None	N/A	N/A	N/A	Accommodation	Room in hostel	Permanent
40	No	None	N/A	N/A	N/A	No	Room in hostel	None

Appendix 3: (Cont.)

Code of Migrant	Registration at migration service	Status	Emergency monetary assistance	Loan	Other help from migration service	Help from migrant association	Present living conditions	Propiska
41	Yes	Refugee	No	No	No	Advice	Room in hostel	Temporary
42	Yes	Forced Migrant	No	No	No	Advice	Room in hostel	Permanent
43	No	None	N/A	N/A	N/A	Material help	House/C.S.	Permanent
44	Yes	Forced Migrant	No	No	Accommodation	No	Room in hostel	Temporary
45	Yes	Forced Migrant	Yes	Yes	Accommodation	Advice	Room in hostel	Temporary
46	Yes	Forced Migrant	Yes	Yes	Accommodation	No	Barracks	Temporary
47	Yes	Forced Migrant	Yes	No	Material help	No	Room in hostel	Permanent
48	Yes	Forced Migrant	Yes	No	Material help	Employment	Room in hostel	Permanent
49	Yes	Forced Migrant	No	No	No	No	Room in hostel	Permanent
50	Yes	Forced Migrant	Yes	No	No	Employment	Room in hostel	Temporary
51	No	None	N/A	N/A	No	No	Room in hostel	Temporary
52	No	None	N/A	N/A	No	Accommodation	Room in hostel	Temporary
53	Yes	Forced Migrant	Yes	No	No	No	Apartment provided by work place	Temporary
54	Yes	Forced Migrant	Yes	No	No	No	Rented apartment	Temporary
55	Yes	Forced Migrant	Yes	No	No	No	Rented house	Permanent
56	Yes	Awaiting decision	N/A	N/A	N/A	No	Room in hostel	Permanent
57	Yes	Awaiting decision	N/A	N/A	N/A	No	Rented apartment	Permanent
58	Yes	Forced Migrant	Yes	No	Accommodation	No	Barracks	Temporary
59	Yes	Forced Migrant	Yes	No	Accommodation	No	Barracks	Permanent

Appendix 3: (Cont.)

Code of Migrant	Registration at migration service	Status	Emergency monetary assistance	Loan	Other help from migration service	Help from migrant association	Present living conditions	Propiska
60	No	None	N/A	N/A	N/A	No	House/C.S.	None
61	Yes	Forced Migrant	Yes	No	No	Material help	Room in hostel	Temporary
62	Yes	Forced Migrant	Yes	No	No	Material help	Room in hostel	Temporary
63	No	N/A	N/A	N/A	N/A	Advice	Private house	Permanent
64	Yes	Forced Migrant	Yes	No	No	No	House provided by work place	Permanent
65	Yes	Forced Migrant	No	Yes	In finding work	No	Private Apartment	Permanent
66	Yes	Forced Migrant	Yes	No	Material help	No	Rented house	Permanent
67	Yes	Forced Migrant	Yes	No	No	No	Rented house	Permanent
68	Yes	Forced Migrant	Yes	No	Material help	Advice	Room in private flat	Permanent
69	Yes	Forced Migrant	Yes	No	No	No	Room in hostel	Permanent
70	Yes	Forced Migrant	Yes	No	In finding accommodation	No	Room in hostel	Permanent
71	Yes	Forced Migrant	Yes	No	Material help	No	Room in hostel	Permanent
72	Yes	Forced Migrant	Yes	No	Material help	Heads a migrant NGO herself	Private apartment	Permanent

Appendix 4

Profiles of Federal Non-governmental Organizations and Regional Migrant Organizations

Moscow

The Civic Assistance Committee
The Civic Assistance Committee (CAC) was created in 1990 following the outbreak of violence in Baku, Azerbaijan, and the arrival of the first refugees in Moscow. The organization was the first non-governmental body concerned with refugees and forced migrants to be created in Russia. Svetlana Gannushkina (an academic and legal expert), Lidiia Grafova (a journalist at *Literaturnaia gazeta*) and Viacheslav Igrunov (a Duma deputy, human rights campaigner and former dissident) make up the joint committee that heads the organization. The primary role of CAC is to serve as a mediating body between refugees, forced migrants and state structures on questions of status, registration and social provision.[1] CAC provides legal/practical information and basic material aid to refugees and forced migrants. The committee holds a twice-weekly reception providing material, humanitarian, medical and legal help for migrants, and has established an education/adaptation centre for migrant and refugee children. It also attempts to influence state policy through lobbying on behalf of migrants and involvement in the formulation of legislation. It has successfully broadened its scope of activity to encompass refugees and asylum seekers from the 'far abroad', and those internally displaced as a result of the Chechen conflicts.

Memorial
The human rights organization *Memorial* is closely linked to CAC. The main focus of the organization is the defence of the legal rights of refugees and forced migrants; it uses the activity of CAC as a base for its more analytical work. *Memorial* is involved in two major programmes with the CAC: a network of

legal consultation points for refugees and forced migrants across the territory of the Russian Federation, set up in 1996: *Migratsiia i pravo* (Migration and Law); and a research programme for the analysis of the situation of refugees and forced migrants in Russia. The legal consultation points, which exist in 49 regions of Russia, provide access to a widespread network of information and advice for a large number of refugees and forced migrants. At the inter-state level, *Memorial* was an active participant in the preparation for the 1996 CIS Geneva Conference and in the follow-up discussions concerning the implementation of the Programme of Action.[2]

Coordinating Council for Aid to Refugees and Forced Migrants

The Coordinating Council for Aid to Refugees and Forced Migrants (CCARFM) evolved from CAC, under the chairmanship of Lidiia Grafova. The council was officially formed in March 1993 with the support of international bodies as an umbrella organization to coordinate 28 separate NGOs and 47 individuals. CCARFM has a dual approach to migration issues: lobbying for migrants' rights and influencing migration policy and legislation; and direct involvement in the resettlement of forced migrants. The organization attempts to bring migration issues into the public arena and to positively influence public opinion. Regular publications are prepared and distributed amongst state and non-state organs. Lidiia Grafova has consistently published articles on refugee and forced migrant issues in the Russian press.

The work of the council as a lobbying pressure group is enhanced through the experience of providing direct assistance and advice to migrants at the level of resettlement. CCARFM holds weekly receptions for forced migrants providing legal, medical and material aid. In 1995 the council published a handbook *Kompas*, updated in 1998, that provides an important source of information for forced migrants and refugees. The handbook details legislation, advice on migrants' rights and information about relevant state and non-state bodies, and is distributed widely to migrant, state and NGO organizations throughout the Russian Federation. CCARFM has been heavily involved in the development of rural compact settlements, both researching the viability of settlements and providing legal and organizational help to a number of individual settlements.

The Forum of Migrant Associations

CCARFM operates as the permanently functioning working apparatus for the Forum of Migrant Associations. This is an umbrella organization for federal level migrant NGOs and the widespread network of migrant associations that exist in the Russian Federation. The member associations of the Forum now number more than 198 in 50 regions of Russia, together with three organizations located in the former republics of Uzbekistan, Kazakstan and Tajikistan. The initiative for its first meeting in April 1996 – which involved regional migrant associations, federal level NGOs, Human Rights organisations, IOM, UNHCR, and State Duma and Ministry representatives – came from leaders of a number of migrant associations and CCARFM. Further meetings of the Forum have been held in April 1998, April 2000 and March 2002. In April 2002, the Forum meetings took the form of two conferences held in the Southern Federal okrug and Volga Federal okrug. The Forum has a central core of federal level NGOs and a permanently acting executive committee elected for a period of two years. The executive committee is made up of 19 leaders of migrant organizations from different regions of Russia.

The initial aims of the forum were to create a general mass movement to foster the idea of the transformation of a chaotic form of migration to that of organized resettlement; and to extend out to the regions of the Russian Federation to provide support for smaller organizations, represent their interests at a federal level and facilitate the development of new associations. The Forum's ongoing activities are: to enable the self-organization of migrant groups and facilitate their growth and development; to create an information network and exchange between migrant organizations and the information-analytical centre in Moscow; and to continue to represent migrants' rights and influence policy and legislation through the mass media, and participation in parliamentary and governmental bodies.[3]

The Compatriots Fund (Russian Fund for Aid to Refugees)
The former deputy of the Committee on Population Migration created the Compatriots Fund in 1991. In 1992 it was allocated 600,000 US dollars by the Ministry of Finance for the creation of workplaces for forced migrants and refugees at compact settlements and in small enterprises, and the organization signed an agreement with the Federal Employment Service for a joint programme of action in the functioning of about 700 migrant associations in different regions of Russia.[4] In 1994 there was a change in its role as state support ceased and it assumed the role of an independent non-governmental organization. Through regional level projects the Fund stresses: the use of migrant initiative and direct participation; the involvement of the local community; and the facilitation of cooperation between organizations and enterprises of forced migrants with state ministries, departments and local administrations. The Fund concluded agreements with local administrations guaranteeing tax and land privileges for migrant organizations and enterprises regarding general resettlement, housing and employment.[5] It supports the idea of migrant communities (*obshchina*): a group of migrants which form a community, made up of a central

'social' organization and commercial enterprises, that collaborates in enterprise production and the construction of housing at a site of settlement.

REGIONAL MIGRANT ORGANIZATIONS IN SAMARA, SARATOV AND NOVOSIBIRSK *OBLASTI*

Saratov oblast'

Saratovskii istochnik
Saratovskii istochnik (Saratov Spring) was the first migrant association to be established in Saratov *oblast'*. The association was created in January 1995 on the basis of a group of 23 families who had arrived from Uzbekistan in 1994 upon the initiative of the migrant group leader and the director of the Saratov TMS. Other groups of migrants from a number of different republics were invited to join, and the association was originally financed with the help of different migrant enterprises for which it provided support. Nine members of staff worked for *Saratovskii istochnik*, including one full-time lawyer. There was some crossover with the staff of the commercial enterprise *Tipografiya AVP Saratovskii istochnik*, which occupied a neighbouring room in the building where the migrant association was located. *Saratovskii istochnik* had received a printing press from UNHCR and created this partner organization that produced information bulletins for forced migrants and the Forum of Migrant Associations and fulfilled commercial orders.

The main work of *Saratovskii istochnik* revolved around a daily reception at the association's headquarters in the centre of the city of Saratov, which provided both general advice and specific legal consultation. The association informed migrants of their rights through the provision of literature they published, and provided information regarding resettlement possibilities in Saratov *oblast'* to potential migrants in the former republics, or to 'scouts' (*razvedchiki*) investigating the possibility of settlement in the region. The organization provided a data-base of job opportunities existing within Saratov *oblast'* to migrants arriving for consultation. In 1995, *Saratovski istochnik* was involved in the implementation of an agreement between the Federal Migration Service and Federal Employment Service that provided funding for the creation of work places for forced migrants in existing enterprises, and for the development of new migrant enterprises on the territory of the *oblast'*. A joint research project with the migration service, employment service and different local level administrations, funded by the Eurasia Foundation, looked at the potential of different regions in the *oblast'* for the creation of work places.[6] However, problems were faced both in the financing of the actual research, and resources for putting the programmes into action.

Vozvrashchenie

Vozvrashchenie (Return) was formed in 1996 to provide support for migrant women and children. Although registered as an independent organization it was originally closely linked with *Saratovskii istochnik* and initially shared their premises, after which it moved to a peripheral region of the city which was fairly inaccessible for migrants. In 1999 the association acquired a new office near to the centre of the city with excellent access to public transport. However, the office was located in a former armaments factory, which made access to the building problematic as an official pass was required and individuals entering had to be accompanied by a member of the association. The accommodation was acquired through one of the businesses that had been set up in the former factory; in return, *Vozvrashchenie* offered the business the use of its fax, telephone, photocopier and computer. The organization employed three paid workers – the head, a secretary and a consultant/migration expert – plus one voluntary worker. The head, the secretary and the voluntary worker were all forced migrants, while the consultant was a former employee of the TMS in Saratov. A qualified lawyer was employed by the organization as part of the *Migratsiia i pravo* network.

The organization provided consultation (general advice, moral/psychological support) and material help (medicine and other material aid) for forced migrants. One of its main objectives was the creation of work places for forced migrants, via cooperation with local businesses, and through concrete programmes which placed employment creation within a wider programme of migrant self-help and self-resettlement. The association was particularly involved at a number of migrant 'compact settlement' sites, where it negotiated on behalf of the migrants in trying to secure help from the TMS and district administrations in order to alleviate the difficult situations existing at the sites. It also had close links with the local press, specifically with a journalist who worked on the local paper *Saratovskii vesti* and wrote a UNHCR-funded page devoted to migration issues. The head of *Vozvrashchenie* was also involved in the work of Danko S, the implementing partner of UNHCR/Opportunity International's micro-credit programme in Saratov *oblast'*, as one of the independent experts responsible for decisions on the granting of micro-credit loans to forced migrants and refugees.

Komitet bezhentsev iz Chechnii

The *Komitet bezhentsev iz Chechnii* (the Committee of Refugees from Chechnia) was created in March 1997 to provide assistance to the large numbers of forced migrants and refugees from Chechnia who had arrived on the territory of Saratov *oblast'*. The *Komitet* was closely linked with *Saratovskii istochnik* and worked at the premises of that organization until acquiring its own accommodation from the city administration in October 1998. Although the premises were situated on a main trolley-bus line they were quite a distance from the centre, which was seen as a problem by representatives of the organization in terms of migrant access. However, the association saw the move as important in that it represented a break from a previous sense of dependence upon *Saratovskii istochnik*.

The association had nine full-time workers, all of whom were forced migrants from Chechnia. A daily consultation and weekly legal consultation with a qualified lawyer (funded by a Soros grant) were held at the headquarters; these consultations were attended by migrants from both Saratov city and the districts of the *oblast'*. The organization had also set up a number of 'social councils' at migrant settlement sites in the districts of Saratov *oblast'*. The *Komitet* particularly visited regions where there were high numbers of forced migrants and refugees from Chechnia. Although focused upon the special needs of refugees and forced migrants from Chechnia, the association was open to all migrants.

Samara oblast'

Samarskii pereselenets

Samarskii pereselenets (the Samara migrant/resettler) was officially registered in 1997, but had been active since 1995; registration was delayed until 1997 due to lack of money. The association was established independently of any state structures; in fact it was formed in reaction to problems with the Samara migration service experienced by the head of the organization after she arrived from Tajikistan in 1993. The staff of *Samarskii pereselenets* comprised five paid employees who were forced migrants, plus other volunteers who were migrants in a hostel where the association was originally located. The original location of the organization impeded its work; until November 1999 there was no phone line, and contact had to be made through the hostel warden. The lack of strict consultation hours also placed great pressure on the association's workers, and consultations usually took place in the evenings after the working day had finished. However, in 2000 the organization acquired an office in a centrally located building from the property committee of the Saratov city administration.

At this new location, the association provided daily consultations offering information and 'moral support'. In 2002, *Samarskii pereselenets* became part of the *Migratsiia i pravo* network, and established an informal network of communication with potential migrants coming from the other former Soviet republics.

Knowledge about the association was passed by word of mouth or in the form of written information (including copies of *Kompas*, the book produced by the Forum of Migrant Associations containing information about migration legislation, migrants' rights, and governmental and non-governmental structures concerned with migration), by migrants who had come to the *oblast'* on exploratory trips and were returning to the former republics, and by information posted at consulates in the other former republics.

Novosibirsk oblast'

Ruka pomishchi

Ruka pomoshchi (Helping Hand) was set up by a group of three unemployed women – one a forced migrant, the other two local residents – on a retraining scheme run by the regional employment service. The head of the organization wrote a business plan for the creation of a body that would provide information and consultation services for forced migrants; as a result the organization was subsidized by the employment service for a year, via individual grants to each of the three founding members. Following this, *Ruka pomishchi* received financial support from *Nemetskii dom* (the 'German House'), due to its interest in assisting ethnic German Russian forced migrants arriving at Novosibirsk *oblast'*, but this funding ceased in August 2002. In addition to the three paid members, there were two volunteers one of whom was a forced migrant. The organization was located in a central region of Novosibirsk city, where it held daily consultations for forced migrants. In August 2002, it became part of the *Migratsiia i pravo* network, at this point on a trial basis. A key part of the organization's activity was providing assistance to forced migrants in finding employment, primarily through a computer vacancy-matching data-base that was run in collaboration with the regional employment service. In addition, the organization received Soros funding for a migrant training programme in 'business and entrepreneurial activity'.

Notes

Introduction

1. Throughout the book the terms 'Russian communities' or 'Russian populations' should be taken to include both the ethnic Russian and Russian-speaking populations resident in the Soviet successor states unless 'ethnic Russian' or 'Russian-speaking' is specified.
2. IOM 2002a, p. 5.
3. The use of the term 'return' for the migration movement is accepted as problematic, as are other terms that are frequently employed to describe the Russian communities and their migration, such as 'diaspora' and 'repatriation'. These terms are questioned throughout the text.
4. The term home/land is used to indicate the multiple levels at which 'homeland' may be understood. Two initial divisions that might be suggested are at the macro-level, the wider physical territory of a [national] 'homeland', or at the micro-level, a more immediate 'home' located at the site of everyday lived experience. The dichotomy proves to be far more complex, however, and is explored through the book.
5. The term 'empire' in relation to the Soviet Union is being used descriptively. The book does not engage directly with the debate over whether or not the Soviet Union can be described as an empire. See for example Beissinger 1995; Dunlop 1993b; Levita and Loiberg 1994; Suny 1995.
6. Burawoy and Verdery 1999, pp. 1–2.
7. Other authors have suggested that there is a need to rethink understandings of 'civil society' in the post-socialist context. See for example Dunn and Hann 1996; Hann 2002.
8. In this respect, the book contributes to the literature that deals with issues of Russia and Russian-ness, both historically and in the contemporary context. See for example Hosking 2001; Laitin 1998; Tolz 2001.
9. Wahlbeck (2002, p. 222) suggests that concepts such as transnationalism and diaspora can be informed by empirical studies, and warns that enthusiasm for such concepts (including globalization) could end up in a 'global babble' with no practical relevance for research. Empirical study allows the 'practical effect' on people to be understood.
10. See for example Burawoy and Verdery 1999; Clifford 1998; Hann 2002; Lawson 2000; Malkki 1995; McHugh 2000; Papastergiadis 1998, 2000.
11. A more detailed description of the empirical project is provided in Chapter 1.

Chapter 1: Understanding Migration in Post-Soviet Russia

1. As suggested in the introduction, the term 'home/land' is used to indicate the multiple levels at which 'home' and 'homeland' may be understood: in very provisional terms, as the wider physical territory of a [national] homeland, or 'home' as the site of everyday lived experience.

2. Brah 1996, p. 178; Castles and Miller 1998, p. 1; Papastergiadis 2000, p. 6.

3. Koser and Lutz 1998, p. 1.

4. Castles and Miller 1998, p. 3.

5. Zolberg (cited in Held *et al.* 1999, p. 302) suggests that the increase in numbers of refugees and asylum seekers is predominantly the by-product of two major historical processes: the formation of new states; and confrontation over the social order in both old and new states.

6. As Castles (1998, p. 9) suggests, although in the past both economic and forced migration were male-dominated, women are increasingly playing a major role in all types of migration and in all regions of migration. In particular, some refugee movements, e.g. those from the former Yugoslavia, are predominantly female.

7. Brah 1996, p. 179; Castles and Miller 1998, pp. 8–9; Held *et al.* 1999, pp. 297–304; Koser and Lutz 1998, pp. 1–3; Portes *et al.* 1999. Castles and Miller identify the majority of these characteristics. However, as Tesfahuney (1998, p. 513) rightly points out, they omit a number of emerging significant trends in international migration and its control, those of 'securitization', and 'racialization' and 'criminalization'.

8. Brah 1996, p. 178; Castles and Miller 1998, p. 12; Koser and Lutz 1998, p. 1.

9. Held *et al.* 1999, p. 299.

10. Mitchneck and Plane 1995, p. 22; Robertson 1996, p. 113; Zaionchkovskaia *et al.* 1993, p. 206.

11. Chinn and Kaiser 1996.

12. The term 'far abroad' is used to refer to those countries that are outside the borders of the former Soviet Union; the term 'near abroad' is used to refer to the other former non-Russian republics of the former Soviet Union.

13. Heleniak 1999, p. 2; Zaionchkovskaia *et al.* 1993, p. 205.

14. Held *et al.* 1999, p. 285.

15. Castles and Miller 1998, p. 9; Codagnone 1998b, p. 39.

16. Codagnone 1998b, p. 55.

17. Zolberg 1989, p. 414.

18. Heleniak 1999, p. 5.

19. Zaionchkovskaia *et al.* 1993, p. 206.

20. Vishnevskii and Zaionchkovskaia 1994, p. 257.

21. Codagnone 1998a, pp. 47, 48.

22. The terms 'returnees', 'refugees', 'forced migrants', 'economic migrants' are used here as broad descriptive categories. However, the difficulty of using such categories to define migrants is acknowledged and is explored throughout the text.

23. Codagnone 1998a, pp. 16–17.

24. By the end of 2001, 141,002 forced migrants who had fled Chechnia as a result of the

conflict had been registered by the Federal Migration Service (*Goskomstat* 2000, p. 113; *Goskomstat* 2002c; *Goskomstat* is the State Statistics Committee). UNHCR estimates 250,000 persons are currently involuntarily displaced as a result of the conflict in various republics of the Northern Caucasus (*http://www.unhcr.ch/ cgi-bin/texis/ vtx/publ/opendoc.pdf?idi=3ddceb8611&tbl=MEDIA*, 2003).

25. Internal movements within the Russian Federation, apart from the refugee movements from the Chechen conflict, have received little attention in the west. However, between 1990 and 1996 about 23 million people changed their residence, either within the same region (12.5 million) or moving from one region to another (10.6 million) (Codagnone 1998a, p. 51). Movement from the 'Far North' has been particularly high. From the 16 regions defined as the 'Far North', over 12 per cent of the population migrated out of the region between 1991 and 2001. From Magadan and Chukotka, 43 and 61 per cent of their populations respectively have left in the past decade (Heleniak 2002).

26. Codagnone 1998b, pp. 42–4; Heleniak 1999, pp. 15–16.

27. Reports are constantly appearing in the Russian media about the growth in organized crime, drug trafficking, smuggling, prostitution, rackets, fraudulent housing schemes, related to the migration inflow (specifically of individuals of Caucasian and Central Asian origin, and of Chinese, Vietnamese, Korean, Afghan and Pakistan nationality) across its 'unprotected' borders, and concerning actions carried out by the Ministry of Internal Affairs against 'illegal' migrants in defence of Russian 'security' and 'stability'. 'Construction' of such a stereotype is feeding into popular perceptions and negatively impacting upon the reception of migrants at the regional level (Vitkovskaia 2002).

28. On 24 January 2002, the Russian newspaper *Nezavisimaia Gazeta* reported that at the end of 2001, around 5 million illegal migrants lived in Russia, and in reality this figure could reach 15 million (Ukolov 2002). The latter figures were based on results of research conducted by the International Organization of Migration in Moscow during May 2001. Recent official government figures estimate the number at around 5 million (Popova 2002b).

29. Codagnone 1998a, p. 5.

30. *Goskomstat* 2002a, p. 22. 77.4 per cent of these emigrants went to Germany, 21.5 per cent to Israel and just 1.1 per cent to Greece. Other significant emigration movements were to Canada, China and the USA (1.5 per cent, 2.5 per cent and 8.4 per cent respectively of the overall total).

31. Oberg and Boubnova 1995, p. 245.

32. As King and Melvin (2000, pp. 118–19) suggest, the figure of 25 million is dubious since who counts as Russian is still very much undecided. They also object to the use of terms such as 'Russian', 'Russian speakers', Russian 'diaspora', and prefer the label 'russified settler communities' primarily because the term does not assume homogeneity across the group or prioritize issues of ethnicity or language. The present study agrees with this criticism and a constant re-evaluation of the constitution of, and labels applied to, the group is integral to the research.

33. Heleniak 1999, p. 11; Messina 1994a, p. 627.
34. The nature of the historical, centre-to-periphery, migratory movements of Russians is looked at in more detail in Chapter 2.
35. Zaionchkovskaia 1996, p. 7.
36. Heleniak 1999, p. 11.
37. Codagnone 1998b, p. 48; Zaionchkovskaia 1996, p. 7.
38. Codagnone 1998a, p. 13.
39. Rowland 1993, p. 171.
40. Codagnone 1998b, p. 46; Messina 1994a, p. 631.
41. Chapters 2 and 3 explore this interplay of causal factors in more detail.
42. *Goskomstat* 2000, p. 113, *Goskomstat* 2002b, p. 128. Since 1994, Tajikistan has been the only former republic to experience open conflict in the form of civil/clan warfare.
43. Codagnone 1998a, p. 13.
44. The Federal Migration Service (FMS) was the official government body set up to deal with migration issues in July 1992. Its formation and development is looked at in more detail in Chapter 2.
45. Federal Migration Service 1998; *Goskomstat* 1998, p. 68; *Goskomstat* 2000, p. 113; *Goskomstat* 2002a, p. 128. The majority of registered returnees have been awarded 'forced migrant' status. The status is awarded to those individuals who are entitled to Russian citizenship, and who have been forced to leave their former place of residence due to persecution or violence on the grounds of race, nationality, religion, affiliation to a particular social group or political conviction. 'Refugee' status was originally available to those Russian returnees who did not hold Russian citizenship at the time of arrival. The amendments to the Russian law on refugees that were introduced in June 1997 made refugee status more difficult to acquire, and in practice it was no longer awarded to returnees who did not possess, but who were entitled to, Russian citizenship.
46. See Appendix 1 for a discussion of the limitations of statistics concerning forced migrants and refugees.
47. On 4 January 2001 Russian migration officials stated that more than 8 million people had arrived in the Russian Federation from the former Soviet republics since 1991 (RFE/RL Newsline 2001a). Other estimates put this figure as high as 10 million (IOM 2002a, p. 5). Over the period 1995–2001 approximately 2.25 million ethnic Russian and Russian-speaking migrants have been *officially* recorded by the Ministry of Internal Affairs of the Russian Federation as having registered at places of residence upon arrival (*Goskomstat* 2002a, p. 363).
48. See for example Tolz 2001. This issue is explored in greater detail in Chapter 2.
49. Giddens 1984.
50. Goss and Lindquist 1995; Wright 1995.
51. Codagnone 1998a; Phizacklea 1996; Pilkington 1998a; Pilkington and Phizacklea 1999; Schwarz 1997. Giddens' theory of structuration is utilized to inform understandings of migration and the interaction between 'agency' and 'structure', while taking account of qualifications of both the theory itself and its application to

post-Soviet migration. Pilkington and Phizacklea, in particular, qualify the use of the theory and draw on the work of Derek Layder (1997) in developing their critique.

52. The term 'migration system' can be closely compared with, and draws upon, the idea of a 'migrant institution' employed by Goss and Lindquist (1995).

53. Phizacklea 1996; Richmond 1993, p. 12; Richmond 1998, pp. 19–20.

54. Pilkington and Phizacklea 1999, p. 96.

55. Codagnone (1998a, p. 48) suggests that the presence of institutional links between the former republics and the Russian Federation are an important reason in explaining why migrants mainly choose to migrate to Russia rather than to the west, where such institutional links are absent.

56. Brubaker 1995; Codagnone 1998b; Messina 1994; *Migratsiia bedstvie ili blago* 1996; Vishnevskii and Zaionchkovskaia 1994, p. 246.

57. Codagnone 1998b, pp. 39, 48; Messina 1994, p. 627; Vishnevskii and Zaionchkovskaia 1994, p. 249; Zaionchkovskaia 1996, p. 10.

58. Vishnevskii and Zaionchkovskaia 1994, p. 249; Vitkovskaia 1999a, p. 53.

59. For examples of academic frameworks see Abdulatipov 1994; Brubaker 1999; Dunlop 1993a.

60. Brah 1996, p. 182.

61. The factors leading to migration will be explored at both a macro and micro level in Chapters 2 and 3.

62. A case that brought this question to light was the status determination of Cuban and Haitian refugees in the United States in 1979–80 (Suhrke 1995, p. 203).

63. Codagnone 1998b, p. 41.

64. Koser 1998 cited in Al-Ali, Black and Koser 2001, p. 616.

65. Held *et al.* 1999, p. 303; Suhrke 1995, p. 203.

66. Brubaker 1998; Codagnone 1998a; Pilkington and Phizacklea 1999.

67. Pilkington 1998, p. 16; Vitkovskaia 1999a, p. 54.

68. Robertson 1996, p. 124.

69. Brubaker 1998, p. 1061.

70. Held *et al.* 1999, p. 285.

71. Schwarz 1997, p. 3. Meznaric (1995) has suggested an analytical framework for analysing the experience of Croatia and the evolution of a migration regime. Some parallels may be drawn with Russia as both countries have similar institutional legacies and no migration structures previously existed. Meznaric stresses the need for research and policy making within the area of refugee studies to be informed by the contextual variables of local situations.

72. Although the process of institutionalization involves the creation of new institutions, integral to the migration regime are national/regional governments that are central to informing migration policy and debate, and to influencing the nature of additional institutions that are formed.

73. A comparative study of reception policies of Chilean and Vietnamese refugees in France and Britain demonstrated that how the influx was viewed, whether as a temporary occurrence or long-term, affected the provision. In this case Britain saw

the process as temporary and responded with an ad hoc approach, whereas France interpreted the situation as long term so attempted to create a positive infrastructure (Joy 1995, p. 18).

74. Nagel 2002, pp. 975–6.
75. Koser 1993.
76. Studies of migration stress that the global context in which the movement of populations is taking place is integral to any analysis of migration movement, where there is a need to link analysis of the global context to the level of a specific case study (Escalona and Black 1995, p. 384; Suhrke 1995, p. 206).
77. Held *et al.* 1999, p. 67. The operation of non-governmental organizations (international, national and regional) is explored in Chapter 5.
78. An example of a perception of the Russian migration space was the UK government's idea, broached in spring 2003, to place 'offshore transit processing centres' in Russia (and other countries beyond the 'new' EU) to handle applications from asylum seekers trying to get to Britain. This was part of an effort to reduce the numbers of asylum seekers/asylum applications. The idea, opposed by UNHCR and other international organizations, failed to appreciate the migration challenges Russia itself is facing, and the still embryonic nature of institutional and legislative frameworks.
79. Escalona and Black 1995, pp. 379, 383.
80. Bourdieu cited in Tucker 1998, p. 71; Layder 1994, p. 142.
81. May 1996, pp. 116–17.
82. Koser and Lutz 1998, p. 4.
83. These levels of 'involvement' may tentatively be compared with Castells' (1997, pp. 355–7) discussion of the transformation of identities within his 'network society'. He suggests that the loss of 'legitimizing' identities, which existed through attachments to a legitimate government, and institutions and organizations of 'civil society', results in the emergence of either communal 'resistance identities' which do not communicate with the state except to struggle and negotiate on behalf of their specific interests, or 'project identities' which emerge from 'resistance identities' with the aim of transforming the social order around them, resulting in the possible reconstruction of a new civil society, and eventually a new state.
84. The question of networks will be explored in detail in Chapter 6, where parallels are drawn with wider tendencies within post-Soviet Russian society to depend upon social networks of family, friends and acquaintances inherited from the Soviet era, and to adapt these to the needs of the post-Soviet present.
85. This approach agrees with the recommendation of Portes, Guarnizo and Landolt (1999, p. 220) who, while deeming it appropriate to define the individual and his/her support networks as proper units of analysis, stress that such an approach does not deny the importance and reality of broader structures, in fact, it is seen as the most efficient way of learning about wider institutional underpinnings and structural effects.
86. Vertovec 1999, p. 449. Wahlbeck (2002, p. 222) argues that transnationalism and diaspora provide conceptual tools through which to understand the specific experiences

of displacement and transnational social relations of refugees and how they relate to their country of origin. The nature of these ties is bound to differ from those of labour migrants to which the body of transnational literature has traditionally been applied.

87. The body of literature that addresses these questions is constantly expanding. For some insightful texts and reviews of current research see: Al-Ali, Black and Koser 2001; Faist 2000; Kivisto 2001; Nagel 2001, 2002; Papastergiadis 2000; Portes, Guarnizo and Landolt 1999; Vertovec 1999; 2001; Wahlbeck 2002.

88. Wahlbeck 2002, p. 222.

89. Wahlbeck (2002, p. 234) argues a similar case for the concept of diaspora to help to understand the 'transnational reality' in which refugees are forced to live: 'in refugees own experiences, homeland and country of exiles, as well as time before and time after migration, constitute a continuous and coherent lived experience'.

90. Berger 1974 cited in Morley and Robins 1993, p. 4; Said 1979, p. 18, cited in Gupta and Ferguson 1992, p. 9.

91. Clifford 1994, p. 307; Morley and Robins 1993, p. 27.

92. Clifford 1988 cited in Gupta and Ferguson 1992, p. 9; Clifford 1994, p. 307. Malkki (1992, pp. 37–8) notes that accepting a generalized condition of homelessness does not negate the importance of place in the construction of identities; instead 'deterritorialization' and identity are intimately linked.

93. Anderson 1983 cited in Malkki 1992, p. 26.

94. Drought 2000, p. 336; Pilkington 1998b, p. 99.

95. Pilkington 1998b, p. 100.

96. Morley 2000, p. 18.

97. Malkki 1992, p. 37.

98. Douglas cited in Morley 2000, p. 16. This echoes well with Faist's thesis of (transnational) space (cited in Kivisto 2001, p. 566): 'Space here does not only refer to physical features, but also to larger opportunity structures, the social life and the subjective images, values, and meanings that the specific and limited place represents to migrants. Space is thus different from place in that it encompasses or spans various territorial locations. It includes two or more places. Space has a social meaning that extends beyond simple territoriality; only with concrete social or symbolic ties does it gain meaning for potential migrants.'

99. A number of studies have been critical of studies of transnationalism on these grounds. See for example, Nagel 2002, p. 981; Vertovec 1999, p. 455; Wahlbeck 2002, pp. 232–3.

100. Brah 1996, p. 3. Tuan (1996, p. 15) suggests two similar levels of 'homeland' and 'home' with specific reference to China: T'ien, as the formal, imperial core of Chinese civilization, and Tu as the soil, locality, homestead, hearth – location of childhood experiences, local customs and practices, and the unique qualities of 'place'.

101. Brah 1996, p. 197.

102. For a more detailed description of the methodological issues and ethical concerns that arose during the research see the author's doctoral thesis (Flynn 2001).

103. Berg 1998, p. 121; Burawoy *et al.* 1991, pp. 1–9.
104. This principal study was conducted as part of research for the author's doctoral the-sis 'Global Frameworks, Local Realities: Migrant Resettlement in the Russian Feder-ation' (University of Birmingham, 2001). The PhD was partly funded by an ESRC doctoral studentship.
105. The particular themes that emerged from the doctoral study, and which were ex-plored further in Novosibirsk, were meanings of 'home' and 'homeland', and the use of personal networks amongst returning migrants. Funding for the research came from an ESRC post-doctoral fellowship award (Award Number TO26 27 1017).
106. The combination of micro-level analysis, an awareness of the wider structural environment, and the use of the regional case studies to inform theoretical under-standing of the whole migration process, reflects what Burawoy labels the 'extended case method'. See Burawoy *et al.* 1991.
107. A press review was carried out at the national and regional levels. Four central newspapers were reviewed for the period March 1996 to mid 2002. These were *Izvestiia, Segodnia* (which ceased publication in April 2001), *Nezavizimaia Gazeta* and *Literaturnaia Gazeta.* In the two main case study regions a comparative press analysis was conducted for the period January 1999–August 1999. However, in both regions a general press review preceded and extended the comparative press analy-sis period. The regional papers were in Saratov: *Saratovskie vesti, Saratov, Komu chto,* and in Samara: *Samaraskie izvestiia, Samarskaia gazeta, Samarskoe obozrenie.*
108. For example, the idea of *doma* ('at home') emerged from initial conversations with migrants in 1997, when the researcher was exploring the idea of 'return', i.e. repatri-ation to a historical homeland (*rodina*) which reflected key Russian political, aca-demic and media discourses concerning the process at the time. This idea was then redefined to include that of being 'at home' as signified by the term *doma.* The con-cept of *doma* was then incorporated into and explored through later migrant inter-views.
109. See Appendix 2 for a detailed overview of the migrant settlement sites in Saratov, Samara and Novosibirsk *oblasti.*
110. See Appendix 3 for a collation of the socio-demographic data gathered.
111. Lawson 2000, p. 174.
112. Ibid, p. 176.
113. McRobbie (1982, p. 51) observes, 'the fact that it is uncommented on text carries par-ticular connotations, seeming the more pure the less it is edited. In this way the in-termediary activities fade into the background and fail to be recognized for what they are: activities which are as ideologically loaded and as saturated with "the sub-jective factor" as anything else'.

Chapter 2: Constructions of the 'Homeland' by the Russian State

1. Dixon 1996, p. 50; Kolstø 1995, p. 14; Levita and Loiberg 1994, p. 3; Melvin 1998, p. 29.
2. As a percentage of the whole Russian population, the numbers of Russians in the territories of the later Soviet republics rose from 0.1 per cent in the eighteenth century

to 1.9 per cent in 1897. Migration was a significant factor in this growth (Kolstø 1995, p. 15).

3. Kolstø 1995, pp. 18–39; Messina 1994, p. 621.
4. Melvin 1998, p. 30.
5. Hosking cited in Dixon 1996, p. 52; Melvin 1998, pp. 28–30.
6. Melvin 1998, p. 30.
7. Ibid, p. 29.
8. Kolstø 1995, p. 46.
9. Kolstø 1995, p. 48; Messina 1994, p. 620.
10. Kolstø 1995, p. 52.
11. Aasland 1996, p. 483; Kolstø 1995, pp. 58, 61.
12. Messina 1994a, p. 623; Schwarz 1997.
13. Kolstø 1995, p. 53.
14. Kolstø 1995, p. 102; Levita and Loiberg 1994, p. 11.
15. Dixon 1996, p. 55.
16. Abdulatipov 1994, p. 39; Kolstø 1995, p. 85.
17. Kolstø 1995, p. 99; Payin 1994, p. 25.
18. Melvin 1998, pp. 29, 34; Zevelev 1996, p. 267.
19. Szporluk 1994 cited in Smith 1999, p. 506.
20. Brubaker 1994, p. 51; Levita and Loiberg 1994, p. 16.
21. Castells 1998, p. 46.
22. Brubaker 1994, p. 68. A study conducted in the late 1980s showed that in contrast to members of the titular nations who mostly referred to their republics as their 'homeland', 70 per cent of Russians in Estonia, Uzbekistan, Georgia and Moldova named the Soviet Union as their 'homeland' (Payin 1994, p. 22). Many of the respondents in the present study also demonstrate this association with the Soviet Union (see Chapter 3).
23. Smith 1999, p. 506.
24. Abdlatipov 1994, p. 40.
25. Melvin 1998, p. 35.
26. Stepputat 1994, p. 177.
27. A colloquium was held in 1978 on 'Ethnic Russia Today: Undergoing Identity Crisis' organized at Columbia University, New York, which discussed the nature of the communities of Russians resident in the non-Russian republics of the Soviet Union and their possible identification as a 'diaspora' (Kolstø 1995, p. 3).
28. Kolstø 1996, p. 614.
29. For a detailed analysis of the application of the term 'diaspora' to the Russian communities in the 'near abroad' and to communities upon 'return' see Pilkington and Flynn 2001.
30. See for example, Bremmer 1994; Chinn and Kaiser 1996; King and Melvin 1998; Kolstø 1995; Laitin 1998; Melvin 1994, 1995; Shlapentokh, Sendich and Payin 1994; Smith 1999.
31. See for example, Diatlov 1994 cited in Gradirovskii 1999, p. 45; Gradirovskii 1999;

Kosmarskaia 1998b, 2002; Lebedeva 1997; Militarev 1999 (Militarev addresses the usage of the term, however does not use it at all in relation to the Russian-speaking communities).

32. Clifford 1994, p. 321.
33. Kolstø 1995, pp. 262–3; Kosmarskaia 1998b, p. 76.
34. Kolstø 1995, pp. 262–3.
35. Kosmarskaia 1998b.
36. Melvin 1998, p. 36.
37. Pilkington 1998b, p. 100.
38. Brubaker 1994, p. 70.
39. Melvin 1998, pp. 36, 40.
40. King and Melvin 2000, p. 120.
41. Codagnone 1998a, p. 30; Tishkov 1996, p. 47.
42. Sadkovskaia 1998.
43. Zevelev 2001, p. 133.
44. Ibid, pp. 133–4.
45. IOM 1999, p. 186. The agreement on dual citizenship with Turkmenistan was curtailed by a joint protocol signed by Russian President Vladimir Putin and Turkmen President Saparmurat Niyazov on 10 April 2003 [at the time of writing the protocol had not been ratified by Russia]. The reasons for the decision were disputed. Putin claimed that those Russians who wished to leave Turkmenistan have already done so. However, in reality there was widespread panic about the protocol amongst Russian residents and many left the country. Subsequently, it was agreed that if Russians chose to keep Russian citizenship, they would be granted Turkmen residence permits guaranteeing them all their previous rights apart from being able to vote, hold government office or serve in the Turkmen armed forces. It was suggested that the real reason for the decision lay with Russia's desire to secure a long-term contract on the sale of Turkmen gas to Russia. President Niyazov was concerned about the security implications of having large numbers of Russian citizens in Turkmenistan and granted the contract in return for the cessation of dual citizenship (RFE/RL 2003a, 2003b).
46. Although the sub-committee brought these two interest groups together, the priorities of the representative bodies of the State Duma and non-governmental organizations regarding the fate of the Russian communities differed. The parliamentary position favoured a policy of promoting integration while the NGO lobby championed the right of Russians to return (Pilkington 1998a, p. 53).
47. Melvin 1998, p. 37; Smith 1999, p. 507. Continued parliamentary concern with the protection of compatriots was reflected in the creation of another organ in November 1996, the Council of Compatriots. The organ is a permanently operating consultative body composed of the representatives of compatriots living abroad (Codagnone 1998a, p. 30). In 1999 the organ was extended to include representatives of Russian communities from the 'far abroad' (Lebedev 1999b).
48. Lebedev 1999a. In the law compatriots are defined 'as persons, born in one state, and

who live or lived in that state, and possess common characteristics of language, religion, cultural heritage, traditions and customs, and also descendants of the indicated persons by a direct line of ancestry'. The term 'compatriots abroad' includes
citizens of the Russian Federation permanently living beyond the borders of its territory, former citizens of the USSR, and now citizens of the 'former states of the
USSR', former emigrants from the Russian empire, the RSFSR, the USSR, and the
post-Soviet Russian Federation, and the direct descendants of the above groups
excluding descendants of the titular nations of foreign states (*Federal'nii zakon* 'O
gosudarstvennoi politike Rossiiskoi Federatsii v otnoshenii sootechestvennikov za
rubezhom', 5 March 1999).

49. The core of the term *sootechestvenniki* is *otechestvo* (fatherland), which is a political
rather than an ethnic concept (Kolstoe 1995, p. 261).

50. Melvin 1998, pp. 36–8. As King and Melvin (2000, p. 113) suggest, the Russian case, like
other new national states in Europe, reveals the discrepancy that can exist between
'the political boundaries of states and the amorphous and ascriptive cultural boundaries of nations'. In these cases there is tension between an inclusive vision of the state
(i.e. where citizenship and nationality coincide), and a more exclusive conception of
the state, as defined by Rogers Brubaker (1996, p. 103) 'of and for a particular ethno-
cultural "core nation" whose language, culture, demographic position, economic
welfare and political hegemony must be protected and promoted by the state'.

51. Kolstø 1995, p. 260. The ethnicization of the Russian media debate on diaspora is
evidenced by the frequent use of the ethnically exclusive terms 'Russians' (*russkie*) or
'ethnic Russians' (*etnicheskie russkie*) to refer to the Russian-speaking minorities in
the former Soviet Union, see Pilkington 1998a, p. 25.

52. King and Melvin 2000, p. 122.

53. 52 million roubles were allocated in the federal budget of 1999 for support of 'compatriots'. A figure of 100 million roubles was allocated in 2000; however, for both
years it is uncertain exactly how this money has been used and at the ground level,
the presence of these resources has not been greatly felt (Sokolova 2000; Tuleev
2000). A further 100 million roubles was allocated for 2001. Galina Vitkovskaia noted
that it is ironic that such a policy is promoted to protect the rights, and support 'compatriots' while they are resident in the former republics, while little is done for them
upon return (Vitkovskaia 1999b).

54. For example, in June 2000, President Putin approved a foreign policy concept that
contained amongst its general principles the aim 'to uphold in every possible way the
rights of Russian citizens and fellow countrymen abroad'. The Parliamentary Committee on CIS Affairs and Relations with Compatriots also continued to push for the
protection of the rights of the ethnic Russian and Russian-speaking populations in
the 'near abroad', witnessed in a statement by the Committee chairman in February
2001 advocating an increase in Russian state protection for these communities
(RFE/RL 2001b).

55. King and Melvin 2000, p. 120.

56. This is explored below. See also Brubaker 1999.

57. During the Soviet period although Russians formed the nucleus of settler communities in the other republics, their ethnic makeup depended heavily upon the region of settlement and always included Ukrainians and Belarusians alongside the Russians in the core group (Melvin 1998, p. 33).
58. Melvin 1998, p. 48.
59. Ibid. Empirical studies confirm this lack of ethnic solidarity among diaspora communities and point to socio-cultural links as providing a possible common, diasporic identity. See Gradirovskii 1999, p. 44; Kudriavtsev 1996, p. 3; Zevelev 1996, p. 279.
60. Smith 1999, p. 78.
61. For more in-depth descriptions of the development of the Russian migration regime, its institutions, policies and legislation, see Codagnone 1998a, 1998b; Pilkington 1998a; Tiskov 1997, 1998.
62. At its maximum size in 1997 the service comprised: a central apparatus of approximately 219 people, 89 territorial migration services (TMS) in each of the subjects of the Russian Federation employing a total of 4,000 workers and additional *raion* branches in some regions subordinate to the *oblast'* service (Kamakin 1998a; Kirillova 1998; Shlichkova 1997).
63. For the full texts of the original 1993 laws see *Vedomosti S"ezda Narodnikh Deputatov RF I Verkhovnogo Soveta RF* 1993, pp. 714–27.
64. The February 1992 Law on Citizenship stated that any resident of the Former Soviet Union is entitled to Russian citizenship if they applied before the end of the year 2000. A new citizenship law was introduced in May 2002 that did not include any special conditions for former residents of the Soviet Union. However, amendments were introduced to the law in November 2003, which reestablished limited privileges. This is discussed later in the chapter.
65. Initially, refugee status was often acquired by those returnees who had arrived in the Russian Federation without Russian citizenship, but who were entitled to citizenship. With amendments to the forced migrant law in 1995, refugees could then apply for forced migrant status upon receipt of Russian citizenship. The practice ceased completely with the introduction of amendments to the refugee law in 1997 (see also Appendix 1).
66. Codagnone 1998a, p. 25; Voronina 1997, p. 35.
67. Kuznechevskii 1997; Maksimov 1998.
68. Gannushkina 1997a, p. 16; Kamakin 1998a.
69. The nature of regional migration regimes is explored in greater detail in Chapter 4.
70. Airapetova 1997, 1999.
71. Russian 'power ministries' are the thirteen Russian federal institutions including the Ministry of Defence that are in control of their own armed formations or special armed divisions and tend to be led by military personnel rather than by civilians (Renz 2003, p. 7).
72. Heleniak (2002) suggests that giving migration regulation to the Ministry of Internal Affairs is seen by some as a willingness to rely more on 'force' to manage Russia's complex immigration scenario.

73. Popova 2002a.
74. Mukomel' 2002.
75. IOM 2001, p. 10; Renz 2003, p. 10.
76. According to Article 1 of the law 'On Forced Migrants', a 'forced migrant' is an individual who has citizenship of the Russian Federation and who has, or intends to, leave his/her place of residence on the territory of another state or on the territory of the Russian Federation as a result of violence or other form of persecution towards him/herself or members of his/her family, or who is under real threat of being subjected to persecution towards him/herself or members of his/her family, or who is under real threat of being subjected to persecution on the grounds of his/her race, nationality, religion, language, affiliation to a particular social group or political conviction in connection with the conducting of hostile campaigns towards individual groups of individuals, mass violations of public order or other circumstances significantly restricting human rights'.

    Point 3 of Article 2 of the Law on Forced Migrants states that persons who may be refused forced migrant status are those 'leaving their place of residence due to economic causes or owing to hunger, epidemic or extreme situations of a natural or technical character' (*Sobranie zakonodatel'stva Rossiskoi Federatsii* 1995, pp. 9317–27).
77. The first version of the forced migrant law spoke of the obligations of the state authorities, i.e. FMS, towards individuals granted such status. The amended version of the law no longer spoke of obligations, and defined the duty of the FMS as conditional upon its powers, i.e. its resources (Codagnone 1998a, p. 29).
78. Gannushkina 1996a, p. 1; Grafova 1995, p. 10.
79. The new Law on Citizenship stipulates that persons applying for Russian citizenship must have been resident on Russian territory, i.e. have received a document of registration of permanent residence (*vid na zhitel'stvo*), for five years before applying (Article 13, point 1a). Article 13, point 2 details those for whom the period might be reduced for one year. However, there are no concessions for former citizens of the USSR, apart from those born on the territory of the RSFSR. For a full version of the law see *Rossiiskaia gazeta http://www.rg.ru/oficial/doc/federal_zak/62-fz.shtm*, 2003. The amendments to the law, introduced in November 2003 allow those who arrived in Russia before 1 July 2002 to receive citizenship without any residency requirement, if they apply before 1 January 2006. (http://www.izvestia.ru/politic/38911, 25 November 2003).
80. Totskii 1996, p. 38.
81. For a full draft of the Federal Migration Programme 1998–2000, see *Sobranie zakonodatel'stva Rossiiskoi Federatsii*, 1997, No. 47, pp. 9517–76.
82. Kirillova 1998; Shapenko 1997. In the budget for the Federal Migration Programme 1998–2000, only 3 per cent of the expenditure was allocated to working directly with migrants from CIS countries, 65 per cent of this was for loans and the construction of housing for migrants (Maksimov 1998).
83. A differentiated loan system was introduced as a resolution to the forced migrant law in 1997. For a full draft of the resolution on loans see *Migratsiia* 1997, pp. 29–31. The

loan system took into account the socio-economic specifics of a region, where the loan was based upon the average cost of housing. More favourable loan terms were offered in areas where resettlement was desired, whereas in overpopulated regions only a minimal loan was available. For example, in 1997 in Altaiskii *krai*, the Urals, Siberia, Pskov, Leningrad and Novgorod *oblasti* forced migrants could receive a ten-year interest-free loan of up to 70 per cent of the cost of housing, in Central Russia 50 per cent. The lowest loan of 1.5 per cent was offered in Moscow (Gorodetskaia 1997).

84. Memorial 1997, p. 29.

85. Pilkington 1998a, p. 36. Sergei Yagodin, the Department Chief of the Russian Federation Human Rights Commission suggests that 'The philosophy of the law "On Forced Migrants" is profoundly ethical: its basic concept is that if the state is unable to assure normal life for its citizens beyond the boundaries of the RF and if it permits violence or other forms of persecution to be used against them, Russia should bear the costs of their resettlement on its own territory' (IOM 2002a, p. 6).

86. This is in contrast to repatriation programmes that exist for Russian Jews returning to Israel, and ethnic German Russians returning to Germany. Claims have been made, however, that the 1992 Citizenship Law created the conditions for the voluntary 'repatriation' of people who were not claiming forced migrant status (*Migratsiia bedstvie ili blago* 1996, p. 35).

87. Vitkovskaia noted that proving discrimination through the presentation of documents is widely regarded as unrealistic. Even regional leaders of the FMS have admitted that if their employees paid strict attention to this clause, then no-one would receive the status (Vitkovskaia 1999b; and see Kornev 1998).

88. Apart from the case of Tajikistan, and internal to the Russian Federation, from the Chechen Republic, the majority of the movements from the former republics since the mid 1990s have not been from regions where there has been open conflict.

89. Codagnone 1998b, pp. 45, 47.

90. Pilkington 1998a, p. 89.

91. These criticisms were made during a round table 'The Migration Policy of Russia: the Ethnic Context' organized by the Moscow Research Programme on Migration at the International Organization of Migration, which took place on 29 April 2002 (IOM 2002b, p. 22).

92. For an in-depth discussion of the development of a repatriation discourse within the Russian migration regime see Pilkington and Flynn 1999.

93. The role of non-governmental actors in this process, and their agenda, is explored in greater detail in Chapter 5.

94. The negative natural population compensated for by the levels of in-migration from the 'near abroad', was officially recognized as around 3 million, but unofficially as high as 8 million. This is indicated by the figures for the actual total population at the end of 1991 being 148,704,300, and at the end of 1998, 146,693,300, so in real terms over this period the actual decline was only 2 million (*Goskomstat* 1999b, p. 18).

95. Goble 2000. Ethnic Russian migrants from the other former Soviet republics were described by President Putin as a 'godsend' (*http://www.strana.ru*, 2001).

96. Smirnova, Alksins 2000a, 2000b.

97. In March 2003 the deputy leader of the State Duma, Vladimir Lukin (a member of the political party *Yabloko*), initiated the setting up of a working group for the development of a repatriation law, which included a Moscow based NGO – the Forum of Migrant Associations – (for a draft outline of the suggested law 'On Repatriation to the Russian Federation' see *http://www.migrant/ru/cgi-bin/vestnik.pl? issue200305/ article4.shtml*, 2003).

98. Renz 2003, p. 3. This reflects tendencies at a global, and particularly western, level of the increasing 'racialization' of migration, where it is not just migration that is the issue but the question of migrant identity, i.e. who and where they come from (Tesfahuney 1998, p. 505).

99. There is evidence of 'Agreements on Voluntary Resettlement' being entered into by Russia and other CIS countries. It is claimed that under these agreements, over 80,000 people from the Kyrgyz Republic, Latvia and Turkmenia have moved to Russia since 1998. Migration authorities estimated that some 60,000 will resettle in 2001–3 (IOM 2002a, p. 8). However, there is very little information about the implementation of these agreements or the accessibility of the programmes, and no migrants interviewed as part of the present study had any knowledge of such agreements.

100. In Chapter 3, empirical data from migrant interviews shows that the majority of migrants had never considered, or thought about, a move back to Russia until the wider circumstances of their lives in the former republics underwent a significant change. A recent opinion poll demonstrated that only 10 per cent of the population of Russian communities in the post-Soviet states regard Russia as their 'homeland' (Tolz 2001, p. 265).

Chapter 3: Leaving 'Home' and 'Homeland'? The Decision to Migrate

1. The verbs *rodit'*/*rodit'sia* mean to give birth/to be born. This linguistic relationship contrasts with for example the German and English terms *Heimat* (*Heim*) or Homeland (Home), which are not associated linguistically with 'birth' or 'place of birth'. *Rodina* also has no linguistic connection with the Russian word for home – *dom*.

2. In the interests of anonymity, when migrant interviews are cited in the text, respondents are referred to only by the identification number assigned them in the data base of socio-demographic details, the region of their resettlement and the year of interview. See Appendix 3 for a full table of migrant socio-demographic data.

3. *Rod* (family, kin) is also the linguistic root of *rodstvennik* (relation, relative), *rodstvo* (kinship) etc. As is seen through the chapter, in tandem with *rodina* being identified as their 'place of birth', migrants consistently related it to being the place of their kin, both past and future.

4. Verdery 1999, pp. 95–6.

5. Brubaker 1994, p. 68; Payin 1994, p. 22.

6. Castells 1997, p. 39.

7. Pilkington 1998b, p. 98.

8. Melvin 1998, p. 30.

9. Brubaker 1999, p. 4.
10. Fried 1963, p. 153.
11. Massey 1992, p. 12.
12. Fried 1963, p. 154. Parekh (1995, p. 267) notes how identity is closely bound up with the environment. When changes in the environment – the loss of a building, a traditional meeting place – occurs, then individuals may draw back into themselves and become isolated and self-contained.
13. An interesting comparison may be made with a study of meanings of home and homeland in Czech nationalist discourse. Czech respondents found it hard not to talk about homeland and home in terms of each other. 'Home' was the place where they were born, brought up, where they had established their own families, had children. 'Homeland' was the familiar space stretching beyond the boundaries of the immediate 'home' and was where they felt 'at home'. These attachments were prioritized over blood and soil, or common ancestry (Holy 1998, p. 128).
14. Ethnic discomfort has been identified in a number of studies as a key motivating factor for migration, e.g. Gritsenko 1999, p. 41; Lapshova et al. 1996, p. 15; Pilkington 1998a, pp. 134–8; Vitkovskaia 1999a, p. 54.
15. Fried 1963, p. 168.
16. Other research has pointed to concern about the future of children; their education and prospects in influencing the decision to migrate, see for example Gritsenko 1999, p. 41; Lapshova et al. 1996, p. 15; Pilkington 1998a, p. 136; Vitkovskaia 1999a, p. 55.
17. This situation was attributed to the implementation of state language policies that had made the titular language obligatory in schools, the closure of Russian-speaking schools, and the departure of Russian speaking teaching staff.
18. Fried 1963, pp. 156, 168.
19. Hall (1990, p. 231) notes how an identity can suddenly become 'historically available' when he discusses an Afro-Caribbean identity becoming available to Jamaican people. In this case, Africa, and the implications of African identity, have to be confronted by the individual.
20. Gritsenko 1999, p. 43; Lebedeva 1995 cited in Gritzenko 1999, p. 43.
21. Jansen 1998, p. 98.
22. Ibid 1998, pp. 94–6.
23. Brubaker (1994, p. 69), in a discussion of Russian minorities in the other former Soviet republics, notes how potential demands of Russian national minorities for collective public rights and (where plausible) territorial autonomy, shaped by the institutional legacy of the Soviet nationality regime, directly challenge successor state elites' claims to unitary 'ownership' of what they now regard as 'their own' polities and territories. Russians had long thought of the same territory, within the Soviet Union, as 'their own' territory.
24. Cohen 1997, p. 191; Payin in Shlapentokh, Sendich and Payin 1994.
25. Laitin cited in Safran 1999, p. 17.
26. Brubaker 1999.
27. Smith 1999.

28. The suggestion that a strong diasporic identity does not exist at present does not dispute that such an identity could emerge over time. The potential for the gradual development of a 'communal identity' and ultimately a Russian 'diaspora' community is hotly disputed in Russia. Kudriavtsev (1996) claims that it is unlikely that a Russian diaspora will evolve and come to play an important role in the former republics precisely because it lacks any singular ethnicity. Voronin (1994, cited in Kosmarskaia 1998b, p. 76) goes still further, arguing that the shift from a 'colonialist-paternalistic' mentality to that of a 'persecuted minority' will push the Russian 'diaspora', in time, into self-liquidation. However, Kosmarskaia (1998b, p. 76) argues, that while one cannot currently talk of 'a diaspora' as such, the conditions for 'diasporization' are in place and thus Russia currently has a 'proto-diaspora'. This 'emergent' diaspora is seen to differ from 'traditional' historical diasporas – or those forming on the basis of migrant communities in the west – in that it takes a loose, fluid form based on informal friendship, professional or family ties and lacks a mono-ethnic basis. Lebedeva (1997) suggests that if this process were to take place, it might coalesce around a number of key social institutions within the former republics and would act as a positive deterrent to further return migration. However, Kosmarskaia (1998b, p. 76) criticizes this approach for ignoring the specifics of the post-Soviet case, where those individuals who decide to 'stay' are unlikely to be involved in any type of official, socio-cultural organization.

29. The presence of family or friends in Saratov, Samara and Novosibirsk was one of the key factors determining choice of that particular region for settlement. This is explored in greater detail in Chapter 6.

30. The fact that historical, political, social and economic institutional links are present between the former republics and the Russian Federation, and are absent between the FSU space and Western Europe, is seen as a reason for the low levels of migration from the former Soviet republics to Western European destinations (Codagnone 1998a, p. 48). No migrants in the present study mentioned the possibility of moving elsewhere from the former republics; however, a number of migrants spoke of trying to move on to Germany or America due to the unsuccessful experience of resettlement in the Russian Federation.

31. Papastergiadis 1998, p. 171.

32. Ganguly (in Morley 2000, p. 49) in a study of the Indian diaspora, suggests that the past becomes increasingly important for people whose perspective on the present is destabilized as a result of enforced displacement. The stories people tell about their pasts 'have more to do with the continuing shoring up of self-understanding than with historical truths'.

33. Jansen 1998, p. 103.

34. One woman [72, 2002, Novosibirsk] related how she, her husband and friends, also migrants who they had become acquainted with since their move from Kazakstan, would get together in the evenings to watch videos of the countryside of their 'homeland'.

35. Hellberg-Hirn (1999, p. 51) suggests a semantic and etymological affinity of the Russian word *dom* with the Indo-European root, meaning 'to build, construct'. She

identifies *dom*, as a notion central for Russian identity, as one's own kernel space, a protected domestic territory surrounded by secure, sometimes thoroughly sealed boundaries.

36. The discrepancy of the female/male respondent ratio in the present study makes any comprehensive gender analysis problematic. However, it was female migrants alone who stressed that Russia would be a place where, above all, the security of their children might be ensured, and a future *rodina* created. The tendency to prioritize the establishment of family 'roots' in a region was also reflected in the narratives of female migrants concerning why their *rodina* was located in the former republics. Women formed the majority of those who stressed the importance of generations of family having been born, and having died and been buried, in a region. It would seem that female migrants articulate their prioritization of the re-creation of 'home' and a future 'homeland' at the very immediate level of the family. A more equal gender balance was seen when migrants spoke of the importance and experience of a normal 'daily' life – employment, friends, apartments – the continuity of which had generated feelings of 'homeland' in the former republic, and which in Russia would be central to the initial re-creation of a 'home'. See Gritshenko 1999, p. 34; Pilkington 1997, p 123; Vitkovskaia 1995 cited in Pilkington 1998a, p. 122, for a more in-depth discussion of why women might prioritize, or express more vocally, concerns about their children's future.
37. Brah 1996, p. 194.
38. Massey 1992, p. 13.
39. Safran 1991, p. 91.
40. Anderson 1991.
41. Smith 1997, p. 75.
42. Kosmarskaia (1998b) examines the situation of Russians in the Kyrgyz Republic who have chosen not to move back to the Russian Federation.
43. Gupta and Ferguson 1992, p. 11.
44. See Pilkington 1998a, 1998b; Pilkington and Flynn 2001. This is explored in more detail in the following chapters, especially Chapter 6.

Chapter 4: 'Return' and Resettlement: Recognition Within the Russian State
1. Federal Migration Service 1998; *Goskomstat* 2000, p. 115; *Goskomstat* 1998, p. 68. Prior to 2001 *Goskomstat* calculated numbers of forced migrants and refugees according to economic region, of which there were 11. It now calculates numbers according to federal *okrug*, of which there are seven. This is the reason why the figures for economic region are only given to January 2000. The comparative figures in the text for the individual *oblasti* are given with relation to the regions that previously made up the economic regions; i.e. the Volga economic region included: Astrakhan, Volgograd, Penza, Samara, Saratov and Ul'ianovsk *oblasti*, and the republics of Kalmikiia and Tatarstan. The Western Siberian economic region included: Kemerov, Novosibirsk, Omsk, Tomsk, Tiumen *oblasti*, the Altai Republic, and Altai *krai*. Samara and Saratov are situated within the Volga Federal *okrug*, and Novosibirsk is within the Siberian

Federal *okrug*. For the period January 2000–January 2002, the Southern Federal *okrug* received the highest numbers of forced migrants and refugees (22,632), the Central Federal *okrug* received the second highest member (22,621), while the Volga Federal *okrug* and Siberian Federal *okrug* received the third (22,387) and fourth (19,591) highest numbers respectively (*Goskomstat* 2002c).

2. *Samarskii oblastnoi komitet gosudarstvennoi statistiki* 1999, p. 3.

3. Pudina 1999c.

4. Kosygina 2002.

5. The regional migration service in Novosibirsk noted that almost all migrants wish to settle in the city. However, despite the availability of employment, migrants face difficulties finding cheap housing and often have to settle in the district towns and rural regions of the *oblast'* in order to resolve the problem of both housing and employment (Novosbirsk Migration Service, 2002a).

6. High levels of in-migration are identified as a key indicator of the economic well-being and health of a region (Heleniak 1997 cited in Bradshaw and Hanson 1998, p. 291; Shaw 1999, p. 100). In studies of economic change Saratov and Samara *oblasti* have been labelled as 'most favoured regions' (Nefedova and Treyvish 1994 in Shaw 1999, p. 100), and as 'high-tech industrial regions' with the potential for economic revival in conditions of a market economy (Hanson 1995, Bradshaw 1996, cited in Shaw 1999, pp. 113–14). Novosibirsk is classed as a 'gateway and hub region', which has a liberal approach to economic reform and enjoys geographical and infrastructural advantages. However, Novosibirsk city, which has close ties to the defence industry, has suffered from the contraction of the engineering industry (Hanson 1995, Bradshaw, 1996, cited in Shaw 1999, p. 113; Shaw 1999, p. 208).

7. Kamakin 1998a; Kirillova 1998; Shlichkova 1997.

8. Svetlana Soboleva (2002), an economist working on migration issues within Western Siberia, suggests that although a migration 'framework' is set by Moscow, the approach within different regions depends primarily upon the head of the regional administration (the governor), and then the head of the migration service.

9. For example, on the territory of Krasnodar *krai* a regional programme was introduced in 2002 that allowed the eviction of individuals resident in the region who were not officially registered (i.e. who in effect had been prevented from acquiring legal status), and their deportation to other regions. The group that suffered primarily from this programme were the Meskhetian Turk communities resident in the *oblast'* and other migrant groups such as Kurds and Armenians. The programme was applauded by other regions and tolerated by federal migration structures (Petrosian 2002; RFE/RL 2002).

10. Representatives of the migration service justified the practice in logistical terms, claiming the migration service was unable to offer temporary or permanent accommodation and would not register an individual who had no fixed address. However, the service did not offer any help to migrants who had nowhere to register; their only solution was for the migrant to travel on to another region (Samara Migration Service 1998).

11. Gannushkina 1997a, p. 16; Memorial 1997.
12. Many regions across the Russian Federation have used the *propiska* system to regulate movement. The most notable examples are Krasnodar *krai*, Moscow city, Moscow *oblast'* and St Petersburg (Grankina 1996). The assistant head of the FMS department for International Cooperation said that the use of the *propiska*, or as he termed it the system of registration, is not to restrict movement but is rather to obtain a register of the population in the interests of security. He stated that every refugee or forced migrant must hold a document which details that they live at a certain place, but did not suggest how this document can be acquired (Federal Migration Service 1999b).
13. Zhirniagin 1998, p. 70.
14. Drought 2000, p. 165; Vitkovskaia 1998a, p. 27.
15. The implementation of a previous regional migration programme for 1996–8 had been severely affected by a lack of resources.
16. Saratov Migration Service 1999b. In 1995–6 Drought (2000, pp. 183–4) identified a more 'restrictive' attitude on the side of the Saratov regional administration, and the efforts of both the migration service and *Saratov istochnik*, one of the migrant associations, to change this. The present study does not cover the earlier period in detail, but it suggests that growing dialogue between the regional administration, the migration service and non-governmental organizations fostered the more receptive regional administration attitude identified in the later period. However, actions by the regional administration are still the deciding factor. In January 1998 Aiatskov replaced the old director of the TMS (with whom he had a difficult relationship) with a government official he favoured. The decision, originally opposed by the FMS, demonstrated the power the regional administration had over the TMS. Nevertheless, the subsequent increased cooperation between the regional administration and migration service facilitated the more receptive approach. It was in January 1998 that Aiatskov also announced the decision for a new regional migration policy for the *oblast'*.
17. As migrant respondents testified, such a demand ignored the conditions in many of the former republics where citizenship was increasingly difficult to obtain.
18. The practice is not universal throughout the Russian migration service, but representatives of the Saratov TMS claimed they had confirmed it with the Federal Ministry of Justice and that it was in full accordance with the law on forced migrants. They stated that as the law defines who can be a forced migrant as a 'Russian citizen', then a person not holding citizenship at time of application is ineligible (Saratov Migration Service 1999b, 1999c, 1999d). The forced migrant law, however, does not clearly state when or where citizenship must be acquired.
19. The deputy director of the Saratov TMS said that those migrants arriving without citizenship could not have been forced to leave, and as 'illegal migrants' they were the responsibility of the Ministry of Internal Affairs and the passport and visa department, rather than of the migration service (Saratov Migration Service 1999d).

20. The *oblast'* loses migrants to Moscow, Krasnodar *krai*, Rostov *oblast'*, and also other regions of Western Siberia: Omsk *oblast'* and Altai *krai* (Soboleva 1996, p. 129).
21. Gorodestkaia 1997. This had been reduced to 50 per cent by 2002.
22. Kalugina 1996, p. 145.
23. In 2002 a seminar focusing upon migration issues was organized by the Economics Institute of the Novosibirsk branch of the Russian Academy of Sciences, which brought together a wide range of actors including representatives of the regional migration service, the employment service, journalists, local NGOs and academics.
24. A regional migration programme, developed in 1995, suggested the *oblast'* would be able to accept 270,000 migrants, i.e. another 200,000 in addition to the number that have arrived, if adequate resources and financing were made available (Novosibirsk Migration Service 2002a).
25. The director of the Saratov migration service noted that in accordance with established norms an individual employee should deal with 150–200 refugees and forced migrants, in Saratov they are responsible for 2,000 (Pudina 1999b). The reduction in the number of *raion* branches had caused difficulties for migrants wishing to visit the service in Samara *oblast'*. The head of a migrant initiative in Sizran related how she had to leave at three in the morning to be on time for the migration service reception in Samara city. The head of the regional migrant organization *Samarskii pereselents* referred to the difficulties of migrants in the regions accessing the service, and described it as serving urban residents but forgetting those in the regions of the *oblast'*.
26. Fedorova 1999.
27. 23 million roubles were required for the implementation of the Samara programme from the *oblast'* budget and nothing was received. Only 10 per cent of the required federal financing was received (Siprov 1999).
28. Borodkin 1996, p. 113.
29. Novosibirsk Migration Service 2002b. The deputy director of the service attributed the lack of funding to the absence of a federal migration policy, which if it existed would necessitate budgetary attention. As stated in Chapter 2, the Federal Migration Programme was liquidated in June 2001 and excluded from a list of financed programmes.
30. This perception of the arriving migrants was present both in the territorial migration service, and amongst academic commentators.
31. Novosibirsk Migration Service 2002a, 2002b.
32. Of the 20 respondents who had neither forced migrant nor refugee status, seven had been refused status due to their ineligibility; five considered the status unnecessary and had not made an application; four had not known of the migration service; and four had made an application for status and were awaiting a decision. This situation reflects estimates that predict the real numbers of ethnic Russian and Russian-speaking migrants arriving from the former republics to the Russian Federation are up to three times higher than those actually registered, especially taking into account that migrants included in this empirical study were often accessed through

structures such as the migration service and migrant associations, where they were more likely to have, or be in the process of applying for, forced migrant status.

33. This migrant was resident with his family in a village in Saratov *oblast'* where migrants were immediately provided with a house, *propiska* and employment upon arrival. The director of the farm initially claimed he had no knowledge of the district migration service, did not encourage arrivees to register and did not consider the involvement of outside state institutions necessary. Four of the nine respondents interviewed at the village had not received official migrant status.

34. Of the 52 respondents who had received official migrant status from the migration service (forced migrant or refugee), 27 had received a one-time payment of emergency monetary help (Saratov: 8; Samara: 11; Novosibirsk: 8) and seven had received a loan for the acquisition, construction or renovation of housing (Saratov: 6; Samara: 0; Novosibirsk: 1).

35. Similar experiences of bureaucracy, indifference and lack of any concrete help from the migration service were found among migrants in a study conducted in Orel and Ul'ianovsk *oblasti* in 1994/95 (Pilkington 1998a, p. 155).

36. 42 of the respondents held a permanent *propiska*, 24 held a temporary *propiska* and six respondents were not registered at all.

37. The head of a migrant association in Novosibirsk city estimated that the cost of a permanent *propiska* could be as high as 700 US dollars (approximately 21,000 rubles). The average monthly salary in Novosibirsk *oblast'* in 2001, across all spheres of the economy, was 2,658 rubles. (*http://www.nso.ru/pasport/pasport.htm#makro, 2003*).

38. A number of migrants resident in hostel accommodation formed 'action groups' made up of migrant families whose central aim was to negotiate for permanent registration in the hostel where they were living. One of these groups had successfully won their court case, while the other was involved in the process at the time of fieldwork in 1999. In both cases the groups had received advice and support from one of the regional migrant organizations (see Chapter 5).

39. Dick Hebdige notes how in many places the state has long demanded a fixed address in exchange for citizenship rights. Absence of this 'fixed address' then leads to the 'common experience of (the homeless) and the migrant'. . . 'to be made to feel out of place' (in Morley 2000, p. 26).

40. Morley 2000, p. 44.

41. Of the number of registered unemployed in the three regions, forced migrants and refugees made up 0.7 per cent of the total in Samara *oblast'* (up to 31.8.99, Samara Federal Employment Service 1999), 0.9 per cent of the total in Saratov *oblast'* (up to 1.1.99, *Pravitel'stvo Saratovskoi oblasti Ministerstvo truda i sotsial'nogo razvitiia* 1999, p. 10), and, in July 2002, 0.4 per cent of the total in Novosibirsk *oblast'* (Novosibirsk Migration Service 2002a). It is difficult to provide any comprehensive statistics. The TMS did not gather these figures, and the number of unemployed forced migrants and refugees registered with the Employment Service at any one time cannot be compared against the total number of forced migrants and refugees who have

arrived in the *oblasti* over the last decade. Also a large number of forced migrants would not register with the Employment Service due to the meagre unemployment benefit and the lack of help in finding a job. In a study conducted in 1999 unemployment among forced migrants was found to be nearly three times higher than among the Russian population as a whole (Vitkovskaia 1999a, p. 19).

42. The educational and professional levels of the respondents reflect the general characteristics of the returnee population in the three regions of study and the Russian Federation as a whole where the educational levels of migrants and numbers of professional and skilled workers exceeds the average levels of the population in the receiving areas (Vitkovskaia 1998b). The majority of the respondents were either graduates (22 individuals) or had secondary specialist education (45 individuals), and had occupied positions in the professional, skilled sector (including teachers, doctors, engineers, technicians, accountants). Of the 72 migrants interviewed, 62 were of working age and ten were pensioners (see Appendix 3 for socio-demographic breakdown).

43. A study by Vitkovskaia (1999a, p. 25) shows that only 40 per cent of employed forced migrants were employed in the same branch as they had been before moving; there was a drop of those engaged in industry and science, especially in villages, and a rise in those employed in agriculture and trade. These tendencies reflect the wider characteristic of de-skilling across the post-Soviet labour market where there has been a move of professional personnel into the informal trading and service sector, and workers have been forced to accept a drop in professional status in order to secure employment (Pilkington 1998a, p. 144).

44. Previous urban/rural status was not included as a question when gathering socio-demographic data. However, the majority of respondents stated either the capital city of the former republic or another large city as the place they had left. A small number of migrants who had been resident in rural areas had arrived from Kazakstan.

45. Research conducted in Novosibirsk shows a lower percentage of migrants employed in rural areas as compared with urban areas (12.7 per cent as compared with 7.4 per cent). However, the study makes the point that migrants in rural areas improve their situation through personal subsistence farming (Novosibirsk Migration Service 2002a). Other research has shown that unemployment levels are higher amongst migrants resident in rural areas and that de-skilling is more likely due to the move from mental and industrial labour to manual, agricultural employment (Pilkington 1998a, p. 144; Vitkovskaia 1998b, p. 8, 1999a, p. 25).

46. The migrants resident in rural areas and without employment were all female. Research points to the gendered nature of unemployment and de-skilling in both urban and rural areas. In rural areas it is particularly difficult for women to find work commensurable with their previous professions. For a detailed discussion of the gendered nature of migrant unemployment see Pilkington 1998a pp. 145–8; Vitkovskaia 1998b, p. 8.

47. Filippova 1997, p. 54; Pilkington 1998a, p. 144; Vitkovsaia 1998b, pp. 6, 10.

48. Pilkington 1998a, p. 144; Vitkovskaia 1999a, p. 23.

49. See Appendix 2 for a description of the different sites of urban and rural resettlement at which the migrant respondents were resident.

50. One female migrant whom the author met on a number of occasions in Saratov *oblast'* over the period 1996–9 had eventually acquired an apartment where all her family members were resident and declared that this represented the beginning of a new period of their life in the region. In a survey conducted in 1997–8 across five regions of Russia, 22 per cent of respondents had their own houses and 71 per cent their own (privatized) apartments before moving, whilst in Russia only 15 per cent of respondents were able to acquire their own housing (Vitkovskaia 1999a, p. 33).

51. This is part of a Soviet legacy of massive underdevelopment of infrastructure, services and transport in rural areas.

52. Research has shown that the availability of housing is one of the prime motivations for migrants in choosing to settle in rural areas (Drought 2000, p. 134; Pilkington 1998a, p. 151; Vitkovskaia 1999a, p. 36).

53. Similar cases have been identified in other regions. Migrants are frequently buying back housing they have built themselves, and the fact that housing is conditional upon continued employment on a farm or rural enterprise means that even if the migrants are dissatisfied with their work, they are unable to seek employment elsewhere (Pilkington 1998a, p. 152; Vitkovskaia 1998b, p. 8, 1999a, p. 29).

54. The size of the loan varied according to the region. In both Saratov and Samara *oblasti* in 1999 the regional coefficient was 0.5, i.e. 50 per cent of the amount of the total average of the cost of housing was provided. In Novosibirsk *oblast'* in 1997, the regional coefficient was 0.7, i.e. 70 per cent of the total cost of housing. This was reduced to 50 per cent by 2002. However, the 'average' cost of housing obviously fluctuated both within a region and over time, and often the loan amount proved insufficient for securing suitable accommodation. The migrants were critical of the perceived bureaucracy, length of process and the meagre amount of the loan, and the need for a large amount of documentation, for two people willing to act as guarantors in the new region of settlement and for applicants' salaries to be of a sufficient level in order to qualify for a loan. Both the directors of the migration services in Samara and Saratov *oblasti* spoke of the need to increase the size of the loans being awarded (Samara Migration Service 1999b; Saratov Migration Service 1999b).

55. Vitkovskaia suggests that there had been a shift in migrant attitudes from seeing the state as the solution to their housing problems to taking responsibility themselves, primarily through the acquisition of employment. However, the low salaries prevent the strategy from working. Pay received by migrants in Russia was found to be on average more than 35 per cent less than that received by the local population, especially in villages (Vitkovskaia 1999a, p. 27). The situation is exacerbated by the difficulties in selling accommodation in the former republic. In the present study where migrants had been able to sell, the gap in prices between the former republic and the Russian Federation meant the money they brought with them was insufficient to purchase any housing. The money was often used for the transportation of themselves and their belongings.

56. Research conducted in Novosibirsk *oblast'* has shown that the policy of the regional migration service to encourage migrants to settle in rural areas has proved unsuitable both to the needs of the region and the migrants themselves whose prior lifestyle, skills and qualifications are more suited to urban life. The local administrations in rural areas where migrant resettlement has taken place have proved unprepared to cope with the arrival of migrants and are unable to provide housing and employment (Kalugina 1996, pp. 151, 155). The policy also ignores the urban concentration of industry, population and accompanying infrastructure in the *oblast'* and the lack of significant rural development and social infrastructure to facilitate resettlement.
57. Humphrey 1996, pp. 70, 73.
58. Ibid, p. 71.

Chapter 5: The Developing Non-governmental Sector
1. The permanent staff (paid and voluntary) of all the organizations varied from three to nine individuals. Chapter 6 looks at perceptions amongst migrants who might have visited organizations on a number of occasions, may have become involved to some extent in their work, or alternatively who had never heard of or were not interested in the organizations.
2. UNHCR 1995, p. 24.
3. Open Society Institute 1998a, p. 4. The Open Society Institute's programme 'Forced Migration Projects' concentrated on issues of forced migration and displacement in the post-Soviet space. At the end of 1999, the programme was suddenly curtailed due to 'strategic consolidation' within the OSI (*http://www.soros.org/fmp2/html/ july1999.html, 2001*).
4. Mikheev 1996.
5. Grafova 1995; Schwarz 1995 in Pilkington 1998a, p. 82.
6. The debate around the impact of western funding bodies and development aid is not engaged with in detail in the book. For a more in-depth discussion of the issue see: Bruno 1998; Hemment 1999; Kay 2000; Thomson 2001.
7. *Migratsiia* 1996, p. 35; Silvestri 1997, p. 7.
8. *Migratsiia* 1996, p. 35.
9. Salova 2002.
10. IOM 1997, pp. 18–21.
11. Between 1993 and November 1997 representatives of the IOM had visited over 150 resettlement sites, of which over 100 were assisted to the amount of approximately 1,000,000 US dollars, (IOM 1997, p. 20).
12. McClain 1999.
13. Other international organizations active in the Russian Federation are Caritas (the International Confederation of Catholic Organizations of Church Charity and Social Help) and the International Red Cross. Caritas acts through the Russian branch of the organization that was set up in Moscow in 1992. The organization has a permanent reception and drop-in centre at the Moscow migration service where it

provides additional social support and emergency material help for both forced migrants from the FSU and refugees from the far abroad. A regional delegation of the International Red Cross opened in Moscow in 1992. The organization has been heavily involved in providing humanitarian assistance to displaced persons particularly in Chechnia, Ingushetia and Northern Ossetia.

14. Helton 1996, p. 53.
15. *Migratsiia* 1996, p. 35.
16. Codagnone 1998a, p. 32; Gannuskina 1999; Vitkovskaia 1999b.
17. UNHCR/IOM 2000, p. 24.
18. Mukomel' and Payin 1997, p. 7; Open Society Institute 1998b, p. 7.
19. Airapetova 1999b.
20. Airapetova 1998; Sanikidze 1998. Sanikidze was the former deputy director of the IOM mission in Moscow, Airapetova is a journalist who has repeatedly written on migration issues for the Russian newspaper *Nezavisimaia gazeta*.
21. Particular criticism was made of associations insisting on the organization of seminars and conferences. It was felt that the resources would be better used for housing construction and direct assistance to migrants (Gannushkina 1999; Sanikadze 1998).
22. The POA called for the 'establishment of civil society in the CIS'. As an independent expert observed, 'this would take more than an inter-governmental process and longer than five years to achieve' (UNHCR/IOM 2000, p. 28).
23. These criticisms have resonance with other studies that have looked at the effect of western funding and the operation of western organizations in the 'development' of post-Soviet Russia. See especially Bruno 1998; Kay 2000, pp. 187–209.
24. The Chief of the IOM Mission in Moscow admitted that there was a problem in gaining true information about what was going on (McClain 1999). Gannushkina (1999) noted the mutual disappointment of both the west and Russia over how cooperation in the field of migration had developed, identifying the problem as one of different perceptions of priorities.
25. UNHCR/IOM 2000, p. 23.
26. FMS 1999b.
27. Kamakin 1998b; Shuikin 1999.
28. For detailed profiles of the federal level non-governmental organizations see Appendix 4.
29. Stephenson (2000) provides a detailed breakdown of the post-Soviet Russian voluntary sector. Two of the 'types' of NGOs she identifies are those rooted in the ex-dissident movement (such as *Memorial* discussed below) that primarily champion human rights, and the NGO sphere which has developed in recent years to care for the most underprivileged, including migrants and refugees. Professionals (teachers, doctors, lawyers etc.), who are able to make an independent living and/or use the resources of western foundations, have created these organizations. The organizations have become a driving force in the voluntary sector working mainly in 'opposition' to the state through lobbying and directing resources to the most needy. Stephenson is critical, however, of the predominantly paternalistic approach that is adopted by

the organizations, which impedes self-organization or the development of self-help initiatives.

30. Codagnone 1998a, p. 31.

31. Grafova 1999.

32. The member associations of the Forum now number more than 198 in 50 regions of Russia, together with three organizations located in the former republics of Uzbekistan, Kazakstan, and Tajikistan (*http://www.migrant.ru/forum/*, 2003).

33. Lidiia Grafova is a member of the Governmental Commission on Affairs of Compatriots Abroad, and together with Svetlana Gannushkina, of the Governmental Commission on Migration Policy. They have also worked with the Parliamentary Committee on CIS Affairs and Relations with Compatriots and in its Sub-committee on Refugee and Forced Migrant Affairs.

34. Initial amendments to both the forced migrant and refugee law were presented to the State Duma in the summer of 1994. Both documents were condemned for being 'anti-refugee' which led to the formation of the Parliamentary Commission 'On Refugees and Forced Migrant Affairs' which included parliamentary deputies and representatives of the FMS, the presidential apparatus, Federation Council, international organizations and Russian NGOs (Pilkington 1998a, p. 54; *Memorial* 1997, p. 8). The discussions led to a thorough reworking of the amendments to the law on forced migrants, which were adopted by the State Duma on 22 November 1995 (see Chapter 2). A new refugee law came into force on 11 June 1997.

35. For more information of the inclusion of the CCARFM and CAC in the earlier repatriation debate see Pilkington and Flynn 1999, p. 179–180.

36. Gannuskina 2002; *http://www.migrant.ru/cgi-bin/vestnik.pl?issue200305/article2 shtml*, 2003. In early 2003, in collaboration with the vice-speaker of the State Duma Vladimir Lukin, the Forum created a working group for the development of a repatriation law.

37. Gannushkina 1999.

38. Ibid.

39. *http://new.migrant.ru/cgi-bin/vestnik.pl?issue2003/article2.shtml*, 2003. Vitkovskaia noted that with the move of the migration service to the MVD, coordination with NGOs would be more difficult due to the 'closed' nature of the organization, and the fact that cooperation with civil society and NGOs necessitates a 'considerable degree of transparency' – such cooperation had just begun to develop in the final period of FMS existence (IOM 2001, pp. 11–12).

40. Filippov 1998.

41. Other studies of NGO activity have noted how competition for grant aid can be divisive and can distort the priorities of voluntary groups (Kay 2000, pp. 202–5; Stephenson 2000, p. 289 and see below).

42. Airapetova 1998.

43. Grafova 1999; Vitkovskaia 1999b. Grafova questioned the political purpose of this council, and claimed that the Communist Party had approached associations within the Forum and made 'empty promises' in order to attract their support.

44. Pilkington 1998a, p. 78.
45. Edwin McClain (1999) attributed the more cooperative relationship to the better understanding on the side of the FMS of the role of NGOs in society, their relationship to the government and their role in migrant provision.
46. In September 1999 a representative of the Fund stated that its work at compact settlement sites was on hold due to no resources being received from either the state, or from international donors (Compatriots Fund 1999).
47. Compatriots Fund 1999.
48. See Appendix 4 for detailed profiles of each of the regional migrant organizations.
49. There were no other associations in the two urban centres of Samara and Saratov. Interviews were conducted with an organization in the urban centre of Engels', situated across the Volga river from Saratov, but it was not looked at in detail. An organization operating in Novosibirsk city, that had been set up to help 'environmental' migrants from the Semipalatinsk region of Kazakstan, was also interviewed. In the regions of the *oblasti* a number of more commercially based organizations, or organizations centred on compact settlement sites, were visited during fieldwork periods.
50. The empirical data that are directly quoted in this chapter are taken from interviews conducted by the author with representatives of the regional migrant organizations. The date and place of interview are given after the quote in brackets. Permission was received to use the interview data in written publications. However, for ethical reasons the decision was made to use directly quoted data in the text sparingly and as far as possible with anonymity.
51. The lawyers employed by *Vozvrashchenie*, the *Komitet bezhentsev iz Chechnii*, and *Samarskii pereselenets* were part of the network of legal consultation points set up by CAC and *Memorial*. The lawyer working at *Ruka pomoshchi* was also part of the network, but at the time of the fieldwork in 2002, the location of the consultation point at the organization was on a trial basis.
52. See for example Kay 2000; Hemment 1999; Henry 2001.
53. Pudina 1999a.
54. Pudina 1999c.
55. Saratov Migration Service 1999b; Saratov Migration Service 1999c.
56. Samara Migration Service 1998.
57. *Samarskii pereselenets* 1999.
58. *Samarskii pereselenets* 2002.
59. *Ruka pomoshchi* 2002.
60. Novosibirsk Migration Service 2002a.
61. In 1999, the then head of the FMS department for Migration Policy and Data Analysis noted the more effective relationship existing between the FMS and NGO sphere and stated that responsibilities and resources for certain tasks could be handed over to the NGO organizations. However, she stressed the need for this to be established on a legal, contractual basis to ensure that responsibilities were adequately and professionally fulfilled (Federal Migration Service 1999a). As yet, in Russia NGOs rarely

receive government funding. Laws are being proposed by the NGO sector to allow 'social contracting out' where the state would commission 'welfare' projects from NGOs (Stephenson 2000, p. 289). However, this idea has been under discussion since 1995 and, as yet, there has been no clear legislative outcome at the federal level (Kay 2000, p. 250).

62. *Vozvrashchenie* 1999.
63. Samara Migration Service 1999c; *Samarskii pereselenets* 1999.
64. *Materiali mezhdunarodnogo seminara* 1999, p. 6.
65. A seminar (organized in February 2002 by the Economics Institutute of the Novosibirsk branch of the Russian Academy of Sciences and funded by the Open Society Institute) brought together a wide range of participants from different spheres. However, in this instance, *Ruka pomoshchi* was not invited to participate.
66. It has been suggested that the Russian migrants could become a source of nationalist support (Brubaker 1995, p. 213), or a willing target of nationalist or communist groups due to their possible marginal position within Russian society. As yet, this has not proved to be a reality. The migrant organizations in this study themselves chose what political factions to approach and lobby.
67. All of the three regional administrations were tolerant of non-governmental activity. The Saratov regional administration consciously supported non-governmental activity and coordination with state structures. A 'Social Partnership Agreement' and the Council of Social Organizations under the *oblast'* Duma were aimed at facilitating state/non-state relations. In Samara *oblast'* there was a tradition of non-governmental activity in the *oblast'*, and a liberal attitude to their registration, evidenced by the large number of non-governmental social organizations. The number of registered 'social' organizations in 1999 was 2,000. However, including unregistered organizations this number could have been as high as 4,500 (*Povol'zhe* 1999). The Governor of Novosibirsk *oblast'*, Viktor Tolokonsk, is the representative of the Siberian branch of the independent organization *Grazhdanskoe obshchestvo* (Civil Society) and declares one of his chief aims to be the strengthening of civil society in the *oblast'*. The participation of social organizations is seen as central to the preparation for a long-term programme for the development of the *oblast'* to the year 2008 (*http://www3.adm.nso.ru/ru/gov/glava/*, 2003).
68. *Povol'zhe*, formed in 1991, became a registered resource centre in 1995 to facilitate the development of a strong regional NGO sector. It offers help with resources, including computers and other technical equipment, and provides opportunities for computer, legal, secretarial and fundraising training. These activities are funded with the help of Western organizations, primarily US Aid, the Eurasia Foundation and the BEARR Trust (UK).
69. *Povol'zhe* 1999.
70. In 1999, these 'official' social organizations numbered 25. They received funding from the *oblast'* budget to fulfil certain tasks. This can be seen as a regional level example of the 'social contracting out' which is being discussed at a federal level (see note 61).

71. *Komitet* 1999.

72. Stephenson (2000, p. 291) suggests that international aid needs to be directed at the running costs of Russian organizations, and not just to particular projects. If organizations are unable to cover these costs, then they are likely to vanish or experience great difficulties in fulfilling their role. An example of this is the start-up grants previously offered by UNHCR, which had been received by *Komitet bezhentsev iz Chechnii* and *Samarskii pereselents*.

73. A lack of state funding is not universal across the NGO sector in Russia. Health promotion NGOs in the area of drugs prevention are able to acquire local state sources of funding. In general, however, their work is very closely associated with the state, or they are in fact quasi-state organizations (Richardson 2001). Stephenson (2000, p. 277) suggests that in post-Soviet Russia dependency upon government funding can significantly undermine the capacity of the voluntary sector to put forward alternative ideas and be an equal partner of the state. However, Kay and Bridger (2003) provide the example of a male crisis centre in Barnaul', Altai *krai*, which has received financial support from the regional administration, but has retained its independence and has proved very successful. State financial support is often assumed to make the organization/initiative quasi-state, but as indicated, this is not always the case.

74. *Saratovskii istochnik* had received financial assistance from certain migrant organizations in return for its support, and its financial position was alleviated slightly by its 'joint role' as a commercial association. Both the *Komitet bezhentsev iz Chechnii* and *Ruka pomoshchi* actively sought business sponsorship for small-scale activities, but their success had been limited.

75. Kay 2000, pp. 190, 194.

76. Kay 2000, pp. 202–3.

77. Nevertheless, a representative of the association noted that even though they had received accreditation from UNHCR, they still found it hard to gain recognition at the regional level (*Samarskii pereselenets* 2002).

78. Kay (2000, pp. 191, 194) notes the tendency of donor organizations to allocate repeat funding to either individuals who have had experience of running projects, or to the same areas which have already been established as 'useful'. Representatives of IOM and UNHCR stressed the importance of already knowing a region, and having established connections and a positive working relationship with the regional administrations and regional migration services. The Saratov migration service had received technical equipment from IOM and UNHCR as part of their federal-wide programme for the institutional development of migration structures, but neither the Samara nor Novosibirsk migration service had received any assistance.

79. Richardson 2001.

80. All the migrant associations, except for *Ruka pomoshchi*, were national members of the 'Forum of Migrant Associations'. *Saratovskii istochnik* had previously been a member of the Forum's Executive Committee, but later became a member of the alternative 'Council of Migrant Associations' under the State Duma.

Chapter 6: Depending on 'Selves': Family, Friendship and Migrant Networks

1. Alapuro 2001; Ledeneva 1998; Lonkila 1999a, 1999b; Piipponen 2001; Piirainen 1997; Rose 1999, 2000; Salmi 2001.
2. Burawoy and Verdery 1999, p. 1.
3. Alapuro and Lonkila 1999, p. 118; Burawoy and Verdery 1999, pp. 1, 3; Hann 1996, p. 14. Burawoy and Verdery prefer the use of the term 'transformation' to 'transition', as rather than suggesting a unilinear process leading to a predicted future, 'transformation' implies a process having multiple trajectories with unintended and unpredicted consequences.
4. Alapuro 2001, p. 24; Burawoy and Verdery 1999, p. 2; Habermas 1987 in Burawoy and Verdery 1999, p. 2.
5. It has proved difficult to adequately translate the term *blat* from Russian. The meaning of the term, when spoken, is 'understood'. In the introduction to her study Ledeneva (1998, p. 1) defines *blat* as 'the use of personal networks and informal contacts to obtain goods and services in short supply and to find a way around formal procedures'.
6. Other significant studies of the use of networks during the Soviet period include Srubar's (1991) work on 'redistribution networks' and Stoyanov's (1992) work on 'social capital' (cited in Lonkila 1999a, pp. 2–6).
7. Ledeneva 1998, p. 175.
8. Alapuro 2001, Lonkila 1999a and 1999b, and Patico 2001, focus on the behaviour and practices of teachers in St Petersburg. Salmi 2001 looks at the health sector and how personal networks are still relevant due to continued scarcity and distrust within the health service. White 2001 considers the use of networks as part of her study of the gendered nature of survival strategies of the local intelligentsia in small-town Russia.
9. Salmi 2001; White 2001. Many authors address the historical context of networks and ask if the present-day dissociation from the state and the reliance on networks rooted in a distrust of the state is inherited from the Soviet era and a tradition of relying on 'selves'? (Ledeneva 1998, p. 85; Piirainen 1997, p. 71).
10. Alapuro and Lonkila 1999, p. 121; Lonkila 1999a, p. 25; Lonkila 1999b, p. 105; Piirainen 1997, pp. 92, 140.
11. Lonkila 1999b, p. 106–8; Patico 2001; Piipponen 2001.
12. Lonkila 1999b, p. 99; Salmi 2001.
13. Ledeneva (1998, pp. 121, 123) defines horizontal ties between people of similar social status or vertical ties between people from different social strata within networks. In the process of network formation Lonkila (1999a, pp. 69–70, 156), drawing on the ideas of Granovetter (1973), suggests that strong ties exist within a 'core' group of family members or friends. However, weak ties which extend beyond this immediate network are essential as they act as bridges to information not available within the immediate network and unite diverse networks.
14. Alapuro 1997 cited in Lonkila 1999a, p. 21; Lonkila 1999b, p. 105.
15. Alapuro 2001, p. 24; Alapuro and Lonkila 1999, p. 135; Piipponen 2001.
16. Boyd 1989, p. 639; Gurak and Caces 1992, p. 160.

17. Boyd 1989, p. 661.
18. Gurak and Caces 1992, p. 152.
19. As described in Chapter 1, the term 'migration system' incorporates the migratory flows of individual migrants, regional, federal and international government institutions and legislative structures, and national and international level organizations and NGOs in the sending and receiving societies, operating within the wider economic, social and political environment.
20. Van Hear 1998, p. 59.
21. Gurak and Caces 1992, p. 163.
22. Boyd 1989, pp. 642, 645.
23. Boyd 1989, p. 639; Gurak and Caces 1992, p. 160. The development and activity of the more formal migrant associations in the three regions of study is described in detail in Chapter 5.
24. Gurak and Caces 1992, p. 161.
25. Criticisms have been made of the household and social network approaches. The models are inclined to idealize the notions of household/family and community as homogenous and all-inclusive. The choice of the household tends to replace the idea of a rational individual with that of a rational household making calculated decisions, and ignores the presence of individual interest. Feminist critiques have accused the approach of 'gender blindness' as it tends to assume that the male head of the household represents the collective interest (Boyd 1989, p. 654; Goss and Lindquist 1995, pp. 327–8). In the same way the networks approach has been criticized for its reproduction of the individual at the group level and a lack of analysis of the actual constitution and boundaries of networks (Goss and Lindquist 1995, p. 330; Snowdon 1990, p. 578).
26. Gurak and Caces 1992, p. 155; Pohjola 1991, p. 439.
27. Zaslavsky 1994, pp. 139–40.
28. Humphrey 1996, pp. 75, 79.
29. Burawoy and Verdery 1999, p. 2.
30. Other factors that were influential in the choice of the region of settlement included the geographical location of the *oblast'* in relation to the region of departure (including direct transport links connecting the two regions), knowledge of possible sources of assistance in the *oblast'*, climatic conditions in the *oblast'*, and the socio-economic conditions existing in the region of arrival. When migrants spoke of other factors influencing the choice of region they were often mentioned in the context of the absence of family or friends in Russia; but in terms of their potential relationship to something from their past, a similar climate, environment, the possibility of employment.
31. See Appendix 3 for a detailed breakdown of the family status of respondents. A significant proportion of migrant respondents were widowed (10), divorced or separated (11) or single (7). However, migration still primarily took place with other family members, e.g. children, sisters, brothers, parents and grandparents.
32. 40 respondents named family links, and 13 friendship links, as the deciding factor.

The importance of the presence of family, friends or acquaintances in the region of settlement is reflected in other studies, both of the resettlement of ethnic Russian and Russian-speaking migrants in the Russian Federation, and in other studies of migrant 'return', where they are identified as a key factor in the attraction to a particular region (Glytsos 1995, p. 162; Hunt 1992, p. 563; Lapshova et al. 1996, p. 7; Pilkington 1998a, p. 125; Vitkovskaia 1999a, p. 55).

33. Only three of the respondents, however, were returning to their region of birth; in all cases this was Samara *oblast'*.

34. A study of migrant resettlement in Orel and Ul'ianovsk *oblasti* identified this tendency, where the presences of family, friends and acquaintances were seen by migrants as networks which would help in the acquisition of residence rights, housing and employment (Pilkington 1998a, p. 125).

35. It was noted in conversations with returnees over the period of empirical study (1997–2002) that the difficulty of bringing family members still resident in the other former republics to Russia was gradually increasing. This was primarily due to the financial difficulties of funding the move, exacerbated by the problems in selling property in the former republics, and the large differential in property prices between the other former republics and Russia. In addition, respondents in Novosibirsk mentioned that the problems of gaining citizenship, specifically since the introduction of the new law in May 2002, were proving to be an impediment to bringing other family members to Russia.

36. The terms 'friend' (*drug/podruga*) and 'acquaintance' (*znakomii*) are used distinctly by the respondents. Friend is used to describe someone who is close and with whom a personal relationship is shared, whereas acquaintance indicates a more distant, businesslike relationship. Respondents were very clear about the difference, and in some cases described the process whereby previous 'acquaintances' had become 'friends'. These levels of attachment reflect well the structure of different networks that have been identified to exist in communist societies: firstly, family and close and trusted friends with whom people socialized and spent free time, and secondly more distant acquaintances with whom people interacted often for the purpose of acquiring something. The two groups overlapped in that friends and family also offered help and services; however, acquaintances were excluded from being part of the closer network (Morjé Howard 2003, p. 28).

37. See Appendix 2 for a full description of the different forms of migrant resettlement in Saratov, Samara and Novosibirsk *oblasti*.

38. The author's research did not address the question of the reception of migrants by the local community, in that interviews were not conducted with representatives of the local population apart from expert interviews with official representatives of mainly state institutions. The findings therefore are based upon migrants' perceptions of the issue, and from ethnographic observation conducted by the author. Other studies of migrant resettlement in the Russian Federation have addressed the question of the reception of migrants amongst the receiver community in more depth (Filippova 1997; Kosmarskaia 1998a; Pilkington 1998a).

39. A study of the 'return' migration of ethnic Greeks to Macedonia demonstrated the generation of similar 'reactive' expressions of 'superiority' due to competition between the returnees and locals for resources (Voutira 1997, p. 120). Other research amongst forced migrant communities in Russia has revealed feelings of 'superiority' vis à vis the local Russian population in the spheres of education, employment and culture, related to how the returnees saw themselves as representatives of the 'brightest and the best' sent out on a mission to raise the cultural and economic levels of the Soviet republics. Upon 'return' this sense of self leads to the expressions of superiority, and disappointment with the local environment and local Russians (Pilkington 1998a, pp. 168–71).

40. This quote is interesting in its use of phrases, i.e. 'people here', 'those people', 'they didn't do that', 'we were gentle, good people'. A division is made between 'us' [we] and 'them' [they] in the former republic, but both are distinguished from 'people here' in Russia. The sentence, however, ends with a common 'we' in the past tense to describe the community 'there' in the former republic.

41. Glytos 1995; Voutira 1997, p. 119–20.

42. Although the security in the quotes implies a positive identification with being a Russian in Russia, respondents rarely articulated this directly. Rather it was the absence of discrimination for being Russian that was implied. Only three respondents directly attributed their 'home' (but not *rodina*) as being in Russia, due to them being Russian. These respondents were all male.

43. Gupta and Ferguson 1992, p. 11.

44. Glytsos 1995, p. 162; Hunt 1992, p. 563.

45. Fried 1963, p. 160. Although the majority of the migrants in the study were contained within some form of family unit, the study acknowledges that insufficient empirical attention was given to the precise nature of the relations (e.g. gender, generational), which existed within the family unit.

46. Castells (1997, p. 41, 1998, p. 68) observes how the post-Soviet environment of widespread socio-economic and political collapse and the weakening of the state has forced dependence upon primary networks and individual survival strategies and has heightened identification at the family level.

47. Goss and Lindquist 1995, p. 330; Snowdon 1990, p. 578.

48. Grafova et al. 1995, p. 3.

49. In Samara *oblast'* during 1998–9, no financial support had been received for the creation of 100 work places at sites of compact settlement envisaged in the Federal Migration Programme (Samara Migration Service 1999c).

50. Gannushkina 1999; Vitkovskaia 1999b.

51. From 1999 state policy offered continued support to existing settlements, however, the formation of new settlements was not encouraged and individual resettlement was prioritized (Federal Migration Service 1999a).

52. See Appendix 2 for a full description of the three compact settlements focused upon in the research.

53. A migrant organization was set up at this compact settlement as a regional filial of

the central migrant organization *Samarskii pereselenets* based in the city of Samara in the summer of 1999 (see Chapter 5).

54. Such divisions and emerging conflicts over time were seen at all the sites of settlement. For example, on an initial visit to the settlement in Samara *oblast* in 1999, the group of migrants appeared to be united. However on a return visit in 2002, due to the worsening situation with employment and accommodation at the site and the lack of any outside help, the group had split and relations between different groups of migrants had worsened.

55. The term *rossianie* refers to citizens of Russia, i.e. a civic rather than ethnic Russian identity.

56. This 'mistrust' could be related to previous experiences of social organizations. Morjé Howard (2003, pp. 26–7), in his study of 'civil society' in post-Communist societies, attributes a lack of participation and suspicion of new social organizations as a legacy of the communist period, where citizens were often forced to join formal mass organizations. In the present day period, he suggests that a certain mistrust of social organizations continues, and citizens, now free to choose whether or not to join, decide not to do so.

57. Voutira (1997, pp. 120–21) in her study of ethnic Greek 'returnees' in Macedonia, has shown how migrant associations and collectives can help with integration, and facilitate the creation of a sense of self-identity and security in the new environment.

Chapter 7: Conclusion: Reconstructing Immediate 'Homes' and Future 'Homelands'

1. Morley 2000, p. 48.
2. Nagel 2001, p. 253.
3. Faist 2000, p. 200; Glick Schiller *et al.* in Kivisto 2001, p. 551.
4. Nagel (2002, p. 981) warns against tendencies in studies of transnationalism to underestimate the desire amongst immigrants to 'be included in the mainstream' at the site of settlement, Vertovec (1999, p. 456) stresses the need to pay attention to everyday changes in people's lives, while Kivisto (2001, p. 571) argues that with time the concerns of the site of settlement will come to dominate as issues from the 'homeland' become more removed.
5. Hall 1990, p. 225. Vertovec (2001, p. 578) addresses the effect of living in social worlds stretched between two or more nation-states and suggests, with reference to Ulf Hannerz (1996), that people's 'experiences gathered in these multiple habitats accumulate to comprise people's cultural repertoires, which in turn influence the construction of identity – or indeed multiple identities'.
6. Heleniak 2002.
7. Ibid 2002.
8. Stark 1992, p. 300.
9. Burawory and Verdery 1999, p. 6.
10. Katherine Verdery (in Hann 2002, p. 20) in a suggested possible comparison of postcolonial and post-socialist theory, highlights the importance for anthropologists of

incorporating the understandings of people who have less privileged positions in their societies than, for example, intellectuals.

11. Stark 1992, p. 301.

12. Burawoy and Verdery 1999, p. 2.

13. However, the revocation of the agreement on dual citizenship between Turkmenistan and the Russian Federation in April 2003, and the effect this had upon the Russian communities, led to significant political and public response within the Russian Federation.

14. Heleniak 2002.

15. Nagel 2002; Tesfahuney 1998.

16. Tesfahuney 1998, pp. 509–10.

17. Mukomel' 2002; Renz 2003, p. 14.

18. Heleniak 2002.

19. Advocates of increased support for the immigration of the Russian communities come from both democratic centrist and leftist political factions. For example, Grigorii Yavlinskii, a member of Yabloko, Anatolii Chekhoev, a member of the Communist Party of the Russian Federation and Egor Gaidar of the Union of Right Forces (SPS), have all spoken out against the restrictive nature of the 2002 citizenship law and the need to encourage in-migration of the Russian communities (*http:// db.ngo.ru/info.nsf/MigrantIndex/NT00004A56*, 2003; Renz 2003) while Vladimir Lukin, also a member of Yabloko, is central to the plan to develop a repatriation law (see Chapter 2).

20. In December 2002 President Putin declared that Russia should attempt to attract immigrants from the former Soviet republics whose population often had the 'same mentality, the same cultural and often religious roots' as Russians and were also Russian-speaking (UNHCR 2002). On a visit to Kazakstan in 2003 the President called the Russian 'diaspora' a 'golden/precious fund' (*zolotoi fond*) (Grafova 2003).

21. The resources allocated to migrant resettlement in the federal budget in 2003 were four times less than those allocated in 2002 (*http://db.ngo/ru/info.nsf/MigrantIndex/NT00004A56*, 2003).

22. Kosmarskaia has conducted ethnographic research into the migratory intentions of Russian communities still resident in the Kyrgyz Republic (1998b). Other useful studies of the Russian communities have tended to be located at the more macro-level, and have addressed the ethnic, socio-economic, political and demographic characteristics of the Russian communities, their identification with their country of residence, their political significance for the Russian state and the possible significance and likelihood of their 'return' to the Russian Federation (for example Barrington 2001; Chinn and Kaiser 1996; Kolstoe 1995; Melvin 1998; Poppe and Hagendoorn 2001, 2003; Smith 1999; Shlapentokh et al. 1994).

23. Heleniak (2002) shows how researchers found that in order for Russia to maintain the same population size as in 1995, there would have to be a net migration of 24.9 million in the first half of the twenty-first century. For the size of the working-age population to remain the same, there would have to be a net migration of 38.5

million. To meet even the lower figure, the entire Russian diaspora (ethnic Russians and Russian-speaking populations) in the other former Soviet republics would have to return, with an average annual influx of between 500,000 and 810,000. The net migration for 2001 was only 72,000.

24. The perception of 'illegal' migration as a threat to the stability and security of the Russian nation, its economy and society is widespread in both media and political discourse and cannot be attributed to particular political groupings.

Appendix 1: Limitations of Statistics Concerning Forced Migrants and Refugees

1. Federal Migration Service 1998; *Goskomstat Rossii* 1998, p. 68; *Goskomstat Rossii* 2000, p. 113.
2. Vitkovskaia 1998a, p. 11.
3. Codagnone 1998a, p. 27.
4. IOM 1999, p. 188; Vitkovskaia 1998a, p. 14.
5. IOM 1999, p. 188.
6. Vitkovskaia 1998a, p. 13.
7. Ibid, p. 14.

Appendix 4: Profiles of Federal Non-governmental Organizations and Regional Migrant Organizations

1. Gannushkina 1997b.
2. *Memorial* 1997a, pp. 4–5.
3. *http://www.migrant.ru/index.php/news/*, 2000.
4. Drought 2000, p. 97; Heradstveit 1993, p. 55; Pilkington 1998a, pp. 78–9.
5. Tishkov 1996, p. 219.
6. *Materialy mezhdunarodnogo seminara* 1999, pp. 26–7.

Bibliography

ENGLISH LANGUAGE SOURCES

Aasland, A, 1996, 'Russians Outside Russia: the New Russian Diaspora' in Smith, G, (ed.), *The Nationalities Question in the post-Soviet States*, London and New York, Longman, pp. 477–97.

Abdulatipov, R, 1994, 'Russian Minorities: the Political Dimension', in Shlapentokh, V, Sendich, M, and Payin, E, (eds), *The New Russian Diaspora : Russian Minorities in the Former Soviet Republics*, Armonk, New York, London, M.E. Sharpe, pp. 37–44.

Alapuro, R, 2001, 'Reflections on Social Networks and Collective Action in Russia' in Webber, S, and Liikanen, I, (eds), *Education and Civic Culture in Post-Communist Countries*, Hampshire, New York, Palgrave, pp. 13–27.

—— and Lonkila, M, 1999, 'Networks, Identity and (In)Action: A comparison between Russian and Finnish Teachers' in Lonkila, M, *Social Networks in Post-Soviet Russia. Continuity and Change in the Everyday Life of St. Petersburg Teachers*, Helsinki, Kikimora Publications, pp. 117–37.

Al-Ali, N, Black, R, and Koser, K, 2001, 'Refugees and Transnationalism: the Experience of Bosnians and Eritreans in Europe', *Journal of Ethnic and Migration Studies*, Vol. 27, No. 4, pp. 615–34.

Anderson, B, 1991, *Imagined Communities*, London, Verso.

Barrington, L, 2001, 'Russian-Speakers in Ukraine and Kazakstan: "Nationality", "Population", or Neither?', *Post-Soviet Affairs*, Vol. 17, No. 2, pp 129–58.

Beissinger, M, 1995, 'The Persisting Ambiguity of Empire', *Post-Soviet Affairs*, Vol. 11, No. 2, pp. 149–84.

Berg, B, 1998, *Qualitative Research Methods for the Social Sciences*, Boston, Allyn and Bacon.

Boyd, M, 1989, 'Family and Personal Networks In International Migration: Recent Developments and New Agendas', *International Migration Review*, Vol. 23, No. 3, pp. 639–69.

Bradshaw, M, and Hanson, P, 1998, 'Understanding Regional Patterns of Economic Change in Russia: An Introduction', *Communist Economies and Economic Transformation*, Vol. 10, No. 3, pp. 285–304.

Brah, A, 1996, *Cartographies of Diaspora, Contesting Identities*, London and New York, Routledge.

Bremmer, I, 1994, 'The Politics of Ethnicity: Russians in the New Ukraine', *Europe-Asia Studies*, Vol. 46, No. 2, pp. 261–83.

Brubaker, R, 1994, 'Nationhood and the National Question in the Soviet Union and Post-Soviet Eurasia: An institutionalist account', *Theory and Society*, Vol. 23, pp. 47–78.

—— 1995, 'Aftermaths of Empire and the Unmixing of Peoples: Historical and Comparative Perspectives', *Ethnic and Racial Studies*, Vol. 18, No. 2, pp. 189–218.

—— 1998, 'Migrations of Ethnic Unmixing in the "New Europe"', *International Migration Review*, Vol. 32, No. 4, pp. 1047–65.

—— 1999, *Accidental Diasporas and External 'Homelands' in Central and Eastern Europe: Past and Present*, Unpublished conference paper presented to the International Conference on Diaspora, Transnational Identities and the Politics of the Homeland, University of California at Berkeley.

Bruno, M, 1998, 'Playing the Co-operation game. Strategies Around International Aid in Post-Socialist Russia', in Bridger, S, and Pine, F, (eds), *Surviving Post-Socialism: Local Strategies and Regional Responses in Eastern Europe and the FSU*, London and New York, Routledge, pp. 170–87.

Burawoy, M, Burton, A, Ferguson, A, Fox, K, Gamson, J, Gartrell, N, Hurst, L, Kirzman, C, Salzinger, L, Schiffman, J, and Shiori, U, 1991, *Ethnography Unbound. Power and Resistance in the Modern Metropolis*, Berkeley and Oxford, University of California Press.

Burawoy, M, and Verdery, K (eds), 1999, *Uncertain Transition. Ethnographies of Change in the Postsocialist World*, Lanham and Oxford, Rowman and Littlefield Publishers Inc.

Castells, M, 1997, *The Power of Identity*, Malden and Oxford, Blackwell Publishers.

—— 1998, *End of Millennium*, Malden and Oxford, Blackwell Publishers.

Castles, S, and Miller, M, 1998, *The Age of Migration*, Basingstoke and London, Macmillan Press Ltd.

Chinn, J, and Kaiser, R, 1996, *Russians as the New Minority: Ethnicity and Nationalism in the Soviet Successor States*, Boulder and Oxford, Westview Press.

Clifford, J, 1994, 'Diasporas', *Cultural Anthropology*, Vol. 9, No. 3, pp. 302–38.

—— 1998, *The Predicament of Culture: Twentieth-Century Ethnography, Literature, and Art*, Cambridge, Mass., Harvard University Press.

Codagnone, C, 1998a, 'New Migration and Migration Politics in post-Soviet Russia', *CEMES Ethnobarometer Working Paper*, No. 2.

—— 1998b, 'The New Migration in Russia in the 1990s', in Koser, K, and Lutz, H, (eds), *The New Migration in Europe*, Basingstoke and London, Macmillan Press Ltd., pp. 39–59.

Cohen, R, 1997, *Global Diasporas: An Introduction*, London, UCL Press.

Dixon, S, 1996, 'The Russians and the Russian Question', in Smith, G, (ed.), *The Nationalities Question in the post-Soviet States*, London and New York, Longman, pp. 47–74.

Drought, B, 2000, *Resettlement in the Russian Federation: a Case Study of Refugees and Forced Migrants from Tadzhikistan*, PhD thesis, Swansea, University of Wales.

Dunlop, J, 1993a, 'Will a Large-Scale Migration of Russians to the Russian Republic Take Place Over the Current Decade', *International Migration Review*, Vol. 27, No. 3, pp. 605–29.

—— 1993b, 'Russia: Confronting a Loss of Empire', in Bremmer, I, and Taras, R, (eds), *Nations and Politics in the Soviet Successor States*, Cambridge, CUP.

Dunn, E, and Hann, C, (eds), 1996, *Civil Society: Challenging Western Models*, London and New York, Routledge.

Escalona, A, and Black, R, 1995, 'Refugees in Western Europe: Bibliographic Review and State of the Art', *Journal of Refugee Studies*, Vol. 8, No. 4, pp. 364–89.

Faist, T, 2000, 'Transnationalization in International Migration: Implications for the Study of Citizenship and Culture', *Ethnic and Racial Studies*, Vol. 23, No. 2, pp. 189–222.

Flynn, M, 2001, *Global Frameworks, Local Realities: Migrant Resettlement in the Russian Federation*, PhD thesis, Birmingham, University of Birmingham.

Fried, M, 1963, 'Grieving for a Lost Home', in Duhl, L, (ed.), *The Urban Condition*, New York and London, Basic Books Inc., pp. 151–71.

Giddens, A, 1984, *The Constitution of Society*, Cambridge, Polity Press.

Glytsos, N, 1995, 'Problems and Policies Regarding the Socio-economic Integration of Returnees and Foreign Workers in Greece', *International Migration*, Vol. 33, pp. 155–73.

Goble, P, 2000, 'Compounding a Demographic Disaster', *RFE/RL Newsline*, Part 1, 20 November.

Goss, J, and Lindquist, B, 1995, 'Conceptualising International Labor Migration: A Structuration Perspective', *International Migration Review*, Vol. 29, No. 2, pp. 317–51.

Grafova, L, Fillipova, E, and Lebedeva, N, 1995, *Compact Settlements of Forced Migrants on the Territory of Russia*, Moscow, Open Society Institute.

Gupta, A, and Ferguson, J, 1992, 'Space, Identity and the Politics of Difference', *Cultural Anthropology*, Vol. 7, No. 1, pp. 6–23.

Gurak, D, and Caces, F, 1992, 'Migration Networks and the Shaping of Migration Systems', in Kritz, M, Lin Lean, L, and Zlotnik, H, (eds), *International Migration Systems A Global Approach*, Oxford, Clarendon Press, pp. 150–76.

Hall, S, 1990, 'Cultural Identity and Diaspora' in Rutherford, J, (ed.), *Identity, Community, Culture, Difference*, London, Lawrence and Wishart, pp. 222–37.

Hann, C, 1996, 'Political society and anthropology' in Dunn, E, and Hann, C, (eds), *Civil Society: Challenging Western Models*, London and New York, Routledge.

—— (ed.), 2002, *Postsocialism: Ideals, Ideologies and Practices in Eurasia*, London, Routledge.

Held, D, McGrew, A, Goldblatt, D, and Perraton, J, 1999, *Global Transformations*, Cambridge, Polity Press.

Heleniak, T, 1999, *The End of an Empire: Migration and the Changing Nationality Composition of the Soviet Successor States*, Unpublished paper presented at the 'Diasporas and Ethnic Migrants in 20th Century Europe', International Conference, Humboldt-Universitat, Berlin.

Heleniak, T, 2002, 'Migration Dilemmas Haunt Post-Soviet Russia', *Migration Information Source*, Migration Policy Institute, October 2002.

Hellbery-Hirn, A, 1999, 'Ambivalent Space: Expressions of Russian Identity', in Smith, J, (ed.), *Beyond the Limits: The Concept of Space in Russian History and Culture*, Helsinki, Suomen Historiallinen Seura.

Helton, A, 1996, 'Lost Opportunities at the CIS Migration Conference', *Transition*, 28 June, pp. 52–4.

Hemment, J, 1999, *Russia's Democratization Industry: Civil Society and the Manufacture of the Third Sector*, Unpublished conference paper presented at the CREES Annual Conference, Windsor.

Henry, L, 2001, 'The Greening of Grassroots Democracy? The Russian Environmental Movement, Foreign Aid and Democratization', *Berkeley Program in Soviet and Post-Soviet Studies Working Paper Series*, Berkeley, University of California.

Heradstveit, D, 1993, *Ethnic Conflicts and Refugees in the Former Soviet Union*, Norwegian Refugee Council Report No. 3.

Holy, L, 1998, 'The Metaphor of "Home" in Czech Nationalist Discourse', in Rapport, N, and Dawson, A, (eds), *Migrants of Identity, Perceptions of Home in a World of Movement*, Oxford and New York, Berg, pp. 111–37.

Hosking, G, 2002, *Russia and the Russians from Earliest Times to 2001*, London, Penguin.

Humphrey, C, 1996, 'Myth-Making, Narratives, and the Dispossessed in Russia', *Cambridge Anthropology*, Vol. 19, No. 2, pp. 70–91.

Hunt, J, 1992, 'The Impact of the 1962 Repatriates from Algeria on the French Labour Market', *Industrial and Labour Relations Review*, Vol. 45, No. 3, pp. 556–72.

International Organization of Migration, 1997, *UNHCCR-IOM Joint Fact-Finding Donor Mission – Russia October 30-November 4 1997*, Moscow, IOM.

—— 1999, *Migration in the CIS 1997–98*, Geneva, IOM.

—— 2001, 'Russia's Migration Policy: Two Views, Two Contexts', *IOM Open Forum Information Series*, Issue 2, September/October.

—— 2002a, 'Management of Migration in the CIS Countries', *IOM Open Forum Information Series*, Issue 3, January.

—— 2002b, 'Immigration Policy of Russia: the Ethnic Context', *IOM Open Forum Information Series*, Issue 5, August.

Jansen, S, 1998, 'Homeless at Home: Narrations of Post-Yugoslav Identities', in Rapport, N, and Dawson, A, (eds), *Migrants of Identity. Perceptions of Home in a World of Movement*, Oxford and New York, Berg, pp. 85–109.

Joy, D, 1995, 'Reception and Settlement Policies: A Comparative Study', in Dello Donne, M, (ed.), *Avenues to Integration: Refugees in Contemporary Europe*, University of Rome, Iper Medium Divisione Editoria, pp. 6–24.

Kay, R, 2000, *Russian Women and their Organizations: Gender, Discrimination and Grassroots Women's Organizations*, Basingstoke and London, Macmillan Press Ltd.

—— and Bridger, S, 2003, 'The Altai Regional Crisis Centre for Men: Supporting Single Fathers in Western Siberia', Unpublished paper presented at the West Coast Seminar Series, University of Glasgow.

King, C, and Melvin, N, 1998, *Nations Abroad: Diaspora Politics and International Relations in the Former Soviet Union*, Boulder, Westview Press.

King, C, and Melvin, N, 2000, 'Diaspora Politics, Ethnic Linkages, Foreign Policy and Security in Eurasia', *International Security*, Vol. 24, No. 3, pp. 109–38.

King, R, (ed.), 1995, *Mass Migration in Europe*, Chichester and New York, John Wiley and Sons, pp. 234–58.

Kivisto, P, 2001, 'Theorising Transnational Immigration: A Critical Review of Current Efforts', *Ethnic and Racial Studies*, Vol. 24, No. 4, pp. 549–77.

Kolstø, P, 1995, *Russians in the Former Soviet Republics*, London, Hurst and Company.

—— 1996, 'The New Russian Diaspora: An Identity of its Own?', *Ethnic and Racial Studies*, Vol. 29, No. 3, pp. 609–39.

Koser, K, 1993, 'Repatriation and Information: A Theoretical Model', in Black, R, and Robinson, V, (eds), *Geography and Refugees Patterns and Processes of Change*, London and New York, Belhaven Press, pp. 171–84.

—— and Lutz, H, (eds), 1998, *The New Migration in Europe, Social Constructions and Social Realities*, Basingstoke and London, Macmillan Press Ltd.

—— 1998, 'The New Migration in Europe: Contexts, Constructions and Realities' in Koser, K, and Lutz, H, (eds), *The New Migration in Europe, Social Constructions and Social Realities*, Basingstoke and London, Macmillan Press Ltd, pp. 1–17.

Laitin, D, 1998, *Identity Formation: The Russian-Speaking Populations in the Near Abroad*, Ithaca, Cornell University Press.

Lawson, V, 2000, 'Arguments within Geographies of Movement: The Theoretical Potential of Migrants' Stories', *Progress in Human Geography*, Vol. 24, No. 2, pp. 173–89.

Layder, D, 1994, *Understanding Social Theory*, London, Sage Publications.

—— 1997, *Modern Social Theory*, London, UCL Press.

Ledeneva, A, 1998, *Russia's Economy of Favours*, Cambridge, Cambridge University Press.

Levita, R, and Loiberg, M, 1994, 'The Empire and the Russians', in Shlapentokh, V, Sendich, M, and Payin, E, (eds), *The New Russian Diaspora : Russian Minorities in the Former Soviet Republics*, New York and London, M.E. Sharpe, pp. 3–20.

Lonkila, M, 1999a, *Social Networks in Post-Soviet Russia. Continuity and Change in the Everyday Life of St. Petersburg Teachers*, Helsinki, Kikimora Publications.

—— 1999b, 'Post-Soviet Russia: A Society of Networks', in *Russia: More Different than Most*, Helsinki, Kikimora Publications, pp. 99–112.

Malkki, L, 1992, 'National Geographic: The Rooting of Peoples and the Territorialization of National Identity Among Scholars and Refugees', *Cultural Anthropology*, Vol. 7, No. 1, pp. 24–44.

—— 1995, *Purity and Exile. Violence, Memory and National Cosmology among Hutu Refugees in Tanzania*, Chicago and London, University of Chicago Press.

Massey, D, 1992, 'A Place Called Home?', *New Formations*, No. 17, pp. 3–15.

May, T, 1996, *Situating Social Theory*, Buckingham, Philadelphia, Open University Press.

McClain, E, 1999, Chief of Mission, IOM, Interview conducted by the author, 15 July, Moscow.

McHugh, K, 2000, 'Inside, Outside, Upside Down, Backward, Forward, Round and Round: A Case for Ethnographic Studies in Migration', *Progress in Human Geography*, 24, 1, pp. 71–89.

McRobbie, A, 1982, 'The Politics of Feminist Research: Between Talk, Text and Action', *Feminist Review*, No. 12, October, pp. 46–57.

Melvin, N, 1994, *'Forging the New Russian Nation*, Discussion Paper 50, London, Royal Institute of International Affairs.

—— 1995, *Russians Beyond Russia's Borders*, London, Pinter/Royal Institute of International Affairs.

—— 1998, 'The Russians: Diaspora and the End of Empire', in King, C, and Melvin, N, (eds), *Nations Abroad : Diaspora Politics and International Relations in the Former Soviet Union*, Boulder, Colorado, Oxford, Westview Press, pp. 27–57.

Messina, C, 1994, 'From Migrants to Refugees: Russian, Soviet and Post-Soviet Migration', *International Journal of Refugee Law*, Vol. 6, No. 4, pp. 620–35.

Meznaric, S, 1995, 'Refugees and Displaced Persons in Croatia', in Dello Donne, M. (ed.), *Avenues to Integration: Refugees in Contemporary Europe*, University of Rome, Iper Medium Divisione Editoria, pp. 206–20.

Mitchneck, B, and Plane, D, 1995, 'Migration Patterns During a Period of Political and Economic Shocks in the Former Soviet Union; A Case Study of Yaroslavl' Oblast', *Professional Geographer*, Vol. 47, No. 1, pp. 17–23.

Morjé Howard, M, 2002, *The Weakness of Civil Society in Post-Communist Europe*, Cambridge, Cambridge University Press.

Morley, D, 2000, *Home Territories. Media, Mobility and Identity*, London and New York, Routledge.

—— and Robins, K, 1993, 'No Place like Heimat: Images of Home(land) in European Culture', in Carter, E, Donald, J, and Squires, J, (eds), *Space and Place, Theories of Identity and Location*, London, Lawrence and Wishart, pp. 3–31.

Nagel, C, 2001, 'Nations Unbound? Migration, Culture and the Limits of the Transnationalism-Diaspora Narrative', *Political Geography*, Vol. 20, No. 2, pp. 247–56.

—— 2002, 'Geopolitics by Another Name: Immigration and the Politics of Assimilation', *Political Geography*, Vol. 21, No. 8, pp. 971–97.

Oberg, S, and Boubnova, H, 1995, 'Ethnicity, Nationality and Migration Potentials in Eastern Europe', in King, R, (ed.), *Mass Migration in Europe*, Chichester and New York, John Wiley and Sons, pp. 234–58.

Open Society Institute, 1998a, *Forced Migration Monitor*, No. 23.

—— 1998b, *Coping with Conflict, A Guide to the Work of Local NGOs in the North Caucasus*, New York, The Forced Migration Projects of the Open Society Institute.

Papastergiadis, N, 1998, *Dialogues in the Diasporas: Essays and Conversations on Cultural Identity*, London, Rivers Oram.

—— 2000, *The Turbulence of Migration*, Cambridge, Polity Press.

Parekh, B, 1995, 'The Concept of National Identity', *New Community*, Vol. 22, No. 2, pp. 255–68.

Patico, J, 2001, 'Raskol'nikov is my Sponsor; or, Exchange Relations and Confrontations with Inequality in Post-Soviet St. Petersburg', Unpublished conference paper presented at the BASEES Annual Conference, Cambridge.

Payin, E, 1994, 'The Disintegration of the Empire and the Fate of the 'Imperial Minority'', in Shlapentokh, V, Sendich, M, and Payin, E, (eds), *The New Russian Diaspora : Russian Minorities in the Former Soviet Republics*, New York and London, M.E. Sharpe, pp. 21–36.

Phizacklea, A, 1996, *Structure and Agency: Conceptualising Forced Migration in the Former Soviet Union*, Unpublished paper produced for INTAS seminar on Post-Soviet Migration and Inter-Ethnic Tension, Moscow.

Piipponen, M, 2001, 'Local Formation of Community and Informal Social Networks', Unpublished conference paper presented at the BASEES Annual Conference, Cambridge.

Piirainen, T, 1997, *Towards a New Social Order in Russia*, Aldershot, Vermont, Dartmouth.

Pilkington, H, 1997, 'For the Sake of the Children: Gender and Migration in the Former Soviet Union', in Buckley M, (ed.), *Post-Soviet Women: from the Baltic to Central Asia*, Cambridge, Cambridge University Press, pp. 119–40.

—— 1998a, *Migration, Displacement and Identity in post-Soviet Russia*, London and New York, Routledge.

—— 1998b, 'Going Home? The Implications of Forced Migration for National Identity Formation in post-Soviet Russia', in Koser, K, and Lutz, H, (eds), *The New Migration in Europe, Social Constructions and Social Realities*, Basingstoke and London, Macmillan Press Ltd, pp. 85–108.

—— and Flynn, M, 1999, 'From "Refugee" to "Repatriate": Russian Repatriation Discourse in the Making', in Black, R, and Koser, K, (eds), *The End of the Refugee Cycle*, Oxford and New York, Berghahn Books, pp. 171–97.

Pohjola, A, 1991, 'Social Networks – Help or Hindrance to the Migrant?', *International Migration*, Vol. 29, No. 3, pp. 435–44.

Poppe, E, and Hagendoorn, L, 2001, 'Types of Identification among Russians in the 'Near Abroad', *Europe-Asia Studies*, Vol. 53, No. 1, pp. 57–71.

—— 2003, 'Titular Identification of Russians in the Former Soviet Republics', *Europe-Asia Studies*, Vol. 55, No. 5, July, pp. 771–88.

Portes, A, Guarnizo, L, and Landolt, P, 1999, 'The Study of Transnationalism: Pitfalls and Promise of an Emergent Research Field', *Ethnic and Racial Studies*, Vol. 22, No. 2, pp. 217–37.

Rapport, N, and Dawson, A, 1998, (eds), *Migrants of Identity, Perceptions of Home in a World of Movement*, Oxford and New York, Berg.

Renz, B, 2003, '*Regulating the Migration Process in Contemporary Russia: Securitization or Normalization*', Unpublished conference paper presented at the BASEES Annual Conference, Cambridge.

RFE/RL Newsline, 2001a, 'Eight Million Immigrants from Former Republics in Decade', Part 1, 5 January.

—— 2001b, 'Moscow Less Interested in CIS, More in Ethnic Russians', Part 1, 12 February.

—— 2003a, 'Protocol Ending Turkmen-Russian Dual Citizenship Published', Part 1, 18 April.

RFE/RL Newsline, 2003b, 'Russian Citizens Can Get Turkmen Residence Permits, Says Ombudsman', Part 1, 15 July.

RFE/RL (UN) Civil Societies, 2002, 'Kalingrad Senator Proffers Krasnodar as Model for Immigration Policy', Vol 3, No. 20, 15 May.

Richardson, E, 2001, 'Health Promotion and the "Third Sector" in Russia', Unpublished conference paper presented at the BASEES Annual Conference, Cambridge.

Richmond, A, 1988, 'Sociological Theories of International Migration: The Case of Refugees', *Current Sociology*, Vol. 36, No. 2, pp. 7–25.

—— 1993, 'Reactive Migration: Sociological Perspectives on Refugee Movements', *Journal of Refugee Studies*, Vol. 6, No. 1, pp. 7–24.

Robertson, L, 1996, 'The Ethnic Composition of Migration in the Former Soviet Union', *Post-Soviet Geography and Economics*, Vol. 37, No. 2, pp. 113–28.

Rose, R, 1999, 'Getting Things Done in an Antimodern Society: Social Capital Networks in Russia', in Dasgupta, P, and Serageldin, I, (eds), *Social Capital: A Multi-faceted Perspective*, Washington, D.C., World Bank, pp. 147–71.

—— 2000, 'Use of Social Capital in Russia: Modern, Pre-Modern and Anti-Modern', *Post-Soviet Affairs*, Vol. 16, No. 1, 2000, pp. 33–57.

Rowland, R, 1993, 'Regional Migration in the Former Soviet Union During the 1980s: The Resurgence of European Regions', in King, R, (ed.), *The New Geography of European Migrations*, London, New York, Belhaven Press, pp. 152–74.

Safran, W, 1991, 'Diasporas in Modern Societies: Myths of Homeland and Return', *Diaspora*, Vol. 5, No. 1, pp. 83–99.

—— 1999, 'Describing and Analyzing Diaspora: An Attempt at Conceptual Cleansing', Unpublished conference paper presented at the International Conference on Diaspora, Transnational Identities and the Politics of the Homeland, University of California at Berkeley.

Salmi, A, 2001, 'Health Through Networks? Teachers, Doctors and Informal Exchange', Unpublished conference paper presented at the BASEES Annual Conference, Cambridge.

Salova, O, 2002, Department for Cooperation with Social Organizations, UNHCR, Interview conducted by the author, Moscow, 5 July 2002.

Schwartz, L, 1993, 'Realignment of Territory and Nationalities: The Potential for Russian In-Migration', *Post-Soviet Geography*, Vol. 34, No. 1, pp. 38–46.

Schwarz, T, 1997, 'Post-Soviet Migration and Ethno-Political Tension: Conceptualizing the Interaction', Unpublished paper produced for INTAS seminar on Post-Soviet Migration and Inter-Ethnic Tension, Birmingham.

Shaw, D, 1999, *Russia in the Modern World, a New Geography*, Oxford, Blackwell Publishers.

Shlapentokh, V, Sendich, M, and Payin, E, (eds), 1994, *The New Russian Diaspora : Russian Minorities in the Former Soviet Republics*, Armonk and London, M.E. Sharpe.

Smith, G, 1997, 'The Russian Diaspora: Identity, Citizenship and Homeland', in Bradshaw, M, (ed.), *Geography and Transition in the Post-Soviet Republics*, Chichester, John Wiley and Sons, pp. 75–88.

Smith, G, 1999, 'Transnational Politics and the Politics of the Russian Diaspora', *Ethnic and Racial Studies*, Vol. 22, No. 3, May, pp. 500–523.

Snowdon, L, 1990, 'Collective versus Mass Behaviour; A Conceptual Framework for Temporary and Permanent Migration in Western Europe and the United States', *International Migration Review*, Vol. 24, No. 3, pp. 577–90.

Sokolova, V, 2000, 'Russia Decides to Give its Fellow Countrymen Some Financial Help', *Current Digest of the Post-Soviet Press*, Vol. 52, No. 43, p. 18.

Stark, D, 1992, 'The Great Transformation? Social Change in Eastern Europe', *Contemporary Sociology*, Vol. 21, No. 3, pp. 299–304.

Stephenson, S, 2000, 'Civil Society and its Agents in the Post-Communist World: The Case of the Russian Voluntary Sector', in Dean, H., Sykes, R. and Woods, R. (eds), *Social Policy Review*, No. 12, pp. 272–94.

Stepputat, F, 1994, 'Repatriation and the Politics of Space: the Case of the Mayan Diaspora and Return Movement', *Journal of Refugee Studies*, Vol. 7, No. 2/3, pp. 175–85.

Suhrke, A, 1995, 'Analysing the Causes of Contemporary Refugee Flows', in Van der Erf, R, and Heering, L, (eds), *Causes of International Migration*, Luxembourg, Luxembourg Office for Official Publications of the European Communities, pp. 201–21.

Suny, R, 1995, 'Ambiguous Categories: States, Empires and Nations', *Post-Soviet Affairs*, Vol. 11, No. 2, pp. 185–96.

Tesfahuney, M, 1998, 'Mobility, Racism and Geopolitics', *Political Geography*, Vol. 17, No. 5, pp. 499–515.

Thomson, K, 2001, *Services for People with Learning Difficulties in the Russian Federation. A Case-Study Approach to the Development of a Post-Communist Welfare System*, PhD thesis, Birmingham, University of Birmingham.

Tolz, V, 2001, *Inventing the Nation: Russia*, London, Arnold.

Tuan, Y, 1996, *Cosmos and Hearth, a Cosmopolite's Viewpoint*, Minneapolis, London, University of Minnesota Press.

Tucker, K, 1998, *Anthony Giddens and Modern Social Theory*, London, Sage.

UNHCR, 1995, *The State of the World's Refugees*, Oxford, Oxford University Press.

—— 2002, 'Russian Immigration Quotas to be Increased in 2003 – Official', *UNHCR World News*, 20 December.

UNHCR/IOM, 2000, *Assessment Report of the Conference Process 1996–2000*, Geneva, UNHCR Centre for Documentation and Research.

Van Hear, N, 1998, *New Diasporas. The Mass Exodus, Dispersal and Regrouping of Migrant Communities*, London, University College of London Press.

Verdery, K, 1999, *The Political Lives of Dead Bodies, Reburial and Postsocialist Change*, New York, Columbia University Press.

Vertovec, S, 1999, 'Conceiving and Researching Transnationalism', *Ethnic and Racial Studies*, Vol. 22, No. 2, p. 447–62.

—— 2001, 'Transnationalism and Identity', *Journal of Ethnic and Migration Studies*, Vol. 27, No. 4, pp. 573–82.

Vishnevskii, A, and Zaionchkovskaia, Z, 1994, 'Emigration from the Former Soviet Union: The Fourth Wave', in Fassmann, H, and Munz, R, (eds), *European Migration in the Late Twentieth Century: Historical Patterns, Actual Trends and Social Implications*, Aldershot, Hants, Edward Elgar Publishing, pp. 239–59.

Vitkovskaia, G, 1998a, *Resettlement of 'Refugees' and 'Forced Migrants' in the Russian Federation*, Geneva, International Organization of Migration.

—— 1998b, 'Hope of Russia', *Migration*, Vol. 2, pp. 5–10.

—— 1999a, *Adaptation and Integration of Forced Migrants in Russia: Efficiency of Various Ways of Settlement*, Moscow, International Organization of Migration.

—— 2002, 'Forced Migration and Migrantophobia in Russia', Unpublished paper presented at workshop Understanding Xenophobia in Eastern Europe, June 21–22, Central European University, Budapest.

Voutira, E, 1997, 'Population Transfers and Resettlement Policies in Inter-war Europe: The Case of Asia Minor refugees in Macedonia from an International and National Perspective', in Mackridge, P, and Yannakakis, E, (eds), *Ourselves and Others: the Development of a Greek Macedonian Cultural Identity Since 1912*, Oxford, New York, Berg, pp. 111–31.

Wahlbeck, O, 2002, 'The Concept of Diaspora as an Analytical Tool in the Study of Refugee Communities', *Journal of Ethnic and Migration Studies*, Vol, 28, No. 2, pp. 221–38.

White, A, 2001, *Women's Survival Strategies in Small-town Russia*, Unpublished paper presented at the CREES Women's Seminar, University of Birmingham.

Wright, C, 1995, 'Gender Awareness in Migration Theory: Synthesizing Actor and Structure in Southern Africa', *Development and Change*, Vol. 26, pp. 771–91.

Zaionchkovskaia, Z, Kocharian, A, and Vitkovskaia, G, 1993, 'Forced Migration and Ethnic Processes in the Former Soviet Union', in Black, R, and Robinson, V, (eds), *Geography and Refugees: Patterns and Processes of Change*, London and New York, Belhaven Press.

Zaslavsky, V, 1994, *The Neo-Stalinist State*, Armonk, New York, M.E. Sharpe.

Zevelev, I, 1996, 'Russia and the Russian Diasporas', *Post-Soviet Affairs*, Vol. 12, No. 3, pp. 265–84.

—— 2001, *Russia and its New Diasporas*, Washington D.C., United States Institute of Peace Press.

Zolberg, A, 1989, 'The Next Waves: Migration Theory for a Changing World', *International Migration Review*, Vol. 23, No. 3, pp. 403–30.

RUSSIAN LANGUAGE SOURCES

Airapetova, N, 1997, 'Migratsionnoi politiki v RF vse eshche net – pretenzii na takoviiu, zaiavliaemie rukovodstvom FMS, predstavliaiutsia maloobosnovannimi', *Nezavisimaia gazeta*, 26 December, p. 3.

—— 1998, 'Kto poedet v Zhenevu?', *Nezavisimaia gazeta*, 6 October, p. 8.

—— 1999a, 'Likvidatsiia FMS vygodna rukovodstve sluzhbi, i vlasti v Rossii dve bedi – beskontrol'nost, i beznakasannost', *Nezavisimaia gazeta*, 23 January, p. 5.

—— 1999b, 'FMS – eto gosudarstvennaia sostavliaiushchaia', *Nezavisimaia gazeta*, 24 June, pp. 1, 5.

Borodkin, F, 1996, 'Novoe velikoe pereselenie narodov – faktor v regional'noi sotsial'noi situatsii', *Oblast' – ekonomika i sotsiologiia*, 1, pp. 100–121.

Compatriots Fund, 1999, Interview conducted by the author with a representative of the Fund, 9 September, Moscow.

Federal Migration Service, 1998, Statistics, Unpublished data.

—— 1999a, Interview conducted by the author with the head of the FMS department for Migration Policy and Data Analysis, 24 September, Moscow.

—— 1999b, Interview conducted by the author with the assistant head of the FMS department for International Cooperation, 23 September, Moscow.

Federal'nii zakon, 1999, 'O gosudarstvennoi politike Rossiiskoi Federatsii v otnoshenii sootechestvennikov za rubezhom', Unpublished document, 5 March.

Fedorova, T, 1999, 'Bezhentsi khotiat normal'no zhit', *Samarskaia gazeta*, 24 June, p. 3.

Filippov, V, 1998, 'Otvergnut'ie gosudarstvom migranty stanoviatsia novoi politicheskoi siloi', *Izvestiia*, 2 September, p. 4.

Filippova, E, 1997, 'Adaptatsiia russkikh vynuzhdennikh migrantov iz novogo zarubezh'ia', in Tishkov, V, (ed.), *Vynuzhdennie migranty: Integratsiia i vozvrashchenie*, Moskva, Institut etnologii i antropologii RAN, pp. 45–74.

Gannushkina, S, 1997a, 'Osnovnie problemi bezhentsev i vynuzhdennikh pereselentsev. Proekt organizatsii seti punktov iuridicheskoi pomoshchi dlia bezhentsev i vynuzhdennikh pereselentsev', in *Memorial, Organisatsiia iuridicheskikh konsul'tatsii dlia bezhentsev i vynuzhdennikh pereselentsev v rorodakh i regionakh Rossii*, Moskva, Zven'ia, pp. 12–20.

Gannuskina, S, 1997b, Head of the Civic Assistance Committee, Interview conducted by the author, 13 November, Moscow.

—— 1999, Interview conducted by the author, 13 September, Moscow.

—— 2002, Interview conducted by the author, 4 July, Moscow.

Goskomstat, 1998, *Regioni Rossii, Statisticheskii sbornik*, Volume 2, Moskva, Goskomstat.

—— 1999a, *Regioni Rossii, Statisticheskii sbornik*, Moskva, Goskomstat.

—— 1999b, *Demograficheskii ezhegodnik rossii*, Moskva, Goskomstat.

—— 2000, *Statisticheskii biulleten. Chislennost' i migratsiia naseleniia rossiiskoi federatsii v 1999 godu*, Moskva, Goskomstat.

—— 2002a, *Demograficheskii ezhegodnik rossii*, Moskva, Goskomstat.

—— 2002b, *Ezhegodnik biulleten*, Moskva, Goskomstat.

—— 2002c, *Statisticheskii biulleten: Chislennost' i migratsiia naseleniia Rossii'skoi Federatsii*, Moskva, Goskomstat.

Gorodetskaia, N, 1997, 'Potok bezhentsev v Rossiiu umen'shilsia', *Nezavisimaia gazeta*, 6 February, p. 2.

Gradirovskii, S, 1999, 'Rossiia i postsovetskii gosudarstva: iskushenie diasporal'noi politikoi', *Diaspory*, No. 2–3, pp. 40–58.

Grafova, L, 1995, *Obshchee delo Rossii, Koordinatsionnii sovet pomoshchi bezhentsam i vynuzhdennim pereselentsam*, Moskva, Koordinatsionnii Sovet.

—— 1999, Head of the CCARFM and President of the Forum of Migrant Organizations, Interview conducted by the author, 22 September, Moscow.

Grafova, L, 2003, 'Vladimir Lukin: "Repatrianty spasut Rossiiu"', *Vestnik Foruma*, No. 5.

Grankina, V, 1996, 'Sud'ba bezhentsev v Rossii', *Nezavisimaia gazeta*, 7 June, p. 3.

Gritsenko, V, 1999, *Russkie sredi russkikh: Problemy adaptatsii vynuzhdennikh migrantov i bezhentsev iz stran blizhnego zarubezh'ia v Rossii*, Moskva, Institut etnologii i antropologii RAN.

Kalugina, Z, 1996, 'Bezhentsy i vynuzhdennie pereselentsy v sel'skom raione: mnenie storon', *Region ekonomika i sotsiologiia*, No. 1, pp. 144–56.

Kamakin, A, 1998a, 'Tat'iana Regent: ia kritikuiu sebia bol'she, chem liuboi zhurnalist', *Nezavisimaia gazeta: Oblast'i*, No. 8, pp. 9–10.

—— 1998b, 'Nelegal'naia migratsiia v strankakh SNG', *Nezavisimaia gazeta*, 12 August, p. 5.

Kirillova, N, 1998, 'Migratsiia v tsivilizovannikh formakh zakonomerna i ekonomicheski vygodna', *Chelovek i Trud*, 3, pp. 4–9.

Komitet bezhentsev iz Chechnii, 1999, Interview conducted by the author with the organization, 19 August, Saratov.

Kornev, V, 1998, 'Chuzhie sredi svoikh', *Izvestiia*, 29 April, p. 4.

Kosmarskaia, N, 1998a, 'Integratsiia vynuzhdennikh pereselentsev v rossiiskoe obshchestvo', in Tishkov, V, (ed.), *Vynuzhdennie migranty i gosudarstvo*, Moskva, Institut etnologii i antropologii RAN, pp. 211–36.

—— 1998b, 'Ia nikuda ne khochu uezhat', zhizhn' v post-sovetskoi Kirgizii glazami russkikh', *Vestnik Evrazii*, No. 1–2, pp. 76–100.

—— 2002, 'Russkie diaspory: politicheskie mifologii i realii massovogo soznaniia', *Diaspory*, Vol. 2, pp. 110–56.

Kosygina, L, 2002, Interview with the head of the *raion* Migration Service, 26 July, Cherepanavo, Novosibirsk oblast'.

Kudriavtsev, V. 1996, 'Lovushka integratsii', *Nezavisimaia Gazeta*, 25 June, p. 3.

Kuznechevskii, V, 1997, 'Pomozhet li otechestvo svoemy "inostrantsu"', *Rossiiskaia gazeta*, 19 December, p. 5.

Lapshova, E, Reprintseva, E, and Rusina, O, 1996, *Otchet po rezul'tatam sotsiologicheskogo issledovaniia po teme: Problemy sotsial'noi adaptatsii migrantov*, Samara, Istoriko-eko-kul'turnaia assotsiatsiia 'Povolzh'e', Sotsiologicheskii tsentr Samarskogo pedagogicheskogo universiteta.

Lebedev, V, 1999a, 'Sootechestvenniki snova v pochete', *Nezavisimaia gazeta: Sodruzhestvo*, No, 4, April, p. 10.

—— 1999b, 'U kazhdogo – svoi sootechestvenniki', *Nezavisimaia gazeta*, 1 December, p. 5.

—— 1997, *Novaia russkaia diaspora. Sotsial'no-psikhologicheskii analiz*, Moskva, Institut etnologii i antropologii RAN.

Maksimov, V, 1998, 'Brounovskoe dvizhenie iz variag v greki', *Ekspert*, 26 January, pp. 48–9.

Materiali mezhdunarodnogo semianara: 'Rasrabotka i realizatsiia regional'nikh migratsionnikh programm', 1999, Saratov, Saratovskii Istochnik.

Memorial, 1997, *Bezhentsi i vynuzhdennie pereselentsi na territorii Rossiiskoi Federatsii*, Moskva, Zven'ia.

Migratsiia, 1996, No. 1.

—— 1997, No. 2.

Migratsiia bedstvie ili blago: materialy kruglogo stola po problemam vynuzhdennoi migratsii v Rossii, 1996, Moskva, Koordinatsionnii sovet pomoshchi bezhentsam i vynuzhdennim pereselentsam, Institut etnologii i antropologii RAN.

Mikheev, V, 1996, 'OON beret pod svoe krilo bezhentsev Rossii', *Izvestiia*, 16 October, p. 3.

Militarev, A, 1999, 'O soderzhanii termina 'diaspora' (k razrabotke definitisii), *Diaspory*, Vol. 1, pp. 24–33.

Mukomel', V, 2002, 'Ia i sem' minuvshikh dnei', *Obshchaia Gazeta*, 11 April 2002, p. 3.

—— and Payin, E, 1997, *Vynuzhdennie Migranti v Gosudarstvakh SNG: Poisk soglasovannikh reshenii v ramkakh sodruzhestva*, Moskva, Tsentr etnopoliticheskikh i regional'nikh issledovanii.

Novosibirsk Migration Service, 2002a, *Informatsiia*, Unpublished informational bulletin.

—— 2002b, Interview conducted by the author with the deputy director, 15 July, Novosibirsk.

Petrosian, A, 2002, 'Pofamil'nai zachistka. Gubernator Kubani provozglasil kampaniiu protiv ethnicheskoi migratsii', *Izvestiia*, 20 March, p. 4.

Pilkington, H, and Phizacklea, A, 1999, 'Postsovetskie migratsii v kontekste zapadnikh migratsionnikh teorii', in Viatkin, A, Kosmarskaia, N, Panarin, S, (eds), *V dvizhenii dobrovol'nom i vynuzhdennom, postsovetskie migratsii v Evrazii*, Moskva, Natalis, pp. 78–98.

—— and Flynn, M, 2001, 'Chuzhie na rodine? Issledovanie "diasporal'noi identichnosti" russkikh vynuzhdennikh pereselentsev', *Diaspory*, No. 2–3, pp. 8–34.

Popova, S, 2002a, 'Nelegalov zastaviat platit' nalogi', *Izvestiia*, 4 April, p. 1.

—— 2002b, 'Retsepty ne doktora no Moma. Rossiia prinimaet migrantov taion i v bol'shikh kolichestvakh, *Izvestiia*, 24 January, p. 4.

Povol'zhe, 1999, Interview conducted by the author with the co-director of the organization, 13 October, Samara.

Pravitel'stvo Saratovskoi oblasti Ministerstvo truda it sotsial'nogo razvitiia, 1999, *Sotsial'nii pasport, Saratovskoi oblasti po sostoianiiu na 1 ianvariia 1999*, Saratov, Saratovskii istochnik.

Pudina, L, 1999a, 'Mir vashemu domu', *Saratovskie vesti*, 25 June, p. 2.

—— 1999b, 'Mir vashemu domu', *Saratovskie vesti*, 26 May, p. 2.

—— 1999c, 'Mir vashemu domu', *Saratovskie vesti*, 12 March, p. 2.

Ruka pomoshchi, 2002, Interview conducted by the author with the organization, 20 July, Novosibirsk.

Sadkovskaia, T, 1998, 'Negrazhdane', *Rossiisskii vesti*, 6 March, pp. 1–2.

Samara Federal Employment Service, 1999, Statistics 1998–1999, Unpublished data.

Samara Migration Service, 1998, Interview conducted by the author with an employee of the Department for Resettlement, 20 April, Samara.

—— 1999a, Statistics 1996–1999, Unpublished data.

—— 1999b, Interview conducted by the author with the director, 12 October, Samara.

Samara Migration Service, 1999c, Interview conducted by the author with a representative of the TMS, 30 September, Samara.

Samarskii oblastnoi komitet gosudarstvennoi statistiki, 1999, *Migratsiia naseleniia Samarskoi oblasti 1998*, Samara, *Goskomstat*.

Samarskii pereselenets, 1999, Interview conducted by the author with the organization, 5 November, Samara.

—— 2002, Interview conducted by the author with the organization, 24 August, Samara.

Sanikidze, G, 1998, 'Kak pomogaet rossii mezhdunarodnie organizatsii', *Nezavisimaia gazeta*, 21 April, p. 8.

Saratov Migration Service, 1999a, Statistics 1992–1999, Unpublished data.

—— 1999b, Interview conducted by the author with the director, 16 August, Saratov.

—— 1999c, Interview conducted by the author with the head of the department for forced migrant and refugee registration, 16 August, Saratov.

—— 1999d, Interview conducted by the author with the deputy director, 28 July, Saratov.

Saratovskii istochnik, 1999, Interview conducted with the organization, 20 August, Saratov.

Shapenko, I, 1997, 'Chto delat' s beshentsami', *Mirovaia ekonomika i mezhdunarodnie otnoshenie*, No. 12, pp. 37–52.

Shlichkova, T, 1997, 'Osobennosti pazrabotki migratsionnikh programm', *Migratsiia*, No. 1, pp. 14–16.

Shuikin, M, 1999, 'Rossiia stanovitsia raem dlia nelegal'nikh immigrantov', *Nezavisimaia gazeta*, 5 February, p. 1.

Silvestri, A, 1997, 'Rol' i deiatel'nost' UVKB OON v Rossiiskoi Federatsii', in *Memorial, Organisatsiia iuridicheskikh konsul'tatsii dlia bezhentsev i vynuzhdennikh pereselentsev v rorodakh i regionakh Rossii*, Moskva, Zven'ia pp. 7–8.

Siprov, V, 1999, 'Kuda bezhat'? Migratsionnaia programme na granits sriva', *Samarskoe obozrenie*, 5 July, p. 3.

Smirnova, S, and Alksins, V, 2000a, 'Nuzhna li Rossii repatriatsiia?', *Nezavisimaia gazeta*, 15 December, p. 3.

—— 2000b, 'Rossiia prinimaet sootechestvennikov', *Nezavisimaia gazeta*, 27 December, p. 10.

Soboleva, S, 1996, 'Vozmozhnie izmeneniia v demograficheskoi situatsii pod vliianiem potoka vynuzhdennikh pereselentsev', *Region ekonomika i sotsiologiia*, No. 1, pp. 122–33.

—— 2002, Interview conducted by the author, 10 July, Novosibirsk.

Sobranie zakonodatel'stva Rossiiskoi Federatsii, 1995, No. 52, pp. 9317–27.

—— 1997a, No. 26, pp. 4930–49.

—— 1997b, No. 47, pp. 9517–76.

Tishkov, V, (ed.), 1996, *Migratsii i novie diaspori v postsovetskikh gosudarstvakh*, Moskva, Institut etnologii i antropologii RAN.

—— (ed.), 1997, *Vynuzhdennie migranti: Integratsiia i Vozvrashchenie*, Moskva, Institut etnologii i antropologii RAN.

Tishkov, V, 1998, *Vynuzhdennie migranti i gosudarstvo*, Moskva, Institut etnologii i antropologii RAN.

Totskii, N, 1996, 'Organizatsionno-pravovie problemy migratsionnoi sluzhby Rossii', *Gosudarstvo i Pravo*, No. 2, pp. 35–43.

Tuleev, A, 2000, 'Programmy poddershki sootechestvennikov ne sushchestvuiet', *Nezavisimaia gazeta*, 18 October, p. 5.

Ukolov, R, 2002, 'Naselenie Rossii prirastaet nelegalami. Na 10 nashikh sootechestvennikov odin nezakonnii immigrant', *Nezavisimaia gazeta*, 24 January, p. 7.

Vedomosti S"ezda Narodnikh Deputatov RF i Verkhovnogo Soveta RF, 1993, No. 12, 25 March, Moskva, Verkhovnii Soviet RF, pp. 714–27.

Vitkovskaia, G, 1999b, Scholar-in-residence, Moscow Carnegie Centre, Interview conducted by the author, 23 September, Moscow.

Voronina, N, 1997, 'Pravovoe regulirovanie migratsii v Rossii', in Tishkov (ed.), *Vynuzhdennie migranti: Integratsiia i Vozvrashchenie*, Moskva, Institut etnologii i antropologii RAN, pp. 33–44.

Vozvrashchenie, 1999, Interview conducted by the author with the organization, 24 August, Saratov.

Zaionchkovskaia, Z, 1996, 'Russkii vopros', *Migratsiia*, No. 1, pp. 7–11.

Zhirniagin, Yu, 1998, 'Problemi migratsii i vosdeisstvie migratsionnikh protsessov na etnikcheskuiu sredu Samarskoi oblasti', *Etnos i Kul'tura*, No. 1–2, pp. 68–73.

WEB BASED SOURCES

http://soros.org/fmp2/html/july1999.html, 20 April 2001.

http://www.strana.ru, 24 December 2001.

http://www.migrant.ru/index.php/news/, 14 August 2000.

http://new.migrant.ru/cgi-bin/vestnik.pl?issue2003/article2.shtml, 17 March 2003.

http://www.migrant/ru/cgi-bin/vestnik.pl?issue200305/article4.shtml, 10 July 2003.

http://www.migrant.ru/cgi-bin/vestnik.pl?issue200305/article2shtml, 10 July 2003.

http://www.migrant.ru/forum/, 15 July 2003.

http://www3.adm.nso.ru/ru/gov/glava/, 18 July 2003.

http://www.rg.ru/oficial/doc/federal_zak/62-fz.shtm, 6 August 2003.

http://www.nso.ru/pasport/pasport.htm#makro, 13 August 2003.

http://www.unhcr.ch/cgi-bin/texis/vtx/publ/opendoc.pdf?id=3ddceb8611&tbl=MEDIA, 26 August 2003.

http://db.ngo.ru/info.nsf/MigrantIndex/NT00004A56, 26 August 2003.

http://www.izvestia.ru/politic/38911, 25 November 2003.

Index

www.ingramcontent.com/pod-product-compliance
Lightning Source LLC
Chambersburg PA
CBHW071641280326
41928CB00068B/2105